THE COMMUNITY WITNESS

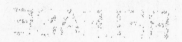

THE COMMUNITY WITNESS

An Exploration of some of the Influences at Work in the New Testament Community and its Writings

HAMISH F. G. SWANSTON

88658

BS538
.S97

SHEED AND WARD: NEW YORK

Nihil obstat: LIONEL SWAIN, S.T.L., L.S.S., Censor.
Imprimatur: ✠ PATRICK CASEY, Vicar General.
Westminster, 6 June 1967.

The Nihil obstat *and* Imprimatur *are a declaration that a book or pamphlet is considered to be free from doctrinal or moral error. It is not implied that those who have granted the* Nihil obstat *and* Imprimatur *agree with the contents, opinions or statements expressed.*

The Old Testament quotations and some of the New Testament quotations are from the *Revised Standard Version of the Bible*, copyright 1946 and 1952.

Library of Congress Catalog Card Number 67-20751

Manufactured in the United States of America

For

MY MOTHER

who first taught me

to say 'Jesus is Lord'

Author's Note

THOUGH it will be immediately evident to those who are acquainted with current writings on the Old and New Testaments that there is little here that is original, I have, after some little hesitation, thought it best not to chronicle by means of either footnotes or bibliography my multifold indebtedness to the work of others, and this not to escape acknowledgements but to render the book less off-putting to the reader I have in mind when publishing this study. There are many with a genuine curiosity about the Scriptures and their meaning who will, I hope, not disdain this 'Just So Story' of 'how the New Testament came to have its shape' because it lacks the imposing apparatus of scholarship. This is not a book for specialists in biblical scholarship; they have provided the material and will not grudge its use to make the Scriptures more accessible to the Christian congregation.

Quotations from the Old Testament are given in the RSV, from the New Testament they are sometimes in the Knox version and sometimes in RSV.

Contents

CONTENTS

III. THE RESURRECTION

'If Christ has not been raised your faith is futile.' The realization of the resurrection as the central moment in God's action among men was so present to the first Christians in everything they did and said that, when they came to write down their accounts of the gospel of Christ, the evangelists were given a tradition seen through 'resurrection-tinted spectacles'. Every act of Jesus in Galilee, Judaea and Jerusalem was understood as a proclamation of the risen Lord.

IV. THE LITURGICAL EXPRESSION OF CHRIST

The first Christians knew that while the Old Testament liturgy brought images of God to the Hebrews, in their New Testament situation they were continually in the presence of the risen Lord who is *'the* image of the invisible God', and who gives intelligibility to their liturgical action. The time when Jesus 'went about doing good' is seen to be the paradigm of all the times when Jesus does good among his people. We have to appreciate something of the Old Testament images if we are to come to an understanding of those sacramental rites which we have received from the liturgy of the first Christian community.

V. LAZARUS   221

In the account of Lazarus come from the grave we can see how the first apologetic led through Old Testament images to an understanding of the resurrection-life among us and thence to the participation and celebration of that life in the sacraments of the Christian community.

I

Preliminaries

1. INSPIRATION

MOST Christians accept that there are some books given to us by God for our encouragement in the Christian life, to help us to see what Christ is doing for us here and now, and what we are to be ourselves. But most also have odd moments of difficulty when it occurs to them that they are not clear in their minds just why they accept these books and no others as coming from God. How do we know that a book is 'inspired by God'?

Of the translations that I suppose most of us habitually used before discovering the Revised Standard Version, neither is satisfactory as a reflection of the original in an important matter. Everything suffers in translation, except of course bishops, but there is something more than usually deceptive in the texture of Douay or Knox. The one turns the prophet Isaiah into an Elizabethan tragedian and the other describes the feeding of the five thousand as if it were an Edwardian picnic complete with hampers. Both, that is, are non-historical. More, they have in common the ability to put us at far remove from any time or place, they present truth in a guise which has evidently no relation to the historical circumstances in which it was realized, a guise which is evidently of God alone since it has so little to do with men.

The liturgical practice of cutting up the text into small bits and rendering these in a quaint chant, sometimes a foreign and always a non-colloquial language, and a formal context persuades many Christians that the word of God has been dictated to bloodless, but doubtless holy, secretaries.

What does Scripture say about itself? What does the Bible show to be normative in a discussion of inspiration? The appeal of Scripture seems to some theologians as a dangerous dissolvent to all

1

our Catholic beliefs, in this case, however, there is much to support the comfortable notion of dictation.

In the New Testament there are many passages which seem to ascribe to God the literary authorship of the text: 'Brethren, the scripture had to be fulfilled, which the Holy Spirit spoke beforehand by the mouth of David . . .' (Acts 1.16). 'The Holy Spirit was right in saying to your fathers through Isaiah the prophet . . .' (Acts 28.25). The Old Testament is even more explicit: 'And Moses wrote all the words of the Lord' (Ex. 24.4). 'And the Lord said to Moses, "Write these words; in accordance with these words I have made a covenant with you and with Israel" ' (Ex. 34.27). 'Thus says the Lord, the God of Israel: Write in a book all the words that I have spoken to you . . . these are the words which the Lord spoke concerning Israel and Judah' (Jer. 30.2). It is not surprising that many have, on this evidence, thought that the only theory of inspiration which does justice to the text is one of direct dictation by God.

Thus Philo, the Hellenistic Jew, is a dictationist of the strict school:

> A prophet says nothing of his own, but everything which he says is strange and prompted by someone else . . . he is a sounding instrument of God's voice, being struck and moved to sound in an invisible manner by him . . . a trance, which proceeds from inspiration, takes violent hold of the man, and madness seizes him, for when the divine light shines the human light sets, for the mind that is in a man is removed from its place at the arrival of the divine spirit, but is again restored to its previous habitation when that Spirit departs, for it is contrary to holy law for what is mortal to dwell with what is immortal . . . even when he appears to be speaking, the inspired one is silent and another is employing his vocal organs, his mouth and tongue, for the explanation of those things that other chooses . . . (*On who is the heir of divine things*, LVIII).

This is a completely worked out theory of inspiration based on the Jewish idea of God, the unimportance of secondary causes and the passivity of man—it is at one with those strange passages in Scripture which so bedevil the dogmatic tracts about free will, like the hardening of Pharaoh's heart by God or the divine plot to entice Ahab to his death at Ramoth-gilead.

Philo takes his theory of human passivity one stage further in his account of our present text when he describes the formation of the Septuagint—the Greek version of the Old Testament made in Egypt during the third and second centuries B.C. The Pharaoh, recounts Philo, preserving the Jewish tradition in this matter, wanted to have in the great library at Alexandria a copy of all the important books of the world and he ordered a translation of the Hebrew writings, and seventy Jewish scholars were commanded to produce a version; Philo describes the process of translation:

> ... considering among themselves how important the business was, to translate laws which had been divinely given by direct inspiration, since they were not able either to take away anything, or to alter anything, but were bound to preserve the original form and character of the whole composition, they looked out for the most completely purified place of all the spots outside the city ... as men inspired they wrote down, not one saying one thing and another another, but everyone of them employed the selfsame nouns and verbs as if some unseen prompter had suggested all their language to them ... (*Life of Moses*, VI).

So that seventy exactly identical versions were produced.

If we are tempted to regard this as a little credulous, symptomatic of the time when the world was young and men behaved like children, or to dismiss Philo as a Jew living under the less perfect earlier covenant, it might be as well to note that St Augustine held the same thesis for the Septuagint and that St Irenaeus thought that direct dictation of the Greek text had happened not only once but twice. He repeats the Hebrew tradition about the translators for the Pharaoh, remarking that the similarity was complete 'so that even the Gentiles saw that the Scriptures had been translated by the inspiration of God' and then says:

> There was nothing astonishing in God having done this—he who when, during the captivity of the people under Nebuchadnezzar, the scriptures had been corrupted and when, after seventy years, the Jews had returned to their own land, then in the time of Artaxerxes, king of the Persians, inspired Esdrah, the priest of the tribe of Levi, to write down again all the words of the former prophets, and to re-establish with the people the Mosaic Law.

He is recounting here a story found in the apocryphal II Esdrah, ch. 14.

So the direct dictationists have a respectable history; they are not merely nineteenth-century obscurantists. I find something attractive in the downright fundamentalist approach to inspiration—there is something endearing in the determination not to be subject to the

3

monstrous tyranny of fact. For it must be evident that those who argue that each word is individually ordered by God's direct intervention have to explain away a great many instances of apparent inconsistency and error.

Is direct dictation, however, necessarily demanded by our Christian understanding of the Scriptures? What is demanded by the phrase 'having God as their author'?

The phrase has come into general and popular use since it was employed first by Leo IX and then more importantly by Clement IV who wrote to Michael Palaeologus in 1267 a profession of faith including the clause: 'We believe also that the one author of the New and Old Testaments of the Law and of the Prophets and the Apostles, is the omnipotent God and Lord.' Even if we accept the word 'author' here in the sense of literary author major difficulties arise.

Our normal criteria for judging literary authorship are concerned with language and style, with the use of words, metaphor and simile, oxymoron and synecdoche, and unless we appropriate these at least to the human author we shall leave him with no claim at all to authorship. The psychology of the inspired writer is a complex affair perhaps, but we need not resort to automation. In fact the history of '*auctor*' in the Councils does not support such an interpretation. Newman some while ago pointed out that the word was used from the earliest times until Trent for a totally different purpose than that of asserting some form of inspiration.

> [It was] directed against the heresy, so early and so late, of Gnostics, Manichees, Priscillianists and Paulicians, that the God of the Old Testament was not the God of the New. On the contrary, in a succession of protests, the Church from the beginning asserts that there is but one God of both Dispensations; that one and the same God is the Author of the one and the other. He who originated the New Covenant also originated the Old. The heresy anathematized was not that the Scriptures were not inspired, but that the God of the New Dispensation was not the God of the Old (*Stray Essays*, privately printed, 1890).

'*Auctor*', here, has the meaning of 'fount' or 'originator' or 'the one who is ultimately responsible' for the existence and economy of our salvation. The word is not being used in a literary context and tells us nothing about the mode of inspiration. The word which is stressed in the references to 'one author of both Testaments' is *one*.

It is necessary therefore to concentrate on what may be said about the human author—if we can define his activity we may be able to say something, at least in a negative way, about the action of God.

We use the word 'inspired' in many contexts, not all of them useful for our purpose. Thus footballers dribbling and cooks icing a cake are sometimes said to be 'inspired', and in a more religious context, Bacci, the seventeenth-century biographer of St Philip Neri, says of the saint's idea of presenting Church history as a response to the Magdeburg 'Centuries', 'By a singular inspiration of God he thought of a method by which he could attack them from a distance' (Bacci, ch. 13), and in the more prosaic *Statuta Generalia* approved for the Oratory in 1962 we find a similar use of the word in an official document of the Holy See: '*Institutum Oratorii Sancti Philippi Nerii ab ipso divina inspiratione in Urbe conditum. . . .*' But this does not really touch our specialist use of the word in the theology of Scripture. Nor, I suppose, need we pay much attention to the grandiloquent invocations of Milton in the writing of *Paradise Lost* and *Paradise Regained*, likening himself in the one to Moses:

Sing Heav'nly Muse, that on the secret top
Of Oreb, or of Sinai, didst inspire
That Shepherd, who first taught the chosen Seed
In the beginning how the Heav'ns and Earth
Rose out of Chaos,

and in the other putting himself in the position of Christ after his baptism in the Jordan:

Thou Spirit who ledst this glorious Eremite
Into the Desert, his Victorious Field
Against the Spiritual Foe, and broughtst him thence
By proof the undoubted Son of God, inspire
As thou art wont, my prompted Song.

Though we may much admire Milton's prosody we may well demur if claims are made for the inspiration of his work in the same sense as they are made for the biblical writings. Indeed such claims are not characteristic of those writers we acknowledge as inspired.

If we examine the prefaces of the biblical writers themselves we find some rather cool descriptions of their work; the making of the book of Ecclesiastes, for example, is described in terms which show no sense at all of any kind of 'inspiration': 'The Preacher taught the people knowledge, weighing and studying and arranging proverbs

5

with great care. The Preacher sought to find pleasing words and uprightly he wrote words of truth' (12.9–10); similarly the historian of II Machabees makes this apology for his work: 'All such things as have been comprised in five books of Jason of Cyrene, we have attempted to abridge into one book . . . we have taken in hand no easy task, yea rather a business full of watching and sweat . . . which if I have done well, and as it becomes the history, it is what I desired; but if not so perfectly, it must be pardoned me' (2.24, 27 and 15.39); and in the famous introduction to his gospel Luke describes his intention to better all previous writers and how this has meant that he has had to put in a great deal of work: 'It seemed good to me also, having diligently attained to all things from the beginning, to write to thee setting them in order, most excellent Theophilus . . .' (1.3).

There is no evidence at all from these writers in favour of any theory of inspiration which suggests that the writer has some mystic intuition of the text. The inspiration of Scripture is a redeeming act of God for men, set in the over-all pattern of the redemptive economy, and carried through in a way consonant with the Incarnation principle of employing nature in the full service of God.

The scriptural writers do not seem, therefore, at all conscious of their work being the result of some take-over by God. They do not feel that their human worrit and fret is a mere charade behind which mask God does everything. They do not, therefore, provide us with a guarantee of inspiration. It is not from the writers themselves that we know which books are inspired. From the writers themselves we learn nothing on this matter. The psychology of the inspired writer is describable only in terms of what is produced. We have no access to a description of how a man is inspired, we have no knowledge, indeed, as to whether God employs one or many modes of inspiration. If we do not know the *how* of inspiration at all, and if we do not know *what* is inspired from the writers themselves, how do we know what is inspired?

St Augustine suggested that the apostles left their disciples a list of the inspired books and that this list is handed down from one generation of the community to another. This has *a priori* attractions as a theory. It places the full emphasis on the activity of the Christian community. The community knows which are inspired because the list of inspired books is framed within the living tradition of the community. A large difficulty against Augustine's theory, however, is the total absence of any historical evidence for the compilation of such a list and the existence of a great deal of historical evidence that the canon of Scripture was not arrived at in this way. Given that the author of II Peter is the apostle (which is by no means proven) we have assurance that Paul wrote some inspired work: 'Our beloved brother Paul wrote to you according to the wisdom given him, speaking of this as he does in all his letters. There are some things in them hard to understand, which the ignorant and unstable twist to their own destruction as they do the *other scriptures*' (3.15–16). But, as Professor Karl Rahner remarks in his paper on *Inspiration*: 'Is it probable that . . . one apostle did not know that his own work was inspired, like some of the smaller writings, the Epistle to Philemon, for example, but that some other apostle did receive an explicit categorical revelation concerning the inspired character of the same piece of writing?'

Are we really to suppose that St John (the last of the apostles to die) in his extreme hours pronounced that these twenty-six books and no others, not the epistle of Barnabas, not the *Pastor* of Hermas, are the inspired Scriptures of God, ranking with the Scriptures of the Hebrews? It is conceivable but not likely. The evidences of history are against such an hypothesis. We have to look more closely at the relation of Scripture to the Christian community and to its precursor the Israelite community if we are to discover the criteria of inspiration. The answer to the question 'How did the list of canonical Scriptures come into being?' can only be realized after an attempt has been made to understand the biblical notion of 'community'.

2. COMMUNITY

The people of Israel knew themselves to be the peculiar of God: 'You will be my people and I will be your God' (Ex. 6.7). They knew that he is a God who acts. When a member of the Israel community came to offer sacrifice he was acknowledging that God was with his people and acting in their history:

A wandering Aramean was my father; and he went down into Egypt and sojourned there, few in number; and there he became a nation, great, mighty, and populous. And the Egyptians treated us harshly, and afflicted us, and laid upon us a hard bondage. Then we cried to the Lord the God of our fathers, and the Lord heard our voice and saw our affliction, our toil, and our oppression; and the Lord brought us out of Egypt with a mighty hand and an outstretched arm, with great terror, with signs and wonders; and he brought us into this place and gave us this land, a land flowing with milk and honey (Deut. 26.5–9).

In this Deuteronomy credal statement two dominant aspects of Hebrew religion are contained. Firstly, the whole history of the people is described as the act of Yahweh. God is looking after the people. Secondly, it is noticeable that the individual member of the people offering his sacrifice has so intimate a union with all other members of his people, not simply with the living but with the dead, that he speaks in a confused series of pronouns and tenses. What happened to 'my father' who was 'few in number' happened to 'us' until 'we cried to the Lord' who was the 'God of our fathers', and he gave 'us' the land of Canaan. The worshipper reciting this creed is presented in a most concrete manner with the fact of his union with all other members of the worshipping community everywhere and at all times. God has worked through history in a progressive manner and the condition of the individual before God depends upon the historical response that the people has made to God's revealing work. To this people, as a people, revelation has been given. Indeed, the people is the creation of the revelation. The reality of Israel is not to be determined by ethnic or economic or even cultural criteria, the reality of Israel is brought about by the saving revelation of Yahweh. There is no people of Israel except the worshipping community.

The Hebrew sense of community is inherited through God's providential working in history by the Christian community. This produces the early Christian sense that all the Old Testament Scriptures were written for the Christian community.

At the same time it must be remembered that the Christians refused to limit their sense of community with men to those who belonged already to the community of revelation. They understood their belonging to the community of revelation to imply a missionary vocation to bring everyone else into that community: 'You are a chosen race, a royal priesthood, a holy nation, God's own people, *that* you may declare the wonderful deeds of him who called you out of darkness into his marvellous light.' (I Pet. 2.9).

The Pauline expression of community in terms of the Body,

although it derives in part from the Old Testament sense of community within revelation, derives also from the Gentile intuition of a man's community with all other men. The Body of Christ is the community of revelation certainly, but it is a universal community. We can understand some part of Paul's thought from Gentile writings as well as from Hebrew. For instance Philip of Macedon's reply to a warning that one of his officers would betray him: 'If part of my body were sick, would I cut it off rather than seek to heal it?' And his horror of punishing other men: 'Whoever was strong enough to amputate the members of his own body without grief and pain?' Or Trajan's remark, also quoted from John of Salisbury's *Policratus*, that a man must be insane if he, having inflamed eyes, prefers to dig them out rather than cure them. These are all rather like Paul's use of the Body image in I Corinthians: 'You are Christ's body, organs of it depending upon each other' (12.27). And he tells his converts that the task of the Christian is to help in 'the building up of the Body of Christ'. The mission of the Christian is to present the revelation of God in Christ to other men. It is this sense of mission in the community which gives the impulse to the production of written testimonies to the work of Christ. The books of the New Testament are community books.

Inspiration is a missionary gift to the Church, a gift given to enable the community to present the traditional understanding of God's activity in the world. The tradition of the Church is the community's experience and understanding of the faith, and it is this tradition which is written in these books.

Our God is a God who saves his community and speaks to his community and charges his community with the spreading of his word. A curious example of our awareness of this community context of revelation is the hesitancy we all feel about the prophecy in Virgil's eclogue, where we understand the messianic truth, but realize that the prophecy is not scripture precisely because it is not given to the community.

Contrariwise, some of the letters of Paul, originally intended for individual recipients, were seen by the early Christian community to be of value to all Christians since these letters recorded our belief and experience in Christ. The letters, therefore, became part of the general round of writings posted from one community to another as public community writings. In general Paul recognized the community

9

setting of his missionary writing; he wrote to the Colossians: 'When this letter has been read among you, have it read also in the church of the Laodiceans, and see that you read also the letter from Laodicea' (4.16). And James sent his letter to all the Christians of the Diaspora: 'to the twelve tribes in the dispersion' (1.1).

This custom of sending letters from one community to another became extremely popular and as a safeguard against forgeries and pseudo-apostolic writings becoming part of the general exchange the community had to vouch for the apostolic character of the writing it was sending on to others. We see this guarantee in the last section of John's gospel where it has become part of the actual text: 'This is the disciple who is bearing witness to these things, and who has written these things, and we know that his testimony is true' (21.24). We have here the beginning of the formation of the Canon of the New Testament.

3. CANONICITY

Canonicity differs from inspiration: it is the communal recognition that a book is in fact inspired. But historically the distinction is not easy to make. Inspiration and canonicity interact. If inspiration is understood as God destining a book from its beginning for his community, then inspiration is only fully effective when the community is moved to put the seal of canonicity upon the book.

The decision that the community made about which books were part of the canon was not made quickly, nor are the criteria adopted by the community for canonicity immediately obvious. Authorship was not one of them. A book might be by an author who was seen to be inspired in other books but yet not be recognized as inspired in that one. The lost epistles of Paul are examples of this.

In the beginning the community which had received letters from the apostles or which had copies of writings such as the gospels or those accounts which Luke mentions at the beginning of his work, kept them and copied them and sent copies to other communities. There grew up small groups of sacred writings, somewhat dependent upon one another but not identical. Greater co-operation had soon to be put into effect since some communities began to question the authority of books which were not included in their own groups of canonical writings. The group round Marcion, for example, about the year 140, accepted only the gospel of Luke and some of the Pauline letters, while on the other hand some communities inflated their holdings by accepting works of doubtful apostolicity. It is at this time that the Gospel of Thomas and the Apocalypse of Peter appear. So it was necessary to make definitive lists of those books which a Christian community ought to accept as containing the inspired word of God. By the end of the second century lists approximating to our own present canon were in circulation. But these lists and those of the next century and a half were all either too short or too long from our modern point of view. Books like the Epistle of Clement or the *Didache* came in, while, until the fourth century, the Roman Church did not accept the Epistle to the Hebrews as being by Paul, the Apocalypse was given hard looks, and the letters of James and John and Peter were considered very doubtful for a long time.

Evidently the Christian community of the first centuries had to work out its canon with diligence. There was no quick way to decide in which books the community had the inspired word of God. This historical progress by slow decisions makes it very difficult to maintain that inspiration is to be recognized either by the inspiring character of the writings themselves, as Calvin supposed, or by their places in the apostolic listing suggested by Augustine. If anyone were able to recognize the inspiration by its content it would have been the men of the first community, and they too would have been the ones to possess the apostolic list. But they worked by neither system. Nor did they adopt any other quick solution to the community problem. They waited patiently, or impatiently in the case of the forgers, for the community to accept any particular book into the canon as inspired Scripture. The community is responsible for the recognition and proclamation of the divine word.

In the historical process the formation of the canon of Scripture is dependent upon the community realizing that a particular book is part of the written tradition properly belonging to the Church. This realization comes about not by some spectacular intervention by God instructing the Pope of Rome, or the bishops in Council, or any individual or group in the Church, that such a book is his in this peculiar way, but by the whole community as a community coming, slowly perhaps, to accept a book as its own, as expressing the faith of the community, and, more particularly, as expressing this faith in a way which is complementary to those books already accepted as destined by God for the community proclamation. It is therefore as destined to the biblical grouping that the Scriptures are inspired by God. Together they present the faith of the community, as a group they have the divine mandate. No human being responds to the whole content of revelation which is given to the community. No author records the full faith of the community in an adequate manner. Disaster follows an exegesis which does not take into account all the writings included by the community in its canon. Disaster follows when either the epistle to the Romans or the epistle of James is read alone, or when the epistle to Philemon is thought to express the totality of Christian thought about slavery and the rights of men. The community has collected the books to form *together* a witness to the living tradition handed down from the apostles' preaching.

The Church of Pentecost produces Scripture for the succeeding generations 'before the death of the last apostles'. If it is now asked why this capacity for receiving and recognizing revelation ceased, we can answer that God has disposed his gifts to his community in ways appropriate to the temporal condition of the community. The founding community needed such gifts as would lead to the formation of the canon of Scripture. It needed to understand that the old covenant writings were written for the instruction of the Christian, and it needed to be able to recognize which contemporary writings were intended by God to fit together into a corporate witness to Christ. But we do not need such gifts. We are willed by God as the conserving community.

Out of time God has the determination to save and from this determination derives the necessity of his communicating somehow with men, the necessity of revelation and the necessity of human response, participating in the divine self-disclosure by recording the acts and words of the Lord in time. The Old Testament was seen by the Pentecost community as a successive record of God's historical intervention. The New Testament was created to show men that God, who spoke in many ways and at many times, now gives us his full expression of himself in the Word made flesh. And the Incarnation happens at one particular temporal moment. Those who at this particular moment receive the fullness of this revelation in Christ have a particular function in the history of the community.

They are to frame the witness which at all times must be given by the community.

If we now ask how it was that the early Christian community recognized that some tradition was part of their community tradition, we shall have to answer that the first Christians must have conceived themselves not as the originators of the tradition but as the witness to the tradition given by Christ. The tradition was living among them because Christ was living among them, they had, as St Paul remarks, 'the mind of Christ', they could know his truth because he was with them speaking it in them.

When, earlier, we argued that the New Testament authors say nothing about the process of inspiration in the production of their writings, there ought perhaps to have been some adversion to the notorious boomerang character of the argument from silence. It may well be that no specific reference in this context was made to the work of the Spirit of Jesus because the writers assumed that they were writing within the context of the Spirit who was acting in multifarious ways in the whole life of the community. The books were realized to be part of the total working of the Spirit among the men of Christ:

> The revelation of the Spirit is imparted to each, to make the best advantage of it. One learns to speak with wisdom, by the power of the Spirit, another to speak with knowledge, with the same Spirit for his rule; one, through the same Spirit, is given faith; another, through the same Spirit, powers of healing . . . but all this is the work of one and the same Spirit, who distributes his gifts as he will to each severally (I Cor. 12.7–11).

It would seem to me very odd that the writer of a gospel should not think his work as much the manifestation of the Spirit in the community as that of the man speaking with tongues, or, if the writer himself were not aware of the action of the Spirit, it would be odd if the community itself did not think the gospel a product of the influence of the Spirit in their community.

So the written word of Scripture was not thought of by the first Christians as simply their testimony to Christ which would, if read in the Spirit, bring men to cry out 'Jesus is Lord'; it was reckoned the living tradition of Christ made manifest by the Spirit among them. Like everything else in the community the written witness had the character of a gift of the Spirit. It will not do, therefore, to

13

speak of the Scriptures in purely human terms of the literary critic, we have to understand them as the Word of God as well as the words of men. Unless we are prepared to do this we shall be for ever undermining our own appreciation of the gospels since we shall be ever wondering how far any particular pericope is the result of an eyewitness testimony directly and how far it is the result of a continual reworking by the worshipping community. We have to realize that both the memorizing of the eyewitness of this event, and the gradually developing cultic shaping of the narrative of the event, take place within the one community by the power of the Spirit.

If I have spent some time in this book considering the various influences at work in the human conditions of the New Testament formation this is because I believe that if we can understand the workings of the human writers of our Scriptures we shall be understanding simultaneously the workings of the Holy Spirit and so shall grow in appreciation of what his word can do in our lives.

4. INERRANCY

From their community character derives the inerrancy of the biblical writings. It cannot be admitted that the God who has created us, redeemed us by the flesh of his Son, and formed us into the community of his Spirit, would allow us to be deceived about his eternal will for his community. We are his people and he guides us in truth. The books he intends as his revelation of himself to his community are, because they are intended for his community, inspired, and so far as they are intended to teach his community, inerrant.

'To err is human', runs the depressing tag, and the assertion of inerrancy brings us up against the problem of the relation of human and divine authorship in the biblical writings. If, as we have already suggested, we can know nothing of the psychology of inspiration, we have yet to consider the sociology of inspiration as it relates to inerrancy. That is, we have to consider how the human authorship and the divine are related to the social function of presenting revelation to the community. In what way must we take into account the humanity of the scriptural writer when considering the community witness of the Bible?

This question comes often enough to the fore when the biblical writings are patient of factual checks against the evidence of archaeological sciences. We cannot today be expected to think in quite the way of Sir Isaac Newton and Archbishop Ussher, who worked out the year and the month, the day and the hour of creation by a complicated fundamentalist mathematics. On the other hand we realize that archaeology will not perform every exegetical function. We find equally far from a proper understanding of the work of inspiration the joy of some exegetes at the discovery that Lysanias *was* tetrarch of Galilee, or that the pool of Bethsaida *did* have five arches, as if the word of God were uncertain without such confirmations. We now see this work as ancillary. Archaeology is preparatory to exegesis, and exegesis preparatory to faith for which the inspired revelation is given to men. God is not a geographer or an astronomer royal, he is not a quick machine for the answers to facts we can discover by natural science. As Augustine put it: 'Christ our Lord did not say "I am sending you the Paraclete" in order to teach you about the course of the sun and the moon. His aim was to make Christians of us, not mathematicians' (*De Act. cum Felice*, 1,10). Or as Cardinal Baronius, the learned and saintly successor of St Philip Neri as Provost of the Roman Oratory, remarked when the heliocentric theory was being discussed among scientists: 'The Scriptures are to teach us not how the heavens go but how to go to heaven'. This happy aphorism is quoted in Galileo's excellent introduction to the methodology of scriptural exegesis, the *Letter to the Grand Duchess Christina*.

So far as the biblical writer is addressing the people of God in the things of God, is making an affirmation within the faith, so far as he is teaching men about God's saving work for men, so far he will be inerrant. While all Scripture is inspired by God much of Scripture, it is immediately apparent, is not didactic in this way, much of it has other purposes, as Paul wrote to his missionary bishop Timothy: 'all scripture is inspired by God and profitable for teaching, for reproof, for correction, and for training in righteousness, that the man of God may be complete, equipped for every good work' (II Tim. 3.16).

5. THE GOSPEL

We know that there once were many more gospels than we possess today—gospels, that is, in the sense of accounts of Christ and his teaching within a loose biographical framework. As Luke writes at the beginning of his work: 'Many have been at pains to set forth the history of what time has brought to fulfilment among us, following the tradition of those first eyewitnesses who gave themselves up to the service of the world' (1.1). It seems almost certain that Luke would be including Mark's gospel amongst his forerunners and seems to mean the reader to regard his own work as much better than that of any of his predecessors.

Today we restrict the word 'gospel' to the four Christian accounts of Christ, *Matthew, Mark, Luke* and *John.* In the first years of the Church there were, of course, no set writings, no 'gospels' in our sense of the word. There was but one gospel of Christ. Very early, however, the word came to have the meaning we now employ. This is demonstrated by the proliferation of pseudo-gospels of Thomas, or Mary, or Philip. All these were attempts to satisfy the demand of Christians who wanted to know more about the biography of Jesus. They had thus departed from the original meaning of gospel as it was used in the first communities who knew only one gospel. Paul before giving his Corinthian converts a short synopsis of the faith of Christians says: 'Here, brethren, is an account of the gospel I preached to you. It was this that was handed on to you; upon this your faith rests' (I Cor. 15.1) and to the fickle-minded Galatians he wrote:

> I am astounded that you should be so quick to desert one who called you to the grace of Christ, and go over to another gospel; this can only mean, that certain people are causing disquiet among you, in their eagerness to pervert the gospel of Christ. Friends, though it were we ourselves, though it were an angel from heaven that should preach to you a gospel other than the gospel we preached to you, a curse upon him! (1.6–8).

Evidently the gospel is thought of as a message which speaks of Christ, a word which brings Christ to the people. It is to be noted that even as early as this Paul assumes that there is a traditional faith which presents the truth to men and which must not be abandoned: 'if anyone preaches to you what is contrary to the tradition you received, a curse upon him!' (Gal. 1.9).

He warns the Colossians of this danger too: 'nothing must shift you away from the hope you found in the gospel you once listened to.

It is a gospel which has been preached to all creation under heaven, and I, Paul, have been brought into its service' (1.23).

There is evidently here no thought of a book and serving a book. Paul is speaking of the news of Christ, the life of Christ which is given to men.

These passages speak of 'the one gospel of Christ' and this is to be understood in two senses. Christ is the author of the gospel—it is his message that the Christian must convey; and Christ is the content of the message—it is his person that is to be made known. There is no gospel without Christ.

Notice, for example, that while John the Baptist exhorts men to repent in preparation for the kingdom, Christ tells his hearers to repent and believe the gospel. The revelation is present to his disciples. Wherever Christ is in the midst of his pupils there is the kingdom.

Throughout the New Testament this dual characteristic of the 'gospel' is maintained. Christians are to preach the gospel and this is the same as preaching Christ and him only, as Paul says. We can see this in the very first sentence of the earliest written gospel we possess: 'The beginning of the gospel of Jesus Christ, the Son of God' (Mk 1.1).

If we are to understand what the term 'gospel' implies we ought to make some effort to understand what it meant to those who first used the word. Some investigation of the Old Testament usages and that of the Roman Gentile world may make more immediate the notion of 'evangelion' that was accepted by the first Christian community who chose the word for the proclamation of their Lord.

The origin of the term 'evangelion' is within the context of a herald's proclamation of the good news, and particularly the good news of a victory. Originally the word was used for the actual messenger who brought the good news. Then the *evangelion* comes to mean the message itself and is used in this sense by Lucian and Appius of the herald's message in Heliodorus when Hydaspes announces his victory over the Persians, and of the cry of the messenger of Marathon. The same usage occurs in II Samuel. David tells the murderers of Ishbosheth that they can expect no reward for their evangelion: 'when one told me, "Behold Saul is dead", and thought he was bringing good news, I seized him and slew him at Ziklag, which was the reward I gave him for his good news' (4.10). David used *evangelion* twice in a sarcastic manner in this passage in order to bring out his fury with those who think he will reward as welcome the news of a murder.

In the sense of a herald bringing good news it is evident that Christ is the 'one gospel' which all will welcome. Indeed the Old Testament sometimes pictures the messianic era as opened out by a herald who brings the good news. The man who asked John the Baptist whether he were the Messiah or no would not have been fully content with the ambiguous answer that he was the herald of the good news. It was an answer capable of bearing more than one meaning. Christ accepted the Old Testament description of himself as the one who brings good news. He is anointed to bring the afflicted the evangelion of the kingdom: 'The Spirit of the Lord God is upon me because the Lord has anointed me to bring good tidings to the afflicted' (Is. 61.1), and he acknowledged this in his reply to the disciples of John the Baptist, using an old Testament quotation about the messianic gospel: 'the poor have the good news preached to them' (Lk. 7.22), and in his choosing this very passage from Isaiah to read in the synagogue at Nazareth as a description of himself: 'Today this scripture has been fulfilled in your hearing' (Lk. 4.21).

The coming of the gospel is the setting up of the kingdom. Mark speaks of both together: 'Jesus came into Galilee, preaching the gospel of God, and saying, "The time is fulfilled, and the kingdom of God is at hand; repent, and believe in the gospel"' (Mk 1.14), and this suggests that the beatitude: 'Blessed are you poor, for yours is the kingdom of God' (Lk. 6.20) means that those who hear the gospel preached, the poor of Isaiah, already possess the kingdom. The men who attend to the herald already in a real sense enjoy the victory.

A word is in place here, I think, about the position of the herald in the Near Eastern society of antiquity. We are accustomed to thinking of a tabard and trumpet person, a man of ceremonial parade, a mere functionary and at best a decorative one. This was not the ancient case at all. In Egypt, for example, the herald was the spokesman of the royal household to the people, and the spokesman of the people to the ruler. The inquiry into the violation of the royal tombs under Ramses IX was entrusted to three high-ranking officials of the Egyptian court: the vizier, the scribe and the herald. The peculiarly death-and-tomb dominated culture of the ancient Egyptians leaves no doubt at all but that this was an extremely responsible commission and in no sense dismissible as merely ceremonial. A similar importance evidently attached to the herald during the period of the Judah monarchy. King Hezechiah sent the chamberlain, the scribe and Yoah, the son of Asaph, the herald, to hear the envoy of the conquering Sennacherib. Evidently the herald was one of the most important members of the government. It is, therefore, as someone of great importance that we should think of the herald in the usage of the Old and New Testaments.

In the New Testament the Christian is often thought of as the herald of Christ. The disciples are sent out as heralds to announce the coming of Christ's kingdom and to proclaim the gospel, they are the harbingers of the kingdom envisaged by Isaiah: 'I give to Jerusalem a herald of good tidings' (41.27), they are to announce the victory of the Lord and the foundation of the new kingdom. In Isaiah the Messiah is preceded by the herald who proclaims his defeat of the power of evil by the force of arms, he is to bring an era, bountiful in prosperity; 'Get you up to a high mountain, O Zion, herald of good tidings; lift up your voice with strength, O Jerusalem, herald of good tidings' (40.9), and the same is true of Isaiah 41.27. A similar passage in Jeremiah, 'Cursed be the man who brought the news to my father, "A son is born to you"' (20.15), implies that evangelion was normally used only of a message which provoked applause and happiness. The same meaning is brought out in II Samuel (18.19–23). There was a battle in the forest of Ephraim and Joab, David's general, gained the victory and Absalom, the rebel son of the king, fled from the field. He was caught by the pursuers and Joab had him killed. Then Ahimaaz, the son of Zadok the priest, volunteered to bring the news to David, and Joab warned him that this was not a good plan because the king would be very angry at the news of the death of his favourite son. But Ahimaaz would not listen to the warning. He ran to the king's fort and the watchman on the tower cried to the king that Ahimaaz was coming, and David said, 'He is a good man and comes with good tidings'. After the battle the messenger brings good tidings, the evangelion.

Again in the famous passage of Isaiah 52.7 Yahweh is thought of as having achieved victory over Babylon and Isaiah pictures a messenger bringing the *evangelion* of the victory:

> How welcome is the runner
> coming over the hill-tops with news
> who announces, 'All is well!'
> who brings good news,
> who announces deliverance,
> who says to Zion,
> 'Your God reigns.'

Isaiah pictures the people of Jerusalem standing on the battlements waiting for the news of the battle and then it seems as if watchman and the ruined watch-towers shout for joy together.

This idea of God as victorious is linked up with the Lord God of Battles and the psalmist's pleasure at the discomfort of their enemies. *Dominus Deus Sabbaoth* that we sing in the Preface has nothing to do with the Sabbath, however much we may pacify its meaning.

It is obvious that in the sense of the good news Christ is the *evangelion*. There is no other news than Christ.

Later in Old Testament usage the *evangelion* became the proclamation of the good will of God in the liturgical assemblies:

> I have told the glad news of deliverance in the great congregation;
> Lo, I have not restrained my lips,
> as thou knowest, O Lord.
> I have not hid thy saving help within my heart,
> I have spoken of thy faithfulness and thy salvation;
> I have not concealed thy steadfast love and thy faithfulness
> from the great congregation (Ps. 40.9–10).

The passage about the messenger which ends with the cry 'Your God reigns' may well be itself a liturgical text. It is possible that it ought to be translated 'God has become King', but either way it would be a parallel passage to several psalm verses:

> Say among the nations: 'The Lord reigns!'   96.10
> The Lord reigns, let the earth rejoice   97.1
> The Lord reigns, let the peoples tremble   99.1

These may represent extracts from the autumnal liturgy of the enthronement festival of Yahweh. Engnell (BJRL 31, 1948) suggests that the 'Ebed Yahweh texts must . . . be characterized as a prophetic remodelling of a liturgical composition belonging to the Annual Festival'. Certainly there is plenty of evidence that the passage from

Isaiah describing the arrival of the royal herald proclaiming the reign of God was well known in Old Testament times—it is quoted in Nahum and is behind several New Testament passages, notably Acts 10.36 and Ephesians 6.15 and is actually quoted by Paul in Romans 10.15 as a description of the Christian evangelist: 'As it is written, "How beautiful are the feet of those who preach good news!" But they have not all heeded the gospel.'

The Old Testament references are always within the context of the cultic ceremonial. Thus Nahum 1.15 (2.1 in the Hebrew) quotes the passage immediately before the command to perform the liturgical rites: 'Behold, on the mountains the feet of him who brings good tidings, who proclaims peace! Keep your feasts, O Judah, fulfil your vows.' And the quotation in Romans is closely associated with Paul's concern that all men should learn to take their place in the liturgical shout of the Christian community and call 'upon the name of the Lord'. News must be announced before the liturgy can take place.

Evangelion, then, is used, in the Old and New Testaments, within contexts which include the arrival of the messenger with good news of God's victory. This is a good part, at least, of the meaning of the word in the first verse of Mark's gospel. Whether one accepts the 'Christus Victor' description that Aulen would give of this gospel or not, it is certainly the case that the opening words of Mark are to be interpreted as a shout of joy because 'the Lord reigns', and that this shout is related to the popular responses in the Christian eucharistic liturgy.

At the same time it would be well to take into account the Gentile culture and its use of *evangelion*. The first Christians were not, after all, Jews of the Jews, knowing nothing of the Graeco-Roman world. They were acquainted with the main features of Roman life. The understanding of the Gentiles of the word may well then be included in the overall Christian concept. The imperial cultus made use of *evangelion* in a way which may have led Mark and his fellow Christians to think of other strands of meaning than the Hebrew when they employed the word.

I have already remarked that Lucian and Appius employ *evangelion* for the good news that is brought by the messenger. It is apparent that just as in the society of Jeremiah the word was often used in connection with the birth of an heir to an Israelite family so in

21

Graeco-Roman society the word, while it could be used for all kinds of situations, especially those of civic celebration, was most often employed on the occasion of the birth of an heir. Theophrastus, in his character of the querulous man (XVII, 7), speaks of him as one who 'when they bring him good news that he has a son born to him' says mournfully and tetchily, 'I have lost half my fortune'. More particularly in the official and courtly circles of the imperial society the word was used for the birth of an heir to the emperor or the accession of a new ruler. It was accompanied by trumpets and purple on the Palatine and the imperial decrees which announced the good news to the provincial governors linked the *evangelion* with the cult of the divine emperor.

It would of course be rash to suggest that Christians of the first centuries would in general be so familiar with this usage that when they spoke of the good news of Jesus Christ they were deliberately opposing the pagan divinization of the ruler. Not many of the Christians would belong to the senatorial or wealthy classes and therefore would have little direct contact with the civic petitions and imperial decrees in which the word appeared. As Paul wrote to his Corinthian converts: 'consider your call, brethren; not many of you were wise according to worldly standards, not many were powerful, not many were of noble birth; but God chose what is foolish in the world to shame the wise, God chose what is weak in the world to shame the strong, God chose what is low and despised in the world' (I Cor. 1.26–8); and he suggests further that 'none of the rulers of this age understood' the gospel.

It would, however, be no less rash to suppose that some of the first Christians would have no knowledge of the imperial ceremonial and its language—Paul's words to the Corinthians acknowledge the presence of some noble and powerful men in the community. So it is not impossible that something of the imperial usage is contained in our Christian use of 'gospel'. I will take a few examples of the imperial *evangelion* and then attempt to show where I think the imperial influence may be descried.

The imperial decree for the province of Asia in the year 9 B.C. celebrating Augustus has this tribute: '(The birthday) of god was, for the world, the beginning (of) the good tidings, brought through his power.'

Similarly, but perhaps less appropriately, the taking of the *toga virilis* by Gaius in 5 B.C. was a time of *evangelion*, and Philo recounts the story of the obsequious ambassadors before Petronius who declared that the Jews had made much of Caligula's accession: 'the happy news proceeded onwards from our city where it had been greeted with joy'.

Again, in a papyrus of A.D. 54, Nero is announced as the hope of all men of good will: 'the Emperor of the world, long expected and hoped for, has been made manifest, and he is the good god of the world'. The proclamation of the good news of Augustus and the divine honours paid to Nero are connected. In the context of the emperor-cult *evangelion* meant the birth or accession of an heir to the divine throne of the world. This resonance would be heard by those Roman Christians who listened to Mark's proclamation of Christ.

The interchange of language here between imperial cult and Christian praise of Christ is not a unique example. The imperial cult titles were certainly appropriated by the Christians for use in their liturgy. Suetonius tells us that Domitian liked to be called '*Dominus et Deus*' which may well have given rise to the Christian acclamation 'My Lord and my God' which John records in his narrative of the resurrection appearances of Christ to his disciples, and which it seems likely was first used in a Christian liturgy. Again, the magistrate examining Polycarp inquired of the old bishop: 'What harm is there in saying "Caesar is Lord"?' It may be, as several writers have suggested, that '*Kurios Kaisar*' was a popular shout in the imperial cult. Certainly 'Jesus is Lord' was used in the earliest Christian worship as we see in I Corinthians: 'No one can say "Jesus is Lord" except by the Holy Spirit' (12.3), and again in Romans: 'You confess with your lips that "Jesus is Lord"' (10.9), and in Philippians Paul demands that every tongue confess 'Jesus Christ is Lord' (2.11).

The habitual use of the title 'Lord Jesus' led of course to the kind of accusation made against Paul and Silas at Thessalonica: 'they are acting against the decrees of Caesar, saying that there is another king, Jesus' (Acts 17.7).

These indications make it quite likely that Mark had the Gentile use of evangelion in mind when he employed the term at the beginning of his witness to Christ.

For the Gentiles the *evangelion* had to do with divinity and the good news of the birth of a son. For the Hebrews it was connected with the proclamation of God's victory. The Christians appear to have taken over both these meanings and to have seen in their combination a proclamation of Jesus as Son of God and Victor. They appear too to have employed the regal shout of the good news in their liturgy. The gospel led on to the proclamation of Christ in the liturgy, and the liturgy influenced the final form of the written witness to the gospel.

6. TRADITION

Since the New Testament is made up of writings composed at various places during the first hundred years of Christianity, and which despite their diversity have the common aim of putting across to others what Christ means, it is not surprising that one writer seems to have access to an element of the community tradition which was not available to the others, or that the same piece of traditional material appears in different contexts.

An example of the first of these is the saying recorded in Paul's preaching at Ephesus that Christ told his disciples that 'It is more blessed to give than to receive', which does not appear in the gospels and seems to have been preserved by only one community tradition. Of the use of a piece of traditional material in several contexts there are many examples: thus in the image of the Second Coming shared by Matthew and Paul, Matthew has: 'Watch, therefore, for you do not know on what day your Lord is coming. But know this, that if the householder had known in what part of the night the thief was coming, he would not have let his house be broken into' (24.42); and Paul has this version: 'You yourselves know well that the day of the Lord will come like a thief in the night' (I Thess. 5.2); again Matthew writes of the disciple: 'the labourer deserves his food' (10.10), which is reframed in I Corinthians as 'those who proclaim the gospel should live by the gospel' (9.14); and among the many similarities between Matthew's Sermon on the Mount and the Epistle of James, there is this command about swearing: 'Do not swear at all, either by heaven . . . or by earth . . . Let what you say be simply "Yes" or "No", anything more than this comes from evil' (Mt. 5.34–7); and 'Do not swear, either by heaven or by earth or with any other oath, but let your "yes" be "yes", and your "no" be "no" that you may not fall under condemnation' (Jas 5.12).

It is of little importance to decide temporal priorities between Matthew and the Epistles, for even if we managed, as we have not yet managed to do, to produce a chronological table of the New Testament writings relative to each other, we would not then have made a table of the traditions from which those writings derived. It may well be that a later writing used an earlier tradition than that of an earlier writing. We have simply to be content with the recognition of a community tradition from which these writings came. They belong to the community rather than to the individual responsible for the final writing out of the tradition. They belong to the community not simply because they were the result of the community meditation and proclamation of Christ but because they are designed to be read not by individuals but by the community met for the liturgical celebration of Christ. As Bishop Robinson has written:

> It may be said that the Epistles and the Apocalypse represent the contributions of the apostles and prophets respectively to the primitive liturgical gathering. If the New Testament Epistles are the apostolic liturgical sermons, the Apocalypse may well be a series of prophecies for the Christian assembly on the Lord's day.

The New Testament writers wrote in order that men may come to believe in Christ and to enter his kingdom through the liturgical celebration of his presence among them. This is made explicit in the opening of John's first epistle:

> That which was from the beginning, which we have heard, which we have seen with our eyes, which we have looked upon and touched with our hands, concerning the word of life—the life was made manifest, and we saw it, and testify to it, and proclaim to you the eternal life which was with the Father and was made manifest to us—that which we have seen and heard we proclaim also to you, so that you may have fellowship with us; and our fellowship is with the Father and with his Son Jesus Christ. And we are writing this that our joy may be complete (1.1–4).

The gospels and epistles are, therefore, not mere histories. They are preachments. Their purpose is to involve a man in the community of Christ. The fact of Christ is primary. This gives Christianity its historical reality, and a foundation for the claim to work in the real world of 'telegrams and anger'. Without the person of Jesus there is no content for Christianity. As Karl Adam wrote over a decade ago:

> All other religions that have demonstrably been founded by an historical personality do not regard their founder as the content, the object of their faith, but simply as its mediator. The faith itself does not coincide with the figure of the founder, but can be presented independently of this figure and separated entirely from him. It is so in Buddhism, and in Islam. In all these religions, the founder is not at the centre but on the periphery of the religious interest. At the centre is his doctrine.

Other religions are concerned with an ethic and a doctrine. Christianity is about a person. Christianity is Christ. Hence the biographical structure at the centre of the tradition. The gospel which is Christ is presented in biographical terms in the tradition. We are a people centred on a person, holding a doctrine of a person, believing that certain events happened about this person in our history.

At the same time, however, the Christ of Faith, though certainly the 'historical Jesus', is not seen in quite the same manner by modern Christians or any of those who even in the first community professed belief in Christ, as he was seen by his contemporaries in Galilee, Judaea and Jerusalem. He is seen now through faith. We do not simply believe that Jesus died, we believe in his resurrection. That is why, perhaps, Professor C. K. Barrett can describe the Epistle to the Romans as 'the plainest gospel of all'. The tradition is not simply biographical, it is also, and primarily, about the life of the Spirit of Jesus in his community.

The Community Life which derived from the experience of Christ initially was dominated by three influences: liturgy, history and Scripture. Of these the most immediate was liturgy since it was performed by the Christians themselves, the most necessary was history, since liturgy would have been meaningless without the event of Christ, and the most explanatory of what they were doing was Scripture.

The writers present their material within an already formed tradition of interpretation, they write as missionaries for that interpretation: 'These things are written that you may believe that Jesus is the Christ, the Son of God, and that believing you may have life in his name' (Jn 20.31). The New Testament writers had to order the already existing tradition into a pattern which would make it possible for the pagan to understand the tradition, and which would challenge the Christian to further the work of the Lord. The writers of the gospels and epistles were creative editors of the community tradition. Of course there are varying degrees of community influence at work in the various writings. The epistles of Paul, for example, are mainly the product of one man's interpretation of Christ as he himself had found him in the community. These epistles are early works before the community tradition was fully formed. So too, probably, is the first version of the gospel of John with its intensely personal sacramental shape for the account of Christ, and its evidence of fresh knowledge of the Palestine of Christ's time.

The publication of the Qumran texts has made it evident that the fourth gospel has far more literary affinities with the writings of the Dead Sea sect than have the synoptic gospels. This can only be adequately accounted for by some contact before the destruction of the settlement which took place in A.D. 68. John's gospel, therefore, at least in its first version, must have been composed in a Palestinian community of the primitive Church. To account for those elements in John's gospel which appear to demand a later date Père Boismard suggested, in *Revue Biblique*, April 1962, that it might well be that St Luke edited the final version of the fourth gospel, and he analysed several passages which lent support to this thesis. It is not, of course, yet possible to determine whether the personalist and sacramental frame of the fourth gospel is to be regarded as primitive or whether this is the form worked out by the last editor. With regard to the synoptic gospels a similar difficulty occurs. Rawlinson, in the Introduction to his commentary on Mark, found it impossible to suppose that there existed in the pre-Marcan community 'anything like a chronological outline of our Lord's Ministry, or an itinerary of his movements', and concluded that 'it is just the framework and the arrangement of the materials of our gospels which ought to be set down to the account of the Evangelist'. I would think, however, that Dibelius was right to assert the existence of a determined framework of Christian apologetic in a biographical form early in the history of the community.

The community tradition was obviously well formed when the later synoptic gospels were composed within the accepted biographical frame. Of these the Biblical Commission's Instruction 'Concerning the historical truth of the Gospels' said in 1964, the glorious events of Christ were 'committed to writing by the sacred authors in four Gospels for the benefit of the churches, with a method suited to the peculiar purpose which each set for himself. From the many things handed down they selected some things, reduced others to a synthesis, others they made plain as they kept in mind the situation of the churches'.

The whole emphasis in this statement is rightly placed on the primary nature of the community tradition and of the demands which the community situation made on the writers of the New Testament books.

If a piece of writing did not express the tradition of the community then it would not survive in the community. The writings we possess are survivors from a large body of such writings, they have been subjected to the community test and have been found by the community to express the tradition. It may even be that the most part of this body of writings has been lost. There is certainly evidence for the disappearance of some of Paul's writings. From internal evidence we can judge that he wrote more than two letters to the Corinthian community. These letters are lost to us because the community did not think them necessary for the preservation of the tradition of Christ. The letters which survive do so because, taken together, they express the traditional faith of the Christian community. The loss of the others may be regretted on devotional or antiquarian grounds, but we must not lament them as if they contained some truth of God properly belonging to the community. It is precisely because they were not necessary for the preservation and promulgation of the tradition that they were not preserved themselves. If we now found a lost Corinthian epistle it would be an interesting relic, and of rather more interest than the cloak Paul left at Troas, but it would not reveal to us a truth necessary for salvation, it would not be a missing part of the inviolate tradition.

It is to be remarked that in the passages from the various community traditions cited at the beginning of this section what was common to all the pericopes was a deriving of their content from the life and preaching of Christ. When Matthew and James argue that swearing by all kinds of sacred things is wrong they are not representing themselves as the authors of an ethic, they are claiming that the wrong was pointed out by Christ. This is the case both in the form of direct quotation used in the Sermon on the Mount tradition, and in the commandment form used in the epistle of James. The Lord is behind both pronouncements. It is noticeable in the James quotation that it follows hard upon a reference to the story of Job's endurance being 'the fulfilment of the Lord'. Christ is at the centre of all the doctrine propounded in the epistle. Christ is himself the tradition.

In accepting the tradition, therefore, we are accepting Christ, and in this acceptance we are following upon the example of the first community. Tradition is not simply the stories about Christ; it is the way in which we meet Christ himself. The gospels are not historical records of what has happened, not this alone certainly, not this chiefly certainly. They are the meeting places of the Christian with Christ. It is for this reason that the Christian community has always and everywhere been ready to nominate these writings as the Word of God, a title belonging properly and only to Christ.

Just as there is only one Gospel which is Christ, so the several gospels are Christ, the Word. If we appreciate this we can understand why it is that the Book of the Gospels is enthroned at the meeting of a General Council: Christ in his community.

Since the tradition is not simply about the Lord, but 'from the Lord' and indeed is the Lord, it is not the result of creative invention in the community. It would have been unthinkable for the members who gathered in the eucharistic community to have so disregarded the sacred character of their reality as to invent stories for the tradition. The emphasis must have been on the eyewitness, as in the primitive credal statement in I Corinthians: 'he appeared to Cephas, then to the twelve, then he appeared to more than five hundred brethren at once' (15.5–6); or the preface to Luke's gospel, in which the evangelist says he has put together the witness he could gather from 'those who from the beginning were eyewitnesses'. We can see this demand for eyewitness qualifications for the proclamation of Christ in the account of the primitive community before Pentecost. For the election of an apostle to take the place of Judas Peter says to the community: 'One of the men who have accompanied us during all the time that the Lord Jesus went in and out among us, beginning from the baptism of John until the day when he was taken up from us—one of these men must become with us a witness to his resurrection' (Acts 1.21–2).

The necessary condition for the apostleship is that the man shall have been present at the events to which he is to witness. The tradition is an eyewitness tradition. Of course no one witness would have been present at every event of Jesus, no one man is the custodian

29

of the tradition. The tradition is conveyed in the community witness. This is evident, again, from the preface to Luke's gospel; the writer is bringing together into one witness the several testimonies of witnesses. It is not, therefore, conceivable that within such a community the tradition could be made up of individual inventions.

It may well be that during the course of this exploration of the New Testament writings it seems that there is an undue emphasis on the human characteristics of the writings; this is to a great extent inevitable. In speaking of the tradition we have either to talk in terms of the community being given a gift by the Lord, or of the community actualizing this gift, and to do the first without the second would cause as many difficulties as the reverse; witness the confusion that is generated by Paul's references to the 'tradition' he has 'received from the Lord' about which controversy rages as to whether he means that there was some direct revelation from Christ or whether he is thinking of the tradition as mediated by the community. Paul would not regard these as alternative ways of thinking. To speak of the way in which the community formulated the tradition is to speak of the way that the tradition is from God.

In the community the living tradition of Christ is newly realized each time a man comes to accept the Baptism of the Lord, each time the community celebrates the event of Christ at the reading of the written witness, each time the community gathers to celebrate the presence of the living Christ in the Eucharist. In these, and so many other circumstances, the Spirit enlivens and the tradition is handed down to the followers. This is what the first community understood by the 'apostolic succession' in the Church.

It becomes quickly evident in any reading of the New Testament writings that behind these epistles and gospels there is a definite body of witness, a well-defined entity which can be received and handed on, a tradition.

In the Pauline epistles there are many instances of the apostle's determination to hand on faithfully the community truth; to the Thessalonians he writes: 'stand firm and hold to the traditions which you were taught by us, either by word of mouth or by letter' (II Thess. 2.15); they are to avoid anyone who is living in a way 'not in accord with the tradition you received from us' (II Thess. 3.6); he recommends the Corinthians because they 'maintain the traditions

30

even as I have delivered them to you' (I Cor. 11.2), and he thinks of this as the only way of leading a Christian life in the community: 'I delivered to you as of first importance what I also received' (I Cor. 15.3).

Similar instances of Paul's concern for the handing on of 'the tradition' occur in his letters to the Galatians, Colossians and Philippians. In the writings of Paul's friend and disciple, Luke, an equal emphasis on the authority of tradition has already been noted. His gospel, he says, is compiled from an ordering of the accounts of Jesus' actions 'just as they were delivered to us by those who from the beginning were eyewitnesses and ministers of the word' (1.2).

The tradition is preserved until our time, it is handed down to us. We who now belong to the traditional community may well therefore expect to understand our heritage. And often enough we are disappointed. If the New Testament writers were representatives of a culture quite other than our own then we should be ready to pay careful attention to the sources of that culture and make ourselves deliberately aware of the thought-patterns behind its representative writings. But we do not, most of us, approach the New Testament as if it were the product of an alien people. We approach it as if it were a product of our own culture simply because we are the rightful inheritors through baptism of the scriptural tradition. It is as if a man were to be convinced that he knew how to sail the *Cutty Sark* simply because he had been a purser on a liner and had saved enough to buy a sailing vessel. Our faith is the faith of the first community. We therefore assume that we are immediately able to appreciate the methods adopted by the first community to put our faith across. It is because this is a half-truth, because we can very well appreciate a great deal of the gospel witness, that catastrophes occur. The history of fundamentalist exegesis and theology is the history of man's refusal to admit that those who share the same faith may find quite different ways of expressing it.

We have to remember that though we come to the same Eucharist we come to make our thanksgiving for vastly different worlds than those of the first community, and though we come to the same Lord we are vastly different people.

The paradox remains that if we would understand ourselves we must make the effort to understand the first community. We can only come to a knowledge of ourselves as present members of the community which is ever new, if we accept our dependence and continuity from the community of the past.

It is the intention of this book to present some ways into the first community so that a better understanding of the present community may come about. I have set out three aspects of the first community, three which seem to me the most important for our present understanding: the Old Testament assumptions which they made when speaking of the Lord, the Resurrection pattern of their view of human life in the community, and the way in which they expressed this life in the sacramental liturgy of the community. A study of these three aspects of the community in which we now live, however inadequate, cannot but be useful in our effort to make ourselves in the world today a community witness.

II

The Christian Use of the Old Testament

COLERIDGE in *Biographia Literaria*, at the end of chapter XIII says of the poet's use of past experience: '[The secondary Imagination] dissolves, diffuses, dissipates, in order to re-create; or where this process is rendered impossible, yet still at all events it struggles to idealize and to unify. It is essentially *vital* even as all objects (*as* objects) are essentially fixed and dead.' There is something here which corresponds to Christ's use of the Old Testament. The gospels present us with a re-vitalization of the old images and concepts so that their new meaning is loyal to the past experience but at the same time relevant to the present.

It was, of course, to be expected that the old Scriptures which had conveyed the word of God to men should be a large influence on the content and structure of the new words of revelation. If the Christians had been early tempted to any form of selective Marcionism they would have remembered that it was through 'all the scriptures' that Christ had presented himself on the Emmaus road.

The very mission of the Church is set in an Old Testament context in the last section of Luke's gospel:

'These are my words which I spoke to you, while I was still with you, that everything written about me in the law of Moses and the prophets and the psalms must be fulfilled.'

Then he opened their minds to understand the scriptures and said to them: 'Thus it is written, that the Christ should suffer and on the third day rise from the dead, and that repentance and forgiveness of sins should be preached in his name to all nations, beginning from Jerusalem' (24.44–7).

33

This goes further than the Emmaus passage since it suggests that Christians can only understand themselves and their business in the world through the revelation in the Old Testament. The preaching of the gospel and the forgiveness of sins are said to be fulfilments of the earlier revelation, just as much as the resurrection of the Lord.

It is noticeable that at the beginning of Romans, Paul describes the 'gospel' that he is to preach in Old Testament terms, for him there is no gospel other than the fulfilment of the Old Testament promise. We do not begin without a heritage and a design, we are not starting again but moving forward through the revealed plan of God. To preach this one truth he was called: 'Paul, a servant of Jesus Christ, called to be an apostle, set apart for the gospel of God which he promised beforehand through his prophets in the holy scriptures, the gospel concerning his Son, who was descended from David according to the flesh' (Rom. 1.1–3), and he leads through a catena of Old Testament passages showing how the Gentiles have inherited the promise that the Jews rejected, until at the end he says that while the truth of God was 'kept secret for long ages' from the Gentiles, now it is revealed 'through writings of the prophets' and 'is made known to all nations'.

His defence at the trial before Festus and Agrippa is couched in the same terms. The gospel is understood in just the way Luke understands it in the Emmaus narrative: 'I stand here testifying both to small and great, saying nothing but what the prophets and Moses said would come to pass: that the Christ must suffer, and that, by being the first to rise from the dead, he would proclaim light both to the people and to the Gentiles' (Acts 26.22–3). Indeed he goes further in Galatians 3.8 when he speaks of the coming of the Gentiles to faith as the fulfilment of God's promise to Abraham that he would be the cause of blessing to all men. He says that God revealed the gospel to Abraham: 'It is men of faith who are the sons of Abraham. And the scripture, foreseeing that God would justify the Gentiles by faith, preached the gospel beforehand to Abraham, saying, "In you shall all the nations be blessed". So then, those who are men of faith are blessed with Abraham who had faith' (3.7–9).

Similarly I Peter opens with a description of the Old Testament as a Christocentric work written for the Christian community: 'Salvation was the aim and quest of the prophets, and the grace of which they prophesied has been reserved for you. The Spirit of Christ was in them, making known to them the sufferings which Christ's cause brings with it, and the glory that crowns them; when was it to be, and how was the time of it to be recognized? It was revealed to them that their errand was not to their own age, it was to you' (1.10–12), and the Gospel of Thomas (c. A.D. 140) Logion 52 has: 'His disciples said to him: Twenty-four prophets spoke in Israel and they all spoke in thee.'

We have a pictorial representation of the Christian realization that it is only through the Old Testament writings that Christ can be properly seen in the narrative of the transfiguration. The disciples for a moment see Christ as he always is, and they see at the same time that Moses and Elijah are close to him and talking to him: 'He was transfigured before them, and his face shone like the sun, and his garments become white as light. And behold, there appeared to them Moses and Elijah, talking with him' (Mt. 17.2–3). The Old Testament figures are guides to the presence of Christ. They speak of him. The description of the transfiguration in II Peter, whether it is by the apostle or not does not affect this point since it is the interpretation not the establishing of the historicity of the event which I am discussing, makes the point more emphatically. The author is vitally concerned that the two prime sources of assurance, Old Testament witness and sensory perception, should be recognized as testifying to the reality of the transfiguration vision: 'We did not follow cleverly devised myths when we made known to you the power and coming of our Lord Jesus Christ, but we were eyewitnesses of his majesty' (1.16). The senses assure us of the reality of the event: 'We heard this voice borne from heaven' (1.18), and the Old Testament gives us the meaning of the event which makes it credible: 'We have the prophetic word made more sure . . . no prophecy of scripture is a matter of one's own interpretation, because no prophecy ever came by the impulse of man, but man moved by the Holy Spirit spoke from God' (1.19–21).

The authority of the prophetic interpretation of Christ is the authority of God. The Old Testament witness is a divine witness to Christ. We see in the working out of the history of Israel's response to God the history of our salvation. It is as a record of the saving history of God that many passages of the New Testament writings treat of the Old Testament.

1. SAVING HISTORY

Probably the most obvious use of the Old Testament history as a prelude to the work of Christ occurs in the opening chapters of the gospels of Matthew and Luke where the genealogies are given which associate the Christ with his Jewish and Gentile ancestors. These passages have often been a difficulty for readers in the recent past since it is evident that they are not compatible with one another in the way that the family-tree produced at one time by an official of Somerset House and that produced at another time by another official would be compatible and indeed probably identical so far as they covered the same period. But once it is realized that these genealogies have little in common with the literary manners of Somerset House and are really missionary elements of the gospel then the way is clearer for the proper understanding of what is being done in these passages.

The genealogies seem to be deliberately incomplete and to have been set down with slight concern for the niceties of academic history. They preach the message of the gospel, and each preaches its own message. Hence they do not agree in all sections. Professor David Stanley, writing in *Theological Studies*, 1959, describes the purpose of Luke's genealogy in these terms:

> The theological significance of the whole structure [is this]: Jesus who is 'of God' in a way infinitely superior to Adam, is the New Adam whose redemptive act far surpasses in its universality Adam's sinful act and its effect upon the entire human race. By his careful use of the structure of each man being 'of the next' in the genealogy Luke makes it possible to show how Christ is of God and Adam is of God. He is performing the same theological act as is Mark in his account of the temptations and Paul in the section on Christ and Adam in the letter to the Romans.

Of Matthew's intention in this genealogical section of his gospel, Stanley writes:

> The chief purpose of the Matthean genealogy is to show the link between Jesus and the salvation-history of His People. It descends from Abraham, and employs the biblical term 'generated'. Matthew can thus state that Jesus is that 'seed of Abraham' who inherits the divine promise made to that patriarch. He is, moreover, that member of the Davidic dynasty in whom the promise made to David is realized. The extraordinary inclusion of four women in this family tree (Thamar,

Rahab, Ruth and Bethsabee, all probably of non-Jewish origin) reveals Matthew's interest in the salvation of the Gentiles.

If Luke's genealogy can be related to the gospel message of Paul's letter to the Romans, then on Stanley's thesis, which seems fully in accord with the text, Matthew's genealogy can be related to Paul's letter to the Galatians: 'The promises you know of were made to Abraham and his offspring; it does not, by the way, say: To thy descendants, as if it meant a number of people; it says: To thy offspring, in the singular, meaning Christ' (3.16).

The function of the genealogies is therefore exactly the same as the function of all parts of the gospel narratives and of the New Testament writings as a whole. That men should come to know the truth of Christ and to believe in him. The method of the genealogies is exactly the same as the method of many passages in the gospels and epistles. To take as a guide the revelation of the Old Testament and to see Christ as the sum and pinnacle of that revelation. That is, the genealogies are summaries of the salvation history of Israel, and like that history they lead straight to Jesus.

That the notion of salvation history was part of the primitive Christian catechesis is not open to doubt. We can see from those first sermons recorded in Acts how dominant was this notion. The event of Christ is presented as the last of a long-planned series within the design of God. Thus Peter says to the Jews on the first day of Pentecost: 'This man you have put to death; by God's fixed design and foreknowledge, he was betrayed to you' (Acts 2.23). The pointing finger of the Old Testament indicates the death of Jesus as its end, the triumph of the resurrection sets in motion a new era in the saving design of God. Always the pattern is within the intention of God. Always Christ is the one to whom all the rest points and from whom all the rest takes meaning.

This short example in the Pentecost speech of Peter is elaborated in the speech of Stephen before the Council. In this great apology for Jewish Christianity Stephen passes in review the whole history of the working out of God's covenant with Israel:

When the God of glory appeared to our father Abraham, it was while he was still in Mesopotamia, before he took up his dwelling in Charan. . . .

Then he made a covenant with Abraham, the covenant that ordained circumcision.

So it was that he became the father of Isaac . . .
and Isaac of Jacob,
and Jacob of the twelve patriarchs.
The patriarchs, out of jealousy, sold Joseph as a slave, to be taken to Egypt.
[The sojourn in Egypt is dealt with at some length and then Stephen moves to the Exodus.]
Moses led them out, performing wonders and signs in Egypt, and at the Red Sea, and in the wilderness, over a space of forty years.
[The Exodus occupies many more verses and in this telling the emphasis is on the refusal of the Israelites to serve God.]
God dispossessed the Gentiles. . . .
So it was until the time of David. . . .
Solomon built the house for [God]
There was not one of the prophets they did not persecute;
it was death to foretell the coming of that just man, whom you in these times have betrayed and murdered (Acts 7.2–52).

The patriarchs, the kings and the prophets all lead up to the Christ, who is then described in terms of the vision of the book of Daniel, which is included in the final section of the Old Testament among the Jews, the Writings. Salvation is set out in history and leads to Jesus. Therefore Stephen is stoned to death.

Saul was one of those who consented to the death of Stephen. That is, Saul was one of those who recognized the kind of argument that Stephen was advancing and who saw its point. Later Paul was to summarize this concept of salvation history in I Corinthians: 'Christ died for our sins according to the scriptures; he was raised on the third day according to the scriptures' (15.3–4). He is not referring to any particular texts here, simply to the total witness of the Old Testament to the fact of Jesus as the climax of the scriptural testimony.

A suggestion by Plooj in his *Studies in the Testimony Book*, that Paul is here thinking of a collection of texts prepared for Christians who are going to take part in apologetic dialogues with Jews leads us into a discussion of a further possibility in the matter of New Testament citations of Old Testament texts.

2. TESTIMONIES

There are some signs in the New Testament texts of the early existence of a catena of Old Testament passages which might be employed by Christian apologists when confronted with Jewish opponents. A long time ago Rendel Harris suggested that there was from almost the first a catena of short passages for this purpose. This view has suffered from severe criticism by Professor Dodd who is content to suggest that the Old Testament quotations in the New Testament derive from certain limited areas of the texts and that the quotations are generally not to be taken as proofs in themselves but as reminders to a reader or hearer of the whole context from which they have been taken.

At any rate some explanation of the quotation pattern along these lines is necessary to make sense of the evangelists' use of the Old Testament, and certainly obviously necessary in connection with an exegesis of the Pauline use of the Old Testament. These writers, as Barnabas Lindars remarks in *New Testament Apologetic*, inherit the formula-quotations 'without being aware of the issues which underlie the selection of them and are responsible for their text forms'.

Rendel Harris worked from such examples of pattern as the way in which I Peter 2 and Romans 9 use the same texts to speak of Christ as the Stone laid in Zion and the stumbling-block for the Jews, or the way in which Mark wrongly attributes a Malachi quotation to Isaiah, a mistake due to looking at a Testimony book with a group of texts for the same point. If we find other explanations for this kind of thing we may yet acknowledge the workings of this catechetical instrument in the example given by a comparison of the use of Psalm 16.8–11 in Acts 2.25 and 13.33 where Peter and Paul speak of the same verses with what is certainly a striking similarity.

In Acts 2 Peter is addressing the first crowd at Jerusalem on the day of Pentecost:

> God raised him up, having loosed the pangs of death, because it was not possible for him to be held by it. For David says concerning him:
> 'I saw the Lord always before me,
> for he is at my right hand that I may not be shaken;
> therefore my heart was glad, and my tongue rejoiced;
> moreover my flesh will dwell in hope.
> For thou wilt not abandon my soul to Hades,
> nor let thy Holy One see corruption.
> Thou hast made known to me the ways of life;
> thou wilt make me full of gladness with thy presence' (24–8).

Peter shows that it cannot have been of David that the psalmist spoke because everyone knows that David is dead and buried, so it must be that 'he foresaw and spoke of the resurrection of the Christ, that he was not abandoned to Hades, nor did his flesh see corruption. This Jesus God raised up, and of that we are all witnesses' (2.31–2). David is entombed, we have his tomb, Christ is risen, we are witnesses to this, therefore, it is of Christ that David speaks, thus runs the argument.

In Acts 13 Paul quotes the same passage of the Psalm in the synagogue at Antioch of Pisidia, and comments: 'For David, after he had served the counsel of God in his own generation, fell asleep, and was laid with his fathers, and saw corruption; but he whom God raised up saw no corruption'. The commentary is almost exactly that of Peter and shows that at least they were using the same tradition of exegesis and catechesis. Or at least that Luke was familiar with this text-formula and thought it not incongruous that two Christian apologists should use it. Either way we have here a witness to the frequent use of this text-formula in the community within which Luke wrote his account.

A similar example of what appears to be a text-formula of Old Testament passages is to be found at the end of Acts; in chapter 28 Paul cites Isaiah 6:

> Go to this people, and say,
> You shall indeed hear but never understand,
> and you shall indeed see but never perceive.
> For this people's heart has grown dull,
> and their ears are heavy of hearing,
> and their eyes they have closed;
> lest they should perceive with their eyes
> and hear with their ears,
> and understand with their heart,
> and turn for me to heal them (26–7).

Paul maintains that this passage fits perfectly the Jews resident in Rome who will not believe his gospel: 'the Holy Spirit was right in saying to your fathers through the prophets' that you would not hear and therefore 'this salvation of God has been sent to the Gentiles; they will listen'.

Paul had already used this passage from Isaiah when speaking of the refusal of the Jews to accept Christ in Romans 11. He quotes the Isaiah passage and then speaks there of Israel failing 'to obtain

what it sought' and through the sin of the Jews 'salvation has come
to the Gentiles' and he has warned the Gentiles that they are not to
boast of this: 'Lest you be wise in your own conceits, I want you to
understand this mystery, brethren: a hardening has come upon part
of Israel, until the full number of the Gentiles come in, and so all
Israel will be saved' (11.25–6).

The passage too was well known to the evangelists. It is used by
Matthew, Mark and Luke as a preface to the explanation of the
parable of the sower when many of his hearers did not understand
Jesus' intention behind the parable, and it is used of the Jews by
John when he speaks of their witnessing signs but yet did not believe
in Jesus. So that Luke in Acts, Paul in Romans and John in his
gospel certainly use the text with the same meaning and intention:
the Gentiles will inherit the kingdom because the Jews have rejected
Christ. It is noticeable, for instance, that the passage occurs in John
immediately after the incident of the Greek strangers at the Jewish
feast who come to Philip and say, 'Sir, we wish to see Jesus', and
which is the setting of Jesus' saying: 'While you have the light,
believe in the light, that you may become sons of light' (Jn 12.36). So
that the context is of Gentiles coming in order to see and believe
while the Jews walk away from him 'for they loved the praise of
men more than the praise of God'. And in another Marcan passage
in which the passage is cited our Lord is questioning the disciples,
'do you not yet perceive?' He means that they should have faith in
him after the miracles he has done, 'are your hearts hardened?
Having eyes do you not see, having ears do you not hear?' Passages
of this kind can be used in two ways. Either the apologetic is
directed against the Jews, as in this case, or the Old Testament is
employed precisely because this is the way to attract Jews, in which
case the notion of fulfilment predominates. It would be wrong
therefore to assume, as some earlier commentators have done, that
the Testimonies (if they did exist) or the text-formulae were uniformly
anti-Judaic. E. Earle Ellis in *St Paul's Use of the Old Testament*
has shown how positive and creative is Pauline usage in this matter
and that preaching against Jewish objectors was only one of the uses
of the text-formulae.

Another Old Testament grouping which seems to have been
included in the Christian anti-Judaic apologetic is the setting of
passages from Psalms 110 and 8 together:

The Lord says to my Lord,
'Sit at my right hand, till I make your enemies your footstool,'
and:

What is man that thou art mindful of him,
and the son of man that thou dost care for him?
Yet thou hast made him little less than God
and dost crown him with glory and honour.
Thou hast given him dominion over the works of thy hands;
thou hast put all things under his feet.

Obviously the first quotation was employed by the early Christians because it had been so effective as a haggadah question in Mark 12 when Christ asked the Jews to explain how David could be the ancestor of the Messiah and yet be prepared to call the Messiah 'Lord'. But it does appear that there was early in the history of the apologetic of the Church a coupling of these passages. They occur together, and always with Psalm 110 before Psalm 8, in several New Testament writings: I Corinthians 15.25ff; Ephesians 1.20ff; Hebrews 1.13 and 2.6 Always the context is one of proclaiming the lordship and dominion of Christ.

In the Hebrews epistle the passage occurs in a long list of Old Testament quotations. It may not be insignificant that two other of these passages, Psalm 2.7 and II Samuel 7.14, occur with the introduction 'to whom has he said?' in a catena of passages in a work ascribed to Gregory of Nyssa, *Testimonia adversus Judaeos*, I. Rendel Harris, of course, thought it very significant for an explanation of the New Testament instrument but Lindars is quite sure that such late catenae are the first examples of such catenae. It may be, as Professor Birger Gerhardsson says in *Memory and Manuscript*, that the testimonies were midrashic groupings of Jesus-tradition based on association with particular Old Testament texts.

Lest it should be thought that Rendel Harris is entirely discredited it ought to be pointed out that he receives support from Pierre Prigent in *Les Testimonia dans le christianisme primitif*, which is a study of the source materials of the Epistle of Barnabas.

3. THE STRUCTURE OF APOLOGETIC

Whatever our opinion of the existence of the Testimony Books there does seem to be enough evidence to be sure of a general pattern of construction in the early catechesis. The early speeches in Acts have a fourfold framework:

(a) a scriptural reference out of which the catechesis is drawn;
(b) the act of Christ which demands belief as its response;
(c) the acceptance of baptism;
(d) the gift of the Spirit.

Illustration enough of the general line of things will perhaps be afforded by two examples: Peter's first speech in chapter 2 and the encounter of Philip the Deacon and the Ethiopian in chapter 8.

(a) Peter's speech begins with a long quotation from the prophet Joel about the last days and the pouring out of the Spirit;
(b) Peter then speaks of the acts of Christ 'a man attested to you by God with mighty works and wonders and signs';
(c) and after repeating the pattern of (a) and (b) in 2.25–9; 31–3, Peter demands that the people be baptized 'for the forgiveness of sins';
(d) 'and you shall receive the gift of the Holy Spirit'.

The incident of the Eunuch works in just the same pattern:

(a) The Ethiopian is reading a passage from Isaiah in his chariot: 'As a sheep led to the slaughter or a lamb before its shearer is dumb so he opens not his mouth';
(b) the text is explained to him in terms of Christ's work: 'then Philip opened his mouth and beginning with this scripture he told him the good news of Jesus', and the Eunuch wants to be baptized: because he believes 'that Jesus Christ is the Son of God'.
(c) 'See here is water! What is to prevent my being baptized?';
(d) and the Spirit manifests himself in two ways. He snatches up Philip so that he is not heard of until he has preached the gospel in Caesarea and begot four daughters. The Eunuch too receives the gift of the Spirit. He 'went on his way rejoicing'. Western manuscripts have a rearrangement of the text so that the Spirit comes on the Eunuch and an angel catches up the Deacon but there is no need to accept this doubtful reading in order to show the presence of the Spirit with the Eunuch. 'Joy' is the gift of the Spirit in several New Testament passages —Acts 13.52, and I Thess. 1.6 and Romans 14.7 amongst

43

many others—and the narrative as we now have it is simply indicating his presence with the Ethiopian. Professor Lampe, who notices this view in his book *The Seal of the Spirit*, discards it in the end: 'I am inclined to think that Luke has an insufficient appreciation of the Spirit as the inner principle of the ordinary believer's life in Christ to make him interested in whether or not the average convert partakes of it.' At any rate it is certainly the case, as Lampe himself suggests, that the baptism of the Ethiopian is seen as in the pattern of Christ's own baptism when the Spirit is described as descending as the Ethiopian and Philip come out of the water.

Dibelius, in his *Formgeschichte des Evangeliums*, noticed certain other passages in Acts which seem to be outlines of the apostolic preaching. It would seem from these that not only were certain passages from the Old Testament collected together as catechetical instruction-helps, and used within a set framework of convert classes, but the whole gospel was written within a frame already determined by the experience of the community. Further, it is evident that the Old Testament exposition was thought to be an integral part of this apologetic pattern.

Dibelius suggested that several editions of the framework existed simultaneously, and thought that I Corinthians 11 and 15 employed fragments of such outlines, while fuller ones were to be found in Acts 10 and 13. I would like to treat the Corinthian material in a different section, since I think that these are primarily not catechetical in a direct sense, but liturgical fragments, but certainly I would agree that the Acts sections have every indication of having been agreed synopses of the Christian historical faith.

An indication that the passages in Acts that Dibelius refers to are among the most primitive in the book is to be found in their vocabulary and grammatical structure. They savour very much of semitisms and these are indications of an Aramaic original. This would suggest that there is something in these passages which derives from the first preaching of the apostles. Professor Bruce says of the catechetical outline in Acts 10: 'The Greek is certainly not Luke's free composition; if it were it would be much clearer' and 'the whole passage can be literally translated into grammatical and intelligible Aramaic'. Dr Wilcox in his thorough study of the language of Acts judged that 10.38 was a very odd Greek construction but 'very natural in the Semitic languages' and of 13.28b he wrote, 'it is indefensible as Greek', and that explanations of the text have to deal with peculiarities of idiom which are probably to be explained on the basis of 'original Semitic tradition, probably Aramaic here'. Wilcox is, however, decidedly cautious about suggesting Semitic originals for the speeches and it is significant that while rejecting much that has been claimed in them for semitisms, he elects a short list of 'stronger' examples which includes both 10.38 and three verses in the Pauline speech in 13. And while he is doubtful if Luke himself converted the speeches into Greek he is sure enough to say that 'In so far as appeal to Aramaic may be suggested anywhere it would seem to be most reasonable in the speeches in question, especially that of Paul at Pisidian Antioch.'

Similarly Professor Black's investigation of the *casus pendens* in Acts in his *Aramaic approach to the Gospel and Acts* led him to suppose that seven passages in the book exhibited signs of an Aramaic original, and his few examples included the two passages I am considering here. So linguistic evidence seems to show that these are very early indeed.

What is most striking, perhaps, in Wilcox's book in relation to the material I am discussing is the discovery that whereas there may be doubts about Luke's use of original Aramaic sources for the body of his work, and even for the speeches of Stephen, Peter and Paul, it does seem to be established that Luke did not use the LXX when he was reporting the Old Testament material in these speeches but, as Wilcox says, 'some kind of fixed, possibly written, Greek source for the divergent quotational material'. The material is divergent, of course, from the received text of the LXX which would be in general use among the Christians at the time that Luke was writing and which he would normally be using for his Old Testament quotations. Wilcox goes further and says that this material of the 'Old Testament quotational block' has 'ties with an earlier period in the Church's history'.

What kind of ties? How far back in the history of the Church's missionary activity do these quotations take us? It may be that these Old Testament citations, differing from any extant text yet coherent in themselves and having exactly the same form whenever they appear (for example, the text of Deuteronomy 18.15–18 in Acts

7.37 and 3.22) thus suggesting a set Greek source, indicate an apostolic origin to the speeches as we now have them. Wilcox at the end of his volume commits himself thus far, and it would be rash to go further however much enthusiasm might entice:

> These aberrant Old Testament quotations and allusions may be ultimately traceable to some tradition or traditions of the words of the Apostles, or perhaps even of Paul. The fact that quotations of this type are found not only in what purports to be a formal speech of Paul (13.22) but also in the tradition of what he said to Bar-Jesus at Paphos (13.11) as well as in the letter to the Ephesians (4.8) may well suggest that Luke had some record of what Paul said, or used to say.

It may be that the early Christians used a text similar to that followed by the Dead Sea Sect. Chaim Rabin has pointed out that the Qumran document 4Q Midrashim and the Damascus Covenant give a quotation from Amos in exactly the same text as that of Acts 15.16 and not the text of the Massoretes or the Septuagint which are identical in this passage. It must be kept in mind that Kahle, in *The Cairo Geniza*, makes a good case for the suggestion that the Greek text of the Old Testament was still so unformed at this period that the disagreement of the Septuagint and the other versions with the quotation texts in the New Testament is neither surprising nor significant. With this caution, it is still, I think, useful to examine the structure of the two sermon passages in Acts 10 and 13 in an attempt to discover something of the pattern of the early Christian preaching and, in particular, the use made of the Old Testament in such preaching.

In Acts 10.36–41 Peter is preaching to the gentile Cornelius and his household:

> You know the word which he sent to Israel, preaching good news of peace by Jesus Christ (he is Lord of all), the word which was proclaimed throughout all Judea, beginning from Galilee after the baptism which John preached: how God anointed Jesus of Nazareth with the Holy Spirit and with power; how he went about doing good and healing all that were oppressed by the devil, for God was with him. And we are witnesses to all that he did both in the country of the Jews and in Jerusalem. They put him to death by hanging him on a tree; but God raised him on the third day and made him manifest; not to all the people but to us who were chosen by God as witnesses, who ate and drank with him after he rose from the dead.

This outline is constructed along a simple pattern of events:

(a) the witness of John the Baptist;
(b) the baptism of Jesus and descent of the Spirit;
(c) the Galilean journey and miracles;
(d) the crucifixion;
(e) the resurrection and meals with the disciples.

It is followed by two further sections of the Christian belief: 'And he commanded us to preach to the people, and to testify that he is the one ordained by God to be the judge of the living and the dead. To him all the prophets bear witness that everyone who believes in him receives forgiveness of sins through his name.' These may be analysed thus:

(f) (i) command to preach given to the community;
    (ii) the coming of judgement;
(g) (i) the witness of the prophets of the Old Testament;
    (ii) the forgiveness of sins through Christ.

In Acts 13 Paul preaches an almost identical catechetical structure, the main difference being that a greater stress is placed upon the Old Testament as a witness to Christ. The speech at Antioch of Pisidia begins with an outline of the Old Testament care of God for the people of Israel from Egypt until David, and then moves into the schema outlined above:

(a) 'Before his coming John had preached a baptism of repentance to all the people of Israel';

(b) The baptismal formula of the Adoptionist 'Western' text: 'Thou art my Son, today I have begotten thee.'

(c) 'Those who live in Jerusalem and their rulers . . . did not recognize him nor understand the utterances of the prophets which are read every sabbath.'

(d) 'Though they could charge him with nothing deserving death, yet they asked Pilate to have him killed.'

(e) 'And when they had fulfilled all that was written of him, they took him down from the tree, and laid him in the tomb. But God raised him from the dead; and for many days he appeared to those who came up with him from Galilee to Jerusalem.'

(f) (i) We 'are now his witnesses to the people, and we bring you good news'.

(ii) 'By him every one that believes is freed.'

(g) (i) 'What God promised to the fathers, this he has fulfilled to us his children by raising Jesus' (followed by the quotations already noticed from Psalms 2 and 16).

(ii) 'Let it be known to you, therefore, brethren, that through this man forgiveness of sins is proclaimed to you.'

This is followed by a further reference to the revelation given in the Old Testament and by quotations from Habacuc and Isaiah.

It would seem, then, that the Old Testament was an integral part of the original catechetical mission of the Church, and that if the writing of the New Testament is to be understood in the sense intended by the first Christian community it must be understood as a record of God fulfilling his promise.

The Old Testament is used in these passages, and in many more in Acts and in the Pauline epistles, as an introduction to the sacramental life of the Church. It is on account of the exposition of the Old Testament that the people come to ask for baptism on the first day of Pentecost and that the Eunuch stops his chariot on the road to Jericho.

Exactly the same pattern can be discerned, of course, in the eucharistic liturgy even today and certainly in the early Christian era. The readings from the Old Testament, in the Advent and Lent liturgies particularly, are designed to lead members of the Christian assembly to take their full part in the eucharistic action of the offertory and communion.

It would not be possible here to follow through all the Old Testament references in the New Testament, showing how they are related to the liturgical structure of early Christian worship. I mean to concentrate on one of the most important Old Testament themes and show something of its relation to the structure of New Testament catechesis.

In this I am concerned mainly with the apologetic presenting Christ to Jewish listeners—even the Ethiopian was a pilgrim to Jerusalem and perhaps a proselyte like those present on the first day of Pentecost. Bertil Gartner of Uppsala has shown in *The Areopagus Speech and Natural Revelation* that there are four main elements in the Gentile-focused catechesis:

(i) a valuation of natural revelation;
(ii) an explanation of the nature of God;

(iii) an attack upon idolatry;

(iv) a promise of salvation for all men;

and that these are followed, as the proclamation of Christ must always be followed, by a demand that the hearer answer the claims of the Word and be converted.

A further difference between the apologetic directed towards Jewish listeners and that proposed to Gentiles has been pointed out by Mgr Cerfaux. In his early letters written while he was more familiar with Hebrew popular attitudes Paul led his catechesis to a proclamation of Jesus as the coming Judge. Later, as he travelled among Gentile peoples, Paul concentrated on their concern with death and presented Christ as the one who rescues men from their fear.

4. THE EXODUS IN THE NEW TESTAMENT

In this section I shall set out some of the ways in which the New Testament writers employed the pattern of the Exodus story to put across their appreciation of Christ and his work. Even with such a limitation the material is far too manifold for a proper discussion in detail and I have space for a few suggestions only. The Exodus pattern appears at almost every point of the New Testament narrative and is employed with both dogmatic and moralistic intent.

A. THE EVENT AND THE LANGUAGE

For the first Christian writers the Exodus signified, as it did for all Jews, the continuing redeeming work of God and the continuing promise of his Kingdom. The God who had saved them out of the land of Egypt would be true to himself, he would always save them; the God who had given them the land of Canaan would always give them a land, he would create for them an empire and a dominion over the Gentiles whom he had not redeemed nor invested with a land. The Christians, as much as any Jew, saw the Exodus as the typical case of God's action. The Exodus paradigm therefore presented them with a way of speaking of God's action in Christ.

Reversewise, the Christians saw in Christ the continuing action of God. They saw that in him they were released from their entanglement with the tears of things and their own sin, that in him they were offered a new opportunity, a beginning again with a new life, that they could receive his Spirit and so be freed from the spirit of the world. Christ's action delivered them from themselves and from every enemy. All the other acts of God had been but signs of this manumission, in Christ they had the reality of freedom. In Christ, that is, they had the proper subject of the Exodus language. God's action in Christ gave meaning to the Exodus way of speaking.

We can see this particularly clearly in the language we use of the total work of Christ, when we speak of our 'redemption'. The vocabulary of 'redemption' has often enough among Christian theologians caused doctrinal difficulties. Recognizing that 're-demption' is a word properly used in connection with buying and pawning, men have asked, 'From whom were we bought back?', and found no satisfactory answer. If we have regard to the reasons why the early Christians adopted this vocabulary we shall witness the difficulties vanish away. The early Christians transferred the word and its attendant vocabulary from its original use in the Exodus context, where it was used for the action of God in releasing the Jews from slavery in Egypt, to the Christ context. It is important always that these terms should be understood as integral elements of a meaningful complex of ideas; to take them out of their context and to expect them to explain themselves is to break up the complex and to be left with nothing but difficulties.

To release a slave it was normally necessary to pay a price. The paying for the slave is the slave's redemption. Since the Lord had released Israel from slavery in Egypt he is properly said to have redeemed the nation. This is a commonplace of Old Testament language and concepts. This is true both of the canonical writings and the later Jewish commentaries. Thus Deuteronomy has: 'The Lord brought you out with a mighty hand, and redeemed you from the house of bondage, from the hand of Pharaoh' (7.8); and the Midrash commentary on Psalm 113, where we have the line: 'Praise the Lord! Praise, O slaves of the Lord, praise the name of the Lord', runs thus: 'Thou recoveredst us and broughtest us out to freedom, for we were slaves unto Pharaoh and thou recoveredst us, madest us into slaves unto thee.' The redeemed become the servants of the Lord.

Redemption has a further connotation. In Israelite society the 'redeemer' was the next of kin who restored the wholeness of his family by the bringing back of what belonged to it. To redeem was to act as a kinsman. This is part of the Leviticus law (25.47-9) and is important for the machinery of the story of Ruth (3.12-13; 4.1-6).

This usage was taken over by the Christian writers when they wanted a linguistic and conceptual frame within which to speak of Christ's action. It was evident to the first community of Christians that the work of Christ was a climax of the one work of God, the saving history of Yahweh among his People led up to the final saving work of Christ for all men, and this fulfilment could therefore be spoken of properly in terms of the promise.

We have evidence of this adaptation of the redemption vocabulary from our first records of the community, those liturgical fragments which have survived in the body of the New Testament texts and which have recently been the subject of much study. Bishop Robinson has lately demonstrated that the *Benedictus* song of Zachary was in its first shape a song about Jesus and not about John the Baptist. The christology of this hymn derives some at least of its concepts from the Exodus fulfilment; the Incarnation is spoken of thus: 'Blessed be the Lord God of Israel, for he has visited and redeemed his people' (Lk 1.68). Christ comes to bring men out of the hands of their enemies and to free the captives who sit in dark prisons.

It would seem that the earliest traditions of the community suggested that Christ himself used the Exodus redemptive language to describe his work, at least the first christologies think it proper to employ this frame. Mark and Matthew both have a pericope of Christ describing his own work in such terms: 'The Son of Man also came ... to give his life as a ransom for many' (Mt. 20.28; Mk 10.45). And in the developing theology of Paul the same language is used because the same concept is in mind. Paul writes in his first letter to Timothy of Christ as the one 'who gave himself as a ransom for all' (2.6), and he tells the Corinthians: 'You were bought with a great price; do not become slaves of men' (I Cor. 7.23).

The slave-market language of ransom and buying leads into the language of release and freedom. John writes to his disciples that Christ is the one who brings manumission: 'The truth will make you free ... if the Son makes you free you will be free indeed' (8.32).

The Hebrews have never felt themselves to be free men. The law was given as a limitation of their freedom. They were released from slavery to the Egyptians in order that they might be the slaves of God: 'Let my people go, that they may serve me' (Ex. 7.16), and this is a dominant theme in Hebrew understanding of their position. They belong to the household of God, but as servants of the Lord, not free men. They can even envisage being put on the market again by Yahweh: 'Thou hast sold thy people for a trifle, demanding no high price for them' (Ps. 44.12). The *Magnificat* shows us Mary's realization of the status of the Jew: 'Behold the slave-girl of the Lord' (Lk. 1.38), which is an echo of Psalm 123.2: 'Behold, as the eyes of slaves look to the hands of their master, as the eyes of a slave girl to the hand of her mistress, so our eyes look to the Lord our God.'

Christ, therefore, is born among slaves to make men free: 'God sent forth his Son, born of a woman, born under the law, to redeem those who were under the law, so that we might receive adoption as sons . . . through God you are no longer a slave but a son, and if a son then an heir' (Gal. 4.4–6).

The Hebrew slavery and release is paralleled by the Gentile experience: 'Formerly, when you did not know God you were in bondage to beings that by nature are no gods; but now that you have come to know God, or rather to be known by God, how can you turn back again to the weak and beggarly elemental spirits whose slaves you want to be once more?' (Gal. 4.8–9).

Some New Testament passages do speak as if by our redemption we had become the slaves of God but in general the language is concerned with 'freedom'. The old redemption certainly effected a change of masters, and God was obviously a better master than the Lord of Egypt, but this was itself a sign of the incomplete nature of the Exodus event. The work of Christ reaches a plenitude of effect in the conferring of real freedom upon his people: 'Now I do not call you servants any longer but my friends' (Jn 15.15). The Exodus has arrived in its totality.

Thus the event and the language come together for the first time and the language and the life are one in Christ. The insight of Wittgenstein that to imagine a language is to imagine a way of life is at this point at any rate exactly the case.

The doctrine of Christ and his work expressed in Exodus terms leads on to a doctrine of the Christian and his work, and this too is expressed in Exodus terms. This is because of two important Christian concepts. Firstly we have always to bear in mind that Christ is the Christian, what he does we all do in him; if this were not the case then Christ died and rose in vain. We die and rise in him, and there-fore can share his present glory. Secondly, and this is perhaps simply another way of putting the same truth, the Christian is Christ. We have all to do what he has done and is doing.

When we use the Exodus language we are, therefore, not accepting simply a way of talking which can be distinguished from our way of acting, we are committing ourselves to a way of living. Wittgen-stein's insight ought perhaps to be inverted and we ought to say that to have a way of life is to bring a language into being. The Christian understanding of Christ demands an expression in action and in word. The word Christians found is that of the Exodus event. The language is essential if we would speak in New Testament terms. If we would share the excitement and commitment of the New Testament writers we must make efforts to understand their language. Of course we do not ourselves have to communicate Christ through this same language. We are not to present Christ as the result of antiquarian activity. But we have to know what we are translating so that how-ever we may change the words of men we do not omit the Word of God.

In this section I shall first of all say something of the way in which the early Christian community saw the relation between Christ and the Exodus as being not simply signified and signification but as identical reality; and then go on to speak of the way in which they thought of the Exodus pattern working itself out in their own lives through Christ.

B. THE REAL PRESENCE OF CHRIST IN THE EXODUS

The first Christians did not simply transfer the redemptive imagery from an Old Testament event to a New Testament event. They did not think of themselves as performing a literary manipu-lation at all. They thought only of the continuing reality of God's action in Christ. The early community saw much more than symbols, hints and shadows of Christ's person and work in the Exodus narrative, they saw Christ himself.

How difficult this is for present Christians to understand and stomach is brought out in the history of a verse in the Epistle of Jude. The Vulgate, following here the best manuscripts, has this: '*Jesus populum de terra Aegypti salvans*'. This reading sets forth the complete identity of the one who brought them out of Egypt and the Jesus who has brought them out of sin by his death and resurrection. This is too difficult for most translators. The Jerusalem Bible puts this in a footnote and substitutes (on less satisfying manuscript authority) *le Seigneur* in the text. The footnote suggests that the 'Jesus' ought to be explained away as a reference to 'Christ in his divine pre-existence', and that *le Seigneur* here refers to God the Father. Thus having put away the reading 'Jesus' and having defended themselves from rearguard attack by talk of 'the pre-existent Christ', the Jerusalem Bible translators have then moved further away from this position by suggesting that the text does not refer to Christ at all. All this is quite understandable from our present theological standpoint, but it is not a proper presentation of the author of *Jude* and his community. R. A. Knox goes further and suggests 'Saviour'. The Revised Standard Version is more cautious though no less muddling by its employment of 'he who saved a people', and the New English Bible has 'the Lord'. Of course one can well understand the perplexity of these translators when confronted with the suggestion that Jesus led the Exodus, but it is a little alarming to discover that there is no manuscript ground at all for the Knox or RSV reading, or for the Jerusalem Bible gloss about 'God the Father'. It would have been better to leave the text alone and subscribe to Professor A. T. Hanson's ironical remark in *Jesus Christ in the Old Testament*: 'We may express a certain amount of relief that Jude is probably one of the later books of the NT to be written, and is on the periphery rather than at the heart of the record of revelation.' But we must also bear in mind Professor Hanson's description of the New Testament community's notion of the continuity of Jesus' work: 'They knew of Jesus who had lived and died and risen from the dead, and who was present with them in the Church's life. They find essentially the same characteristics of that Jesus in the history of the Jewish people before the incarnation.' It is within this consciousness of the work of Jesus at all times that we must understand the passage in Jude, or those in Hebrews or I Corinthians which speak in a way we find strange and off-putting.

At all events we must avoid turning into the blind alley of typology thinking it to be an escape-route in such cases. The difference between typological structures and those with which I am dealing here is well brought out in the Exodus pattern of Rylands Papyrus Gr.7: 'Lo! the virgin has borne Emmanuel: He came down from heaven and saved the people that were astray from the land of Egypt'. The difference between typology and our subject can be illustrated by the two ways in which this papyrus fragment can be interpreted. Either the author is speaking of Jesus as the one who led the Israelites out of Egypt in the distant past—in which case he is using the Jude-structure we have just examined, or else he is employing a typological structure and using 'Egypt' as the pattern and indeed synonym for 'sin' from which Christ has rescued the Christians. Both devices were used by the early Christians to speak of the work of Christ, but it does not help to muddle them up together. 'Moses spoke of me' means not simply prophecy, not simply that we can employ the Old Testament as a treasury of types for Christ, but that the one who is spoken of in the Law is the one who was in Galilee and Judaea and Jerusalem and is in the sacraments of the Church. Of course it is not only in the Exodus event that the early Christians saw the action of Jesus in the past. Hanson produces a vast amount of evidence to show the ubiquity of Jesus in the Old Testament period: 'Isaiah said this because he saw his glory and spoke of him' (Jn 12.41), and: 'Your father Abraham rejoiced that he was to see my day: he saw it and was glad' (Jn 8.56). But the evidence is strongest in the working out of the Exodus pattern—another indication of the importance attached to this pattern as relevant to Christ's action in the minds of the early Christian community. Later such thoughts as that of the author of Hebrews of Christ speaking on Sinai and in the Tabernacle became a commonplace of patristic writing, as Hanson shows with reference to Justin, Melito and Irenaeus.

That such apologetic was often employed can be demonstrated from an entirely different piece of evidence. Professor Daube has shown how the orthodox Jews took pains to controvert the Christian assertion of Jesus being present at the Exodus event. He writes of the different modes of presenting the Passover history of deliverance, and he notices some signs of anti-Christian sentiment at work: 'In one variant, an old teaching that in the Exodus God acted himself, not through a messenger, is provided with the contamination "nor through the Word".' Though for so long we have been unaware of this kind of thinking and must now find it strange, we should as a stranger give it welcome, since it is not difficult for Catholics to understand the kind of appreciation of Christ that is at work in this structure. If we are prepared to affirm that the one Jesus who spoke the parables, worked the miracles, died outside the walls of Jerusalem, and ate meals with his disciples after his resurrection from the dead, is present with us in his sacramental activity, we should have little difficulty in appreciating this other, and in some ways supplementary, affirmation of Jesus' presence in the saving history of the Jews. If the one Jesus is pierced by the spear until streams of blood and water flow, and is present in our Eucharist and Baptism, surely we can accept the idea of Paul in I Corinthians where he speaks of the water from the rock which revived the Israelites: 'The Rock was Christ.'

C. THE PRESENCE OF THE EXODUS IN THE LIFE OF CHRIST

The work of Jesus sums up the whole saving activity of God for men. It would, therefore, be strange if there were no recapitulations of the previous works of God in the redemptive experience of Christ, and if there were not reminders of the previous accounts of God's work in the Christian accounts of Jesus. Since, again, it would be impossible to control all the different pieces of material in the New Testament which present the work of Christ in Exodus terms, I shall concentrate on one incident, that of the Temptations of Jesus. The story of the Temptations is eminently suitable for such a consideration since it contains, in the versions given by Luke and Matthew, significant passages from the Old Testament narrative of the escape from Egypt, and because it can in some sense be regarded as the climacteric point of Jesus' redemptive action. Dr Ernest Best in his work on Marcan soteriology, *The Temptation and the Passion*, concludes his study of the Temptation story and its meaning with a strong assertion of its finality as a redemptive act:

> For Mark the Devil is defeated so far as the life of Jesus is concerned at the Temptation; in this conclusive contest Satan is bound and Jesus is thereafter able to reduce to obedience evil-spiritual powers, the demons which possess men and evil-cosmic forces met in sea storms. This encounter with the Devil in the Temptation is the decisive meeting.

Similarly, Hans Conzelmann in his important study of the *Theology of Saint Luke* writes of the Temptation as being a decisive event:

> The Temptation is finished decisively, and the devil departs. A question of principle is involved here, for it means that where Jesus is from now on, there Satan is no more . . . a period free from Satan is now beginning,

56

an epoch of a special kind in the centre of the whole course of redemptive history.

The importance of the incident and the Exodus-nature of its account are therefore both certain. I will use the short Marcan form—which was employed by Luke and Matthew for various developing purposes —as the basis of my commentary on this event: 'He was in the wilderness forty days, tempted by Satan; and he was with the wild beasts; and angels ministered to him' (1.13).

I will begin by setting out the various Exodus elements in this short passage:

(a) Christ is described as being in the wilderness. This area is beyond Jordan in the desert place where the Israelites had wandered. Though there is no direct mention of Exodus reminiscence at this point it cannot be doubted that the first readers of this description would think of the Exodus desert journey.

(b) Jesus is there for forty days. 'Forty' is generally used by the Hebrew writers to signify 'heap' or 'a lot', but its most significant use is in the 'forty years' of the Israelite wandering, and Moses' 'forty days' (Ex. 24.18; 34.28; Deut. 9.9; 10.10).

(c) The actual temptation of Jesus by Satan is elaborated in the Matthew and Luke narratives with a deliberate summoning of Exodus memories which are designed not to bring into focus the old events in the redemption of Israel but to make clear the meaning of Christ's soteriological activity. This particularly is the case of the third gospel writer.

For Luke the Temptations are the Exodus in Christ's experience. He has emphasized every aspect of the Temptation story as he received it which would strengthen the connection between the two events. I have already shown elsewhere that Luke's narrative of the Temptations depends for its structure not on the primitive accounts in the books of Exodus and Deuteronomy and Numbers but on the liturgical accounts contained in Psalm 106. Luke supposes that the psalmist has the right of it, against Hosea and Jeremiah, in describing the journey through the desert as a time of rebellion and ingratitude: 'Many times he delivered them, but they were rebellious in their purposes'; and he has adopted the psalm order of the events and this has resulted in a peculiar ordering of the quotations from Deuteronomy which supply Christ's answers to the temptations.

It is significant that Luke while casting his account of the Temptations in the form of a dialogue between Christ and Satan does not give us any answer of Christ in original words. Christ is totally identified with the old situation and his answers are produced from an understanding of the old situation. It is for this reason, rather than for the subsidiary one of reproducing the form of rabbinical disputation which moved from one quotation to another, that the dialogue is set up in this manner.

The three temptations are these:

  (i) to turn stone into bread;
 (ii) to worship Satan;
(iii) to force God to protect Jesus by a miracle.

Jesus' three replies in the form of quotations from the account of the Exodus journey in Deuteronomy are these:

(i) 'Man shall not live by bread alone' (Deut. 8.3).
(ii) 'You shall worship the Lord your God and him only shall you serve' (Deut. 6.13).
(iii) 'You shall not tempt the Lord your God' (Deut. 6.16).

Evidently Luke did not have access to a verbatim record of the Temptation dialogue. He has so shaped his narrative that it presents the Temptation in the form under which he sees the whole of Jesus' work. He has worked the narrative in terms of the first redemptive act of God among the Hebrews in order that the second shall be properly understood by the Hebrews.

The Jewish contemporaries of Luke understood the Exodus journey as a time of testing for their race. The people who followed Moses, by their decisions for or against Yahweh, prepared the whole course of the covenant-history between Israel and Yahweh. The redemptive work of God for the present Jew was available only through the events of the past Hebrew experience. Similarly Luke is showing the present Christian that his relation with God, and in particular his triumph over the powers of evil, depend on the past event of Christ's resistance to the Temptation. This piece of the gospel narrative, like every other, has a present intention for the lives of the Christians who read it. There is an interest, therefore, in setting out the actual temptations in the desert before which the old People of

God failed. I will refer to them in the descriptions of Psalm 106, since this is the version uppermost in Luke's mind:

(i) The murmuring of the people against God in the wilderness of sin (Ex. 16.2ff). Ps. 106.14: 'They had a wanton craving in the wilderness, and put God to the test in the desert'. This was the time when bread/manna was given to the people.

(ii) The commandment given at Sinai (Ex. 20), after which the people made an idol for themselves. Ps. 106.19: 'They made a calf in Horeb and worshipped a molten image. They exchanged the glory of God for the image of an ox that eats grass.'

(iii) The demand for water at Massah (Ex. 17.1–7). Ps. 106.32: 'They angered him at the waters of Meribah, and it went ill with Moses on their account', cf. also Ps. 95.8: 'Harden not your hearts, as at Meribah, as on the day at Massah in the wilderness, when your fathers tested me and put me to the proof, though they had seen my work.'

The most likely explanation for Luke's use of the Psalm order rather than that of the Exodus or Deuteronomy accounts is not that he saw some peculiar significance in this order—or if he did he does not seem to have made this plain—but that this was the one he was most familiar with. The historical accounts were not so immediate to his mind as the one sung in the synagogue and temple liturgy. I shall point out later how other sections of the New Testament narratives depend on the Hebrew and early Christian liturgies for their structure. This is but one example of what is now generally recognized as a universally present principle of the New Testament writers.

The main point, however, is not the precise order of the Temptation responses of Christ, but their general significance in the presentation of the Christian faith. I do not wish to elaborate at this juncture the meaning of the incident itself, though much might be said of the way in which Christ, while guided by the Spirit, could resist the temptations, and of what this suggests for the understanding of the situation of the Christian who enjoys the gift of the Spirit within a world of temptations. I want merely to stress that Mark, Luke and Matthew, all three, thought that this was best understood within Exodus terms. The only language they recognize as adequate to the experience they wish to convey is that of the Old Testament experience. Christ in these Temptation narratives is presented as the new Israel who succeeds where the old Israel failed, and as the proper exemplar of the Christian disciple who meets the same temptations as the old Israel and Christ.

(d) He was with the wild beasts.

The wild beasts do not form part of the original tradition of the Exodus as set down in the books of Exodus, Numbers and Deuteronomy, but they are part of the tradition recorded in Isaiah and the Psalms.

In Isaiah 43 there is a passage describing the way that is made by the Lord through the waters of the Red Sea and the desert which brings in the notion of wild animals taking part in the praise of creation because of the redemptive work of the Exodus: 'I will make a way in the wilderness and rivers in the desert. The wild beasts will honour me, the jackals and the ostriches.' And in Psalm 91.11ff.—the very same passage as that quoted by Satan in the Luke Temptation narrative—the psalmist speaks of the way in which the Messiah will be protected:

> He will give his angels charge of you
>   to guard you in all your ways.
> On their hands they will bear you up,
>   lest you dash your foot against a stone.
> You will tread on the lion and the adder,
>   the young lion and the serpent you will trample under foot.

If, as seems at least probable, Mark is suggesting by this part of the Tempation narrative that Christ has tamed the wild beasts and can now treat the lion and the serpent with friendly ease, then we may have here another dual emphasis on Egyptian matters and the triumphant day that Christ has brought for men.

The lion and the serpent, taken together, have a significance for the Hebrews which they do not have for us. In the book of Amos there is a description of the way in which the Israelites continually watch and wait for the Day of the Lord when all evil will, they think, come to an end and God will reign and they will have a marvellous kingdom. He tells the people that they have behaved so ill, they have so much forsaken the covenant made at Sinai, that the coming of the Lord will not be like that at all:

> Why would you have the day of the Lord?
> It is darkness and not light;
>   as if a man fled from a lion,

and a bear met him;
Or went into the house and leaned with his hand
against the wall,
and a serpent bit him.
Is not the day of the Lord darkness, and not light,
and gloom with no brightness in it? (5.18–20)

The same notion is behind Psalm 104.20–21: 'Thou makest darkness, and it is night when all the beasts of the forest creep forth, and the young lions roar for their prey.' In these passages Yahweh is thought of as being very much like the Egyptian God Aton, the god of the sun worshipped by Amen-hotep IV. In the 'long hymn' to Aton, from the tomb of Eye at Tell-el-Amarna, there is a description of this god as the one who turns day into night and night into day, first of all 'Every lion is crept forth from his den; All creeping things, they sting. Darkness (is a shroud) and the earth is in stillness', but at dawn 'All beasts are content with their pasturage.' The victorious god turns the beasts into domestic animals. There is surely a likeness here to the description of Christ as the one who can live with the wild beasts. Gradually through the medium of the Old Testament writers the attributes of the Egyptian god have been brought to their fulfilling resolution in Christ.

The first Christians may not, of course, have been able to work all this out, and it is extremely doubtful whether Mark had any open sense of what was happening, but certainly it may be suggested that the old myth of a god who has to bring peace and harmony to the animals and men is at the back of Mark's mind. And it is interesting that the remote starting-point for this usage came from an Egyptian source.

More interesting perhaps is that by reference to the Amos passage we can view the Marcan Tempation narrative as presenting us with a version of Christ's bringing us the Day of the Lord by his triumph.

(e) The angels here lead onto the angels who serve Christ in the wilderness. It was part of the Hebrew tradition that the Exodus route was marked out by angels.

In Stephen's speech in chapter 7 of Acts the Hebrew tradition is recounted in synopsis. The account of Moses' leadership of the people begins with his encounter with the burning bush: 'an angel appeared to him in the wilderness of Mount Sinai in a flame of fire in a bush', and he was made leader because God sent him 'as both ruler and deliverer by the hand of the angel', and gave him the Law through the angel: 'this is he who was in the congregation in the wilderness with the angel who spoke to him at Mount Sinai.'

All this is derived from the narratives of the Exodus when 'the angel of the Lord went before the host of Israel' (Ex. 14.19) and fulfilled the covenant with them: as in Exodus 23.20ff; 'Behold I send an angel before you, to guard you on your way and bring you to the place which I have prepared. Give heed to him and hearken to his voice.'

In every section of this verse, therefore, the Exodus tradition is operative and it must be concluded that the community from which Mark wrote and for which he wrote had a high estimate of the value of the Exodus narrative as a catechetical subject for Christians. I have made this extended reference to the Temptation narrative because it seemed wisest to show how the Exodus pattern influenced in detail the writing of the New Testament rather than to show how the general system of New Testament images derives from the Exodus event. The treatment of a particular example, though it leaves the case open to a charge of careful selection of the evidence, does at least allow of a full presentation of the case. It would have been possible to choose many another incident to make the point. The Temptation narrative is not an isolated piece of writing in this respect. The life of Christ is ever understood by the evangelists to be expressed properly in Exodus language.

Of course the evangelists were not simply trying to put Christ into an Exodus system for purely literary reasons, they were not indulging in an esoteric game of references. There is nothing of the intellectual gnostic about these writers. They held it to be true that Christ could only be described in Exodus terms because he was the completion of the Exodus event. For them Christ was the Exodus. With the elabora-ation of this point I shall be concerned in the next section.

D. THE EXODUS IN CHRIST

The distinguishing characteristic of Hebrew religious experience was the emphasis put upon the covenant of Yahweh with his People. This covenant was renewed at various stages of their history but was primarily established in the Sinai event. The Hebrew religion was therefore about an alliance or treaty with Yahweh.

The distinguishing characteristic of Christian religious experience is the emphasis placed upon the person of Christ, in his very person the covenant is established. Our religion is about Christ. It is not, therefore, surprising that the evangelists should put across their commitment to Christ in the terms used by the old writers of the Covenant event. What the Sinai event is to Hebrew religion the Incarnation is to Christianity. Further, Jesus is presented by the first Christians as taking up into himself all that is meant by the covenant with the Hebrews; there is now only one covenant, one way to the Father, and that is through the person of Christ.

This is what is meant by the continual assertion that the whole of the Old Testament speaks of Christ. It is not simply that many passages can be adapted to a prophetic use and brought into connection with specific events of Jesus' life. It is not this merely. The first Christians understood that whenever the old community spoke of the covenant, whenever, that is, they spoke of their relation with Yahweh, they were speaking of Christ. To accept the old witness properly is to be led on to accept the new witness in Christ.

This is put negatively in the gospels of both Luke and John. To refuse to listen to Christ and to commit oneself to him argues that one has never listened to the old community and has never been a faithful member of the old covenant society. In Luke's gospel, at the end of the parable of the Rich Man and the Beggar Lazarus, the solemn warning comes: 'If they do not hear Moses and the prophets, neither will they be convinced if some one should rise from the dead' (16.31).

The resurrection of Christ will not bring faith to men who have already ignored the testimony of the Old Testament. In John's gospel the same point is made in the dispute after the healing of the man at the pool of Bethesda. Jesus says to the Jewish leaders: 'Do not think that I shall accuse you to the Father; it is Moses who accuses you, on whom you have set your hope. If you believed Moses you would believe me, for he wrote of me. But if you do not believe his writings, how will you believe my words?' (5.45–7).

The continuity of witness and the subsuming of the old witness into that of Christ is particularly the theme of the first verses of John's gospel. John presents the Word of God in three ways, always stressing that it is the one Word of which he speaks, revealed in three ways to men. He begins by asserting the divine creativity of the

63

Word and then moves through the Word given in the Law of Moses to the Word made flesh in Christ. The witness is one, at the same time it is progressive: 'For the Law was given through Moses; grace and truth came through Jesus Christ' (1.17).

In the person of Christ the Law is hypostatized. This is characteristic of John's method of speaking of Christ. He uses the Exodus vocabulary to describe Christ not in terms of simile but in terms of identification: 'I am the light of the world' (8.12), he writes, and we are to understand that the sign of the pillar of fire that led the Hebrews through the desert into the promised land has been actualized in Jesus; 'If any one thirst, let him come to me and drink' (7.37), and we are to realize that the water which flowed out of the rock and quenched the thirst of the dying men has become Jesus and that we are to drink him; 'I am the bread of life' (6.48), and we are to accept the strange notion that the bread he gives us is himself, that the manna in the desert which kept the men alive in their journey is fulfilled more marvellously in the Eucharist. In Christ the pillar of fire, the water from the rock, and the manna from heaven have not simply become one, they have become one person. It is this which conveys to us the movement from a covenant only to be expressed in various signs to a personal covenant in the Lord Jesus.

The movement is not limited to the major signs of the old covenant but applies to many of its details. For example, when Jesus is speaking to Nicodemus about the work of the Son of Man he employs the Exodus image of the bronze serpent and moves its significance into the event of the Crucifixion: 'As Moses lifted up the serpent in the wilderness, so must the Son of man be lifted up, that whoever believes in him may have eternal life' (3.14–15). The same idea is present in the passage in chapter eight where he tells the Pharisees: 'When you have lifted up the Son of Man, then you will know that I am he' (8.28). And John himself provides the commentary in chapter twelve: 'I, when I am lifted up from the earth, will draw all men unto myself. He said this to show by what death he was to die. The crowd answered him: "We have heard from the law that the Christ remains for ever. How can you say that the Son of man must be lifted up?"' (12.32–4).

It is interesting to notice what part of this incident John thinks needs to be explained to his first readers. The Jews are said to know already what the Law says, they will be equipped to recognize the references to the bronze serpent, but they do not know of the coming crucifixion event. John has therefore to point out the connection between them and to do so within the pattern of Christ's continuing presence. The commentary he provides in these passages is therefore shaped thus:

(i) The sign of the Nehustan serpent is fulfilled in Christ's person.

(ii) The Law says that the Christ will be for ever.

(iii) Christ says it is through the crucifixion that he will be for ever.

(iv) Because of the crucifixion of Christ the Christian can be for ever, whoever believes in the lifted-up Christ will have eternal life.

The significance of this bronze serpent sign is not readily understood by modern readers and since the point cannot be made without some historical information I shall have to digress for a moment.

In the early eighth century B.C. the Temple worship had become much adulterated by pagan elements. One of these was a Nehustan or bronze serpent which derived originally from a totally pagan cult ceremonial but which had been accepted at some forgotten time into the sanctuary. Because all things must have a reason the Hebrews asked themselves what this equivocal object was doing in their Temple and it would seem likely that someone fetched out an old story or perhaps even invented a new one to explain its presence. This story was designed to fit into the already accepted history of the people as a further incident on the Exodus journey as was set within the tradition in Numbers 21. There the people are grumbling that their food is uneatable and scarce at that, and they have no water; they are immediately punished by God for their rebellious thoughts:

> Then the Lord sent fiery serpents among the people and they bit the people, so that many people of Israel died. And the people came to Moses and said: 'We have sinned, for we have spoken against the Lord and against you; pray to the Lord that he may take away the serpents from us.'
>
> So Moses prayed for the people. And the Lord said to Moses: 'Make a fiery serpent and set it on a pole; and if a serpent bite any man he would look at the bronze serpent and live' (Num. 21.6–8).

When the good king Hezekiah came to the throne he cleansed the Temple of the pagan chattels and among them removed the Nehustan: 'he broke in pieces the bronze serpent that Moses had made, for

until those days the people of Israel had burned incense to it'
(II Kings 18.4). Obviously the scribe and his fellow temple-attendants
were not wholly convinced of the Mosaic authorship of the Nehustan,
otherwise they would never have allowed the king to destroy so
famous a relic of their leader. Right-minded men must have agreed
with Hezekiah that this was a dangerous innovation. The later
commentator in the book of Wisdom completed the destruction by
his exegesis of the story which still remained in the text of Numbers.
He calls the serpent a 'sign of salvation' which was not salvific
itself: 'he that turned to it was not saved by the thing he saw, but by
thee, the saviour of all' (Wis. 16.7).

If we return to John's narrative we find that he has employed all
this in his account of the lifting-up of Christ.

John believes, as the author of Wisdom believed, that the old sign
was only a sign, and that at most the sign was a medium of God's
grace. He also believes that this sign like those of the bread and the
water and the light are taken up and made totally real in Christ. The
one who looks towards Christ and believes in him crucified has
eternal life. Christ is the Nehustan who can give life. In the terminology of the Wisdom author, the 'thing' has become 'the saviour
of all'.

The Nehustan is but one of the signs that is summed up at the
crucifixion of Christ. It is but one of those things which are included
in the cry of completion: It is accomplished.

This triumphant cry has been carefully prepared for in the evangelist's writing. John can be shown, I think, to have had the same
thought as Matthew on this matter, and perhaps to have relied on
Matthew here. In the Sermon on the Mount (which, with its repeated
antithesis of 'it was said to you of old . . . but I say to you', is designed
to persuade the Jews that Christ was another Moses giving a Law
on the mountain of Sinai) there comes a reassurance that the old
Law is not to be done away with: 'Do not think that I have come to
set aside the law and the prophets; I have not come to set them
aside, but to bring them to perfection. Believe me, heaven and earth
must disappear sooner than one jot, one flourish disappear from the
law; it must all be accomplished' (Mt. 5.17–18).

John realizes, as much as Matthew, that the whole Law is accomplished. And John sees, and perhaps Matthew did not see, that the
Law is accomplished in Christ's saving death and resurrection. He

records Christ's consciousness of having done all that had to be done in exactly the same terms as he uses for the crucifixion account: 'I have exalted thy glory on earth, by accomplishing the task which thou gavest me to do; now, Father, do thou exalt me at thy own side' (Jn 17.4).

The resurrection is the reward for the lifting-up on earth, and the lifting-up of the crucifixion is the fulfilment of the Law. After the saving act of Christ the Law is in Christ himself. The whole of the first revelation is summed up in the person who is the final revelation. This is emphasized in Mark's gospel also in precisely the words used in the Matthew and John accounts, thus showing the central character of the theme of accomplishment of the Law in the person of Christ.

Mark's account of the Last Day ends with the affirmation: 'Believe me this generation will not have passed away, before all this is accomplished. Though heaven and earth should pass away my words will stand.' In this saying of Mark's tradition the transfer from the old Law to Christ is total. The Matthew tradition of the saying predicates the endurance of heaven and earth of the Law, the Marcan form uses the identical predication of Christ himself. Further, the eschatological event occurs within this generation, everything is to be accomplished in the work of Christ on earth. It is at the crucifixion that this generation sees the fulfilment and accomplishment of the Law and hears the abiding word: 'It is accomplished' (Jn 19.30).

This tradition occurs in another form in Paul's letter to the Romans: 'Christ is the end of the law' (10.4), and perhaps in Ephesians: 'he abolished in his flesh the law of commandments and ordinances, that he might create in himself one new man' (2.15). In each of these cases the person of Christ takes the place of the fulfilled Law of Moses.

It must not be supposed that Matthew's tradition does not reflect this identification of Christ and the Law in quite so developed a form as is shown in these instances. A glance at the structure of the ethic advanced in the Sermon on the Mount in this gospel will reveal two dominant characteristics of this section: (i) that Jesus is to be thought of as presenting a fulfilment of the old Law by his own instructions to his disciples; and (ii) that the fulfilment is primarily in his own person. The Law is comprehended in committal to Jesus: 'Blessed are you when men revile you . . . because of me' (5.11), and the judgement is a realization of Christ: 'There are many who will say to me when that day comes: Master, master, was it not in thy name we prophesied? Was it not in thy name that we performed many miracles? Whereupon I will tell them openly: You were never friends of mine' (7.22–3), and the condemnation is to be separated from him: 'Depart from me, you that traffic in wrongdoing' (7.23).

The new Law is the commandment of Christ and obedience will bring steadfast surety in the day of wrath: 'Whoever, then, hears these commandments of mine and carries them out, is like a wise man who built his house upon rock' (7.24). The new Law of the new covenant is understood by Matthew, at least as much as by those of other traditions, to be summed up in the person of the Lord.

E. THE NEW COVENANT

Vatican II's Constitution on the Sacred Liturgy speaks of 'the renewal in the Eucharist of the covenant between God and man'. It is with this renewal that I intend to deal in this section.

Certainly we can assert that Christ himself recognized the intimate connection between the old covenant situations of Abraham, Moses and David, and the new situation of his eucharistic covenant. We cannot, of course, be certain that we have his exact words of institution of this new covenant, any more than we can be certain we have his exact words in any other place in the New Testament. But we can be sure that we have here, as in every other place in the New Testament, a faithful reflection of Christ's intention. We can assert the existence of the covenant according to the will of Christ and the creation of a new people through this covenant. The eucharistic covenant makes the Church. We have therefore to explore what this covenant means.

Throughout the New Testament the life of Christ is seen in Exodus-covenant terms, and this leads on to a Christian understanding that what is true of Christ is true of his whole Church as a community and of each of the individual members of Christ in the community. The Exodus pattern is to be discerned in the entire sacramental life of the community. It is of Moses and his People that Paul tells his Corinthians: 'These things were done in a figure of us' (I Cor. 10.6). The foundations of sacramental understanding are in the realization of the meaning of the old covenant.

As the author of Hebrews reminds his people, the covenant pattern is of eternal value since it is derived from the eternal reality of God's holy kingdom. He suggests that the worship and tabernacle of the Exodus 'serve as copy and shadow of the heavenly sanctuary; for when Moses was about to erect the tent he was instructed by God, saying, "See that you make everything according to the pattern that was presented to you on the mountain".' (Heb. 8.5). So the Exodus pattern remains ever valid as a sign of God, and so is to be employed in the Christian worship.

It ought, of course, to be borne in mind that Christ does not simply sum up the one Exodus covenant, but is the completion and personalization of all the alliances between God and man which had gone before. Christ the man is the content of the covenant with Adam in the garden when the saviour is promised and the more highly developed covenant scheme of the promise to all men in Noah that the power of God would never be used for the destruction of man. Christ the Jew is the completion of the alliance of Abraham and the Lord, and of Moses and the Israelites with Yahweh in the desert. Christ the king is the completion of the Zion covenant with the royal family of David. Christ is himself the Covenant promised under the figure of the Suffering Servant of Yahweh in II Isaiah: 'I have given you as a covenant to the people' (Is. 42.6; 49.8).

The central notion of the old covenant was the establishment of a relationship between Yahweh and the Israelites, and the manifestation of this relationship by the presence of Yahweh among his People. He says to Moses: 'My presence will go with you' (Ex. 33.14). The relationship makes the people into a reality. It is by the presence of Yahweh that the nation of the covenant is created. This is recognized in Moses' reply: 'Is it not in thy going with us, so that we are distinct, I and thy people, from all other people that are upon the face of the earth?' (33.16). The covenant presence makes the people. We can see immediately how this is our case also. The economy of Christ's saving work is centred upon his presence among us through a new covenant. It is in the covenant act of the Eucharist that Christ is really present among us, and it is the celebration of that Eucharist which brings into actuality the new people of God.

Christ in his own person is a new covenant establishing a new relation of friendship between God and man. That he himself used the word 'covenant' is difficult to ascertain. It would seem most likely that he did not. Paul and the communities which he served were very much aware of the covenant nature of Christ's act and person and may have inserted the word to bring this meaning out when celebrating the Eucharist. Paul speaks of the Christian Apostles as 'ministers of a new covenant' in II Corinthians, and the intricate allegorism of the letter to the Galatians has a simple starting-point in the contrast between the sons of Abraham as a parallel between the old and the new covenant. The new covenant is in Christ and makes us sons of the free. Again in other communities, such as those amongst whom Mark's gospel was written and read, the notion of the covenant proved so strong and the signification of the Exodus narrative so understandable that Mark thrust into his account of the Last Supper a dogmatic reference to the old covenant. Most linguistic experts find that the Marcan phrase, 'my blood of the covenant', is very difficult to put into Aramaic, and Jeremias baldly states that it is impossible. Higgins, in *The Lord's Supper in the New Testament*, summarizes the state of modern opinion on this matter: '[the cup saying in Mark] represents the older strand of tradition, in which, however, the mention of the covenant is a subsequent, though very early addition. The Pauline version, in which the saying is remodelled to make the covenant idea central, is due to Paul's emphasis on the covenant, and to his representation of the Last Supper as the inauguration of a new covenant ratified in the blood of Christ.'

Whether the covenant expression comes from the original saying of Jesus at the Last Supper, or whether it is a faithful addition to the saying which represents the meaning of the original saying, it is clear that the covenant notion is fully present in the narrative. It will be helpful, therefore, to set out the various components of the covenant concept in Hebrew traditions, and particularly those of the Sinai tradition.

The covenant idea is generally a ratification of a treaty, and is thus found in many Near Eastern cultures; as a ratification of alliances accompanied by sacrifice to God and a meal among the participants it is also common. An example of this treaty, sacrifice and meal pattern is presented by the covenant between Laban and Jacob:

> Then Laban said to Jacob, 'See the heap and the pillar, which I have set between you and me. This heap is a witness, and the pillar is a

witness, that I will not pass over this heap to you, and you will not pass over this heap and this pillar to me, for harm. The God of Abraham and the God of Nahor, the God of their father, judge between us.' So Jacob swore by the Fear of his father Isaac, and Jacob offered a sacrifice on the mountain and called his kinsmen to eat bread; and they ate bread and tarried all night on the mountain (Gen. 31.51–4).

This form of civil treaty was employed in the Hebrew expression of God's friendship with their race. The negotiated terms of loyalty and protection were confirmed in the sacrificial meal in which the Lord shared with his People.

The covenant meal is understood as sacrificial in Hebrew tradition from the first, that is, before the Passover covenant was celebrated, but it took a more permanent and liturgical shape in the Passover rite. The Hebrew assembly is described in covenant and sacrificial terms in many passages of the Old Testament, for example in the liturgical hymn, Psalm 50: 'Gather to me my faithful ones, who made a covenant with me by sacrifice' (Ps. 50.5). The sacrificial element of the covenant is generally described in terms of burnt offerings and peace offerings, and these are referred to in the later redactions of the covenant foundation story in Exodus, but here, as in the most primitive accounts, the emphasis is placed mainly on the sharing of blood. Moses divides the blood of the sacrificial animals and throws half of it across the altar of Yahweh and half he sprinkles on the People. The People thus become sharers in the blood of God, they become the family of God. At this point, as would be expected, the ritual prescribed a family meal: 'they beheld God and ate and drank' (Ex. 24.11). The elements of sacrifice and meal are complementary in Hebrew thought.

That the Israelites 'beheld God' is a sign that they have been freed from their sins, and this is brought out by the accompanying verse: 'He did not lay his hand on the chief men of the people.' The elders who eat with God have been cleansed by the covenant sacrifice and the ritual blood sprinkling. This element of the covenant situation is understood by the great canonical prophets, Isaiah and Jeremiah, to be an everlasting mercy. Jeremiah's conception of the new covenant that God will make in the hearts of his people, and which will not depend upon external observances, is primarily one of forgiveness: 'I will forgive their inquity, says the Lord, and I will remember their sin no more' (Jer. 31.34). It is evident that the Christian covenant has

71

fulfilled this and the other signs of the Hebrew relationship with God.

But until Christ comes the People are told to repeat the celebration of the covenant ceremonial. There are several passages in the Old Testament describing the renewal of the covenant between the penitent people and the forgiving Lord, from the primitive tribal assembly at Shechem, described in the book of Joshua, to the royal cultic ceremonies of Hezekiah in II Chronicles and of Josiah in II Kings, and the priestly liturgy of Nehemiah and Ezra, when the people confessed their sins, and offered great sacrifices and then turned to the meal celebration, 'and the joy of Jerusalem was heard afar off'. It is important to notice that even in these instances we have evidence of the freedom with which the Hebrews regarded the form of the renewal of their covenant situation. The tribal leaders, the kings and the priests adapted the ceremonial to their own needs, they felt empowered to present the covenant in various ways. They did not accept a principle of external uniformity but rather one of internal unity. This attitude remained in the early Christian understanding of the Eucharist.

We can discern, therefore, four main features of the Hebrew understanding of the covenant with Yahweh:

(i)   the ceremonial is set within a meal context;
(ii) the meal is considered to be sacrificial and is set up in blood;
(iii) the sharing in the meal frees the participant from sin;
(iv) the ceremony of the covenant is to be repeated but not slavishly copied from the first performance of the rite.

I want now, without going into many details, to demonstrate the presence of these features in the Christian covenant of the Eucharist.

(1) *The Eucharist is a meal*

Despite the present liturgical celebration of the Eucharist which obscures the meal character of the rite, we are all aware of the original context chosen by Christ for his new covenant.

It is to be noted also that the preliminary hints of the covenant that he would establish were given within a meal context by Christ: 'How are we to obtain bread for these folk to eat?' (Jn 6.6), and that this is immediately connected with the Exodus event and its renewal at the Passover: 'It was nearly the time of the Jews' great feast, the paschal feast' (Jn 6.4).

72

The feeding of the multitude opens the way for an explanation of what Christ is to do. And the way is opened in Exodus terms. The multitude said to him: 'What miracle canst thou do? We must see it before we trust thee; what canst thou effect? Our fathers had manna to eat in the desert' (6.30). Jesus tells them that the bread of the desert time was not substantial, the covenant of Sinai could not last: 'Your fathers who ate manna in the desert, died none the less; the bread which comes down from heaven is such that he who eats of it, never dies' (6.59). Like all the other signs its meaning is only fulfilled in his own person: 'I am the living bread that has come down from heaven. If anyone eats of this bread he shall live for ever. And now, what is this bread which I am to give? It is my flesh, given for the life of the world' (6.51–2). This last phrase suggests of course the sacrificial element which is an integral part of the covenant.

The Last Supper itself will be expected to have the shape of the old covenant meal in order that the participants would realize what is happening among them. But the Eucharist we have now does not have all the features of the Passover feast. In our present texts the evangelists have preserved only those elements of the rite which have been invested with a new meaning by Christ. Thus the lamb disappears from the meal because it has been subsumed into the person of Christ who is the 'Lamb of God' and who has taken upon himself the features of this sign in his passion—in the Johannine account of the crucifixion the event takes place at a time when the lambs were being slaughtered in the city, and ritual prohibition recorded in Exodus against the breaking of any of the lamb's bones is transferred to Christ: 'when they came to Jesus, and found him already dead they did not break his legs' (Jn 19.33).

There are traces in the gospel narratives of other features of the Passover meal—the dish of bitter herbs, the unleavened bread, the singing of the Hallel psalms, but of these only the unleavened bread survived into the primitive eucharistic celebration, though perhaps the whole rite may be described as a praise and thanksgiving song of the Hallel type.

(2) *The Eucharist is a sacrifice set up in blood*

Certainly the primitive Christian community saw the Eucharist as a sacrificial celebration of Christ: 'Christ our pasch is sacrificed.

Therefore let us feast' (I Cor. 5.7, Douay), wrote Paul to the Corinthians, stressing the resemblance to the old covenant feasts of the desert journey by saying immediately afterwards that his converts must avoid all evil-doers and servers of idols, for 'you must make an exodus out of this world' (I Cor. 5.10).

The Eucharist is also plainly a covenant in blood. The institution narratives make this obvious: 'This cup is the new testament in my blood which is to be shed for you' (Lk. 22.20). And this is the understanding of all New Testament writers. The author of Hebrews brings out the connection between the resurrection and the covenant in terms of blood: 'the God of Peace brought again from the dead the great shepherd of the sheep, our Lord Jesus Christ, in the blood of the everlasting covenant' (Heb. 13.20); and in I Peter the writer employs the Passover imagery again: '[the elect] give their allegiance to Jesus Christ and (are) sprinkled with his blood' (1.2); and of our being saved he writes that we are bought 'in the precious blood of Christ; no lamb was ever so pure, so spotless a victim' (1.19).

Further, the author of Hebrews has deliberately altered the text of the Septuagint in order to bring out the resemblance between the old Mosaic covenant and the new covenant of the Last Supper. He remembers the eucharistic introduction to the consecration of the cup which was known to Paul and the Corinthian community: '*In the same way also* the cup, after supper saying, "This cup is the new covenant in my blood"' (I Cor. 11.25, RSV). So he has inserted this introductory phrase in the Exodus narrative: '*In the same way also* he sprinkled with blood both the tent and the vessels used in worship' (Heb. 9.21). The parallelism is introduced in order that the meaning of the new covenant may be grasped by those who have celebrated the old covenant, and so that the significance of the old covenant may be realized by those who now celebrate its fulfilment.

At the same time the New Testament writers make it quite clear that there is a difference between the two covenants. Thus the author of Hebrews stresses the radical difference between the High Priest of the levitical order in the Temple who entered the Holy of Holies and offered God blood that he had taken from other victims, and Jesus the High Priest according to the order of Melchizedek who enters the sanctuary of the new covenant and offers his own blood as a sacrificial pledge.

A similar distinction is drawn by Paul in the Epistle to the Romans:

'God has offered him to us as a means of reconciliation, in virtue of faith, ransoming us *with his blood*' (3.25). The distinction again is between the old sacrifices of the blood of bulls and goats and the new sacrifice of Christ on the cross which is made in the blood of Jesus himself: 'it was while we were still sinners that Christ, in his own appointed time, died for us. All the more surely, then, now that we have found justification *through his blood*, shall we be saved' (Rom. 5.8–9). The emphasis in all the New Testament writings is on the personal character of the new covenant in Jesus Christ.

(3) *The Eucharist remits sin*

The passage from Hebrews which has just been quoted goes on to show the connection in the Eucharist of the blood shed by Christ in this new covenant and the remission of sin: 'unless blood is shed there can be no remission of sins' (9.22), and this shedding of blood brings about the new ritual in the new sanctuary: 'it is his own blood, not the blood of goats and calves, that has enabled him to enter, once for all, into the sanctuary' (9.12), and which completes the redeeming work of God begun at the Exodus: 'the ransom he has won lasts for ever' (9.12), and is the very covenant expected by Jeremiah who had said: 'This is the covenant which I shall make with the house of Israel after those days, says the Lord; I will put my law within them, and I will write it upon their hearts; and I will be their God and they shall be my people' (Jer. 31.33; cf. Heb. 6.10).

This prophecy quoted in Hebrews connects by several phrases with the old covenant and leads forward to the concept of the new covenant in Hebrews which is concerned with inward turning to God and the revitalization and simplification of the Jewish ritual law into a worship in Spirit and in Truth: 'shall not the blood of Christ, who offered himself, through the Holy Spirit, as a victim unblemished in God's sight, purify our consciences, and set them free from lifeless observances to serve the living God?' (Heb. 9.14).

It should be noticed here that the author of Hebrews is assuming that in Christ's sacrificial death all the sacrifices of the old covenant society are being fulfilled. He knew that the normal sin-offering in the old Law was certainly not the Passover lamb which does not seem to have any connection with the liberation from sin, but the 'blood of bulls and goats'. Christ dies as the expiatory sacrificial victim but not as the paschal lamb in this account of the redemption.

75

Contrariwise it certainly seems that in John's gospel the account of the death of Christ is written so that men will come to identify the Christ dying on the cross with the lambs being slaughtered in Jerusalem for the celebration of the Passover commemoration.

We need not read these soteriologies separately, they are not necessarily disjunctive. It is probable that no theology of our redemption could enclose the whole meaning. If we read Hebrews and John together here we are presented with Christ as both the saving victim who bears away our sin by his blood, and as the final covenant sign of the Paschal lamb who is present in our new covenant meal. Both these ideas are held within the context of our eucharistic celebration. Indeed it may well be that these two concepts are complementary in rather the way in which the concepts of sacrifice and meal are complementary in any possible theory of the Christian Eucharist.

(4) *The Eucharist is to be repeated*

It is evident from accounts of the Last Supper that the first Christians interpreted Christ as intending a repetition of his covenant sacrificial meal in his community: 'Do this for a commemoration of me' (Lk. 22.19). They knew themselves commanded to repeat the act of Christ. The command to continue the ceremony and to 'proclaim the death of the Lord' corresponds with the Haggadah at the Hebrew Paschal meal.

The Haggadah exemplar may explain several features of our present New Testament history of Jesus. For example, Professor Daube has suggested that the infancy narrative in Matthew's gospel is partly shaped by a Passover recital of Jewish history which took as its starting-point the persecution of Jacob by Laban and Jacob's flight into Egypt to save Israel: 'Our impression is that this is another instance of a narrative concerning Jesus having been formulated at a Christian Passover eve celebration in the first decade after the crucifixion, and having been formulated as part of a general and natural tendency to attach the "tale", "proclamation", "interpretation" of the new redemption to the traditional Haggadah of the old.' It may also be that the narratives of the Passion are so alike in all four gospels because this part of the Christian account of Christ was early fixed by its recital at the Passover-like Eucharist of the first Jewish converts. The form would become inalterable by the liturgical custom, even many of the details would be kept unchanged. This was the view of K. L. Schmidt over fifty years ago: 'In its full extent the Passion Story will have been publicly read in religious worship as a *lectio continua.*'

At the same time it must be remembered that the Hebrews did not feel themselves bound to any one particular form of repetition. There was a variety in the ways in which they expressed their participation in the one enduring covenant. So with the Christian community. In our narratives there seem to be indications of several re-orderings of the material. Jeremias remarks that Mark 14.22 by the opening genitive absolute reveals a join in the text. He supposes that there must once have been an introductory passage which when he came to write up his account of the Last Supper did not suit his purpose. He therefore removed the phrase from the traditional material he had received. Jeremias suggests that the prefatory remark may well have been something like that which introduces the institution pericope in I Corinthians: 'For I received from the Lord what I also delivered to you: the Lord Jesus on the night when he was betrayed' (11.23, RSV).

On this matter Benoit came in 1939 to the conclusion that the Marcan account had signs of a certain patching and revision, 'something approaching a coalition of expressions which derive from different sources', and he summed up his account by suggesting that 'Mark, having reached the central point of the Last Supper narrative, felt he could not do better, in relating it, than to insert in his text, a liturgical narrative, which was already in his time pretty well established and employed in the celebration of the Eucharist.' Benoit then went on to make some general observations about the shape of the early re-ordering of the Last Supper by the renewing Christians: 'the early Christians, when they renewed the celebration of the Last Supper, dropped therefrom all the elements of the paschal ceremony to which our Lord attached no particular significance; they retained only the two gestures which had taken on, by virtue of the Master's words, a new significance.'

Of our two main accounts, Paul's narrative in I Corinthians is certainly written down earlier but the Marcan form reflects an earlier practice. Mark has the simple ritual verbs: he took . . . blessed . . . broke; while Paul and Luke have the developed form: he took . . . gave thanks . . . and broke, in which the eucharistic language has been introduced. The influence of the cultic situation in different communities suggests that in Mark's community the advice of Paul to the Corinthians to separate entirely the meal and the liturgical celebration had been taken very early. In Mark the consecration of the bread and the wine is one unit, but Paul's narrative shows us a tradition in which they were still separate. Both Mark and Paul, therefore, show signs of development and continuing tradition in the new covenant renewal of the community.

F. THE EXODUS AND THE CHRISTIAN LIFE

What is spoken of Christ is spoken of the Christian. In this section I mean to indicate some of the ways in which the members of the first community thought of the Exodus meaning of Christ as working itself out in their own lives and the lives of their communities. Lest it should be supposed that it is mainly in the Johannine corpus that this simile and fulfilment pattern is to be found I will set out examples from the general epistles.

These epistles are commonly concerned in their use of the Exodus pattern with the introduction of a morality exemplar for their people. They assert a resemblance and therefore a meaning between the Egyptian slavery and the conditions of their present community. The Egyptian slavery was one of injustice and hardship created by a luxurious and effete aristocracy. James, in his epistle, threatens the rich man with the punishments that God inflicted on the Egyptian exploiters: 'You have kept back the pay of the workmen who worked on your lands, and there is a cry against you: the Lord of hosts has listened to their complaints. You have feasted here on earth, you have comforted your hearts with luxuries this day, the day that dooms you to slaughter' (5.4), and in I Peter the Christians are told to live among the heathen as the Hebrews lived in Egypt: 'be like strangers and exiles . . . your life among the Gentiles must be beyond reproach' (2.11); like the Israelites in Egypt they are to begin by suffering and obedience to cruel men.

And like the Hebrews of the Passover night they are to understand that their suffering and obedience is a way into the freedom of the servants of God. One part of the Passover liturgy among the Jews opens with the words: 'In the beginning our fathers were slaves of strange slavery, but God has drawn us close to his slavery.' The Passover context includes the famous description in the book of

Joshua of the Exodus and the gaining of the land of Canaan, a description which ends with the exhortation: 'Now therefore fear the Lord, and be his slaves in sincerity and in faithfulness' (24.14); and shows that the change of allegiance here includes the whole process of the Exodus until the Israelites were established as the men of God. It is paralleled in St Paul's 'You were the slaves of sin but you have obeyed from the heart . . . being then made free from sin you became slaves of righteousness' (Rom. 6.17–18). The change of masters is the reality of freedom. A captive bought back becomes his buyer's bondman, the Israelites pass under God's rule because it is he who freed them from the Egyptians.

The combination of service and freedom is brought out well in the recent commentary on the rabbinic treatment of the Hallel, Psalm 113, by Professor Daube in his book on the *Exodus Pattern*. The Psalm begins: 'Praise ye the Lord, O slaves of the Lord,' and upon this verse a comment in the Jewish tradition is, 'Thou recoveredst us and broughtest us out to freedom, for we were slaves unto Pharaoh and thou recoveredst us and madest us slaves unto thee'. So I Peter exhorts us: 'Submit yourselves to every ordinance of man for the Lord's sake . . . as free, and not using your liberty for a cloak of maliciousness, but as slaves of God' (2.13, 16). They journeyed out into the desert not a people who could choose their own way wherever they would go in the world, but a people given a route and a path.

The path was one of promise, and so we too have our promise as II Peter reminds the Christian community: 'Meanwhile we have new heavens and a new earth to look forward to, the dwelling-place of holiness; that is what (the Lord) has promised. These are your expectations' (3.13). But expectations are often not enough. We can see in the Epistle to the Hebrews how near the early Church came to the grumbling attitude of the Israelites in the desert. The early Christians felt somehow caught in a promise-crammed era. They had left the house of worldly slavery, and had responded to the baptismal vocation of an eschatological existence, and now instead of the promised land there is only the journey. They have become tired and want a worldly patterned existence. They are near to apostasy, 'falling from the living God'. They are like the servants in St Matthew's parable, who say to themselves 'the Master is delayed' and begin to beat their fellows and get drunk. Waiting is a trying time, as II Peter reminds them: 'The Lord is not being dilatory over his promise, as some think; he is only giving you more time, because his will is that all of you should attain repentance, not that some should be lost. But the day of the Lord is coming . . . if our Lord stays his hand, count it part of his mercy' (3.9, 15); and again in the epistle of James: 'You must wait patiently, and take courage, the Lord's coming is at hand' (5.8).

The People of Israel did not wait patiently, they did not walk along the path that God had given them. Christians must be more men of God than the Israelites proved themselves: 'meanwhile through your faith the power of God affords you safe conduct till you reach the salvation which is waiting to be disclosed at the end of time' (I Pet. 1.5). The Israelites forsook the path of the living God and contented themselves with a golden calf. But the Christian when confronted with temptation must realize that this is a tempering of his faith 'so that you may give proof of your faith, a much more precious thing than gold' (I Pet. 1.7). The Christians are worth more than any golden relic of past idolatry. They are the people of the new Passover and we must learn from their wretchedness what truth requires of us.

And Jude makes a specific comparison between those Christians who have fallen from their first response to Christ, and the Children of Israel who murmured against God in the wilderness: 'Learn one lesson and you know all. Let me remind you, how the Saviour who had rescued his people from Egypt went on to destroy those who had proved unfaithful' (Jude 5).

So we can see in these epistles the general pattern of the journey in the desert from its beginnings in the slavery under Egypt and the Passover redemption through the various trials of the wilderness and the punishment of those who complained of God's treatment of his people and lost courage and faith in him. The Christian life is a guided way and the way lies through the shadows of the valley and in the waterless places, and yet though all seems futile and unloving, the only unreasonable response is to complain and to cease the journey.

Such a journey can, of course, only be acceptable as a human existence if there is shown to be a city at the end. A pilgrimage without a shrine, a voyage without a dock, a caravan without a trading market, are not human situations because they lack the ground of reason. A religion that was simply a struggle, simply an emotional longing, would not be of use to us. For real men the real God must signpost the way and point towards something.

As the Exodus journey is the meaningful passage of the Hebrews so death is understood by these early writers as the meaningful passage of the Christian. Both can be spoken of in the same language. Thus in II Peter the author speaks of his own coming death: 'Christ has made known to me that I must fold up my tent before long' (1.14). There is here a reference to the prophecy of Peter's death that the Lord makes in the last resurrection appearance of John's gospel and to the folding up of the tents at the end of the Hebrews' journey through the desert. The death of the apostle is like the coming into the promised land of the Hebrews. This is made more explicit in the next sentence where the author writes: 'I will see to it that when I am gone, you shall be able to remember what I have been saying to you' (1.15). The original Greek here for the 'going' of the apostle into death is 'exodos'. The use of 'exodos' to mean the departure into death occurs in only one other place cited by Liddell and Scott. This is the account of transfiguration in Luke's gospel where Moses and Elijah speak to Jesus of his coming passion and death as his exodus. The death of Christ is the coming into the kingdom, the death of the Christian is like unto this. The whole process of being a Christian is made meaningful by our configuration to Christ who sums up in himself the whole of the Law and the Prophets.

At this point we have some indication of the solution to the difficulty that many have felt—why is it that once Christ has defeated the power of evil at the Temptation incident we should still have to undergo our temptations, why is it that once Christ has undergone his Exodus we should still have to go on our wearisome journey? The answer lies in the principle that we have to be conformed to Christ, that we have to experience the experience of Christ if we are to share the glory of Christ.

Thus the Temptation narratives are certainly his perfect triumph over evil but there yet remains our effort and victory. This comes out in the narratives themselves. Christ's victory holds back Satan for a while. As Conzelmann writes in his commentary on Luke: 'What is now beginning [at the Temptations] is not the last times, but the interval between the period of the Law, or of Israel, and the period of the Spirit, or of the Church.' Luke thinks of the Temptations as effecting a hold-up in the world of Satan's activity. This notion is itself connected with the general Exodus view of the Jews. In the book of Jubilees the devil Mastema is described as bound for five days in order to allow the Israelites to escape from Egypt. After the five days, respite the demon is allowed once more to molest the people. The Temptations both announce the final defeat of evil and show how we are to fight that evil in our own Exodus lives.

This is but one of the paradoxes of the Christian belief. We are always having to hold together the notion of Christ's accomplishment and our endurance, of his grace and our merit, of the difference and the likeness between our position and that of the old people of the Exodus. This is the point of the passage in Hebrews that adverts to the comparison we have been making: 'you have not come to what may be touched, a blazing fire, and darkness and gloom, and a tempest, and the sound of a trumpet, and a voice whose words made the hearers entreat that no further messages be spoken to them' (Heb. 12.18–19, RSV); the old fury is departed and we are the friends of Christ, but our friendship is within the language of the old fury; 'you have come to Mount Zion and to the city of the living God, the heavenly Jerusalem, and to innumerable angels in festal gathering and to the assembly of the first-born who are enrolled in heaven, and to a judge who is God of all, and to the spirits of just men made perfect, and to Jesus, the mediator of the new covenant, and to the sprinkled blood that speaks more graciously than the blood of Abel' (Heb. 12.22–4, RSV). In this passage the author of Hebrews moves from the Exodus experience of the Israelites to the Davidic covenant on Mount Zion and the Temple liturgy of that covenant in Jerusalem.

I shall point later to the various ways in which the Temple liturgy influenced the Old Testament narratives and the New Testament conception of Christ and his work, but first I want to say something about the way in which the prime event of that work influenced the early Christians' understanding of the whole life and actions of Christ. That is, I want to bring out the evidence which demonstrates that, above all, the first Christian people understood Christ to be the Risen Lord. The resurrection dominated their view of Christ, and they looked at everything in his life through the resurrection which gave meaning to everything else.

This is the second stage in my description of the images and attitudes which directed the shape of the Christian account of

Christ. First, they were men of the old covenant, they thought and imagined within the old covenant categories; second, they had as the subject of their thoughts and imaginings the explosive event of the resurrection which altered their whole lives in a revolutionary way, and third, they expressed this, as the men of the old covenant had expressed their understanding of God's action, in a liturgical assembly of believers. The pivoting event which gives meaning to the old witness and to the new liturgy is the Paschal Rising of Christ.

III

The Resurrection

A. PREACHING THE EVENT

THE sermons recorded in Acts may not have come down to us in the form of verbatim reports, though this might be plausibly defended on linguistic and exegetical grounds of no mean force, but at any rate the general tone of the sermons seems to be a faithful reflection of the primitive catechesis. Of the elements common to these sermons and those elaborated in the epistles of the New Testament, the most important is the emphasis on the resurrection of Christ. Such an emphasis is the distinguishing mark of apostolic and immediately post-apostolic preaching, whether the sermon be directed towards Gentiles or Hebrews.

The resurrection gave meaning to the Old Testament scriptures. This is brought out not simply by the implicit manner of using such scriptures in the description of Christ and his work, but in the explicit manner of announcing to the disciples that an Old Testament writing is being fulfilled. Thus when Christ speaks of the destruction of the Temple and his own bodily death, John comments: 'when therefore he was raised from the dead his disciples remembered that he had said this; and they believed the scripture' (Jn 2.22); again, the use of the Zechariah quotation in the Palm Sunday narrative prompts this editorial gloss: 'when Jesus was glorified, then they remembered that this had been written of him' (12.16 RSV).

We have already noticed the construction of Peter's first sermon on Pentecost Day with its catena of Old Testament quotations to present the fact of the resurrection. This was to a Hebrew audience (though of course Luke makes every possible use of the diaspora character of the audience in order to make a claim for early universalist activity in the Church). Paul's mission in Athens gives an example of how the Gentile mission was pursued. Paul preaches the doctrine of the creating unknown God and then moves to the demand for repentance and belief in the risen Christ: 'he commands all men everywhere to repent, because he has fixed a day on which he will judge the world in righteousness by a man whom he has appointed, and of this he has given assurance to all men by raising him from the dead' (Acts 17.30–1, RSV). It is the reference to the resurrection that strikes his listeners as odd in Paul's speech and which is critical for their attitudes: 'when they heard of the resurrection of the dead, some mocked; but others said, "We will hear you again about this"' (Acts 17.32, RSV). The resurrection is difficult for the philosophers to take, they go away, politely or not.

Further instances of the early apologetic being founded on the resurrection occur throughout the New Testament. Paul writes to his Corinthian community of the resurrection as the central truth which gives meaning to the whole of our Christian activity and which leads us on to the possession of the kingdom of God for ever:

> If Christ has not been raised, then our preaching is in vain and your faith is in vain. We are even found to be misrepresenting God, because we testified of God that he raised Christ, whom he did not raise if it be true that the dead are not raised. For if the dead are not raised, then Christ has not been raised. If Christ has not been raised, your faith is futile and you are still in your sins. Then those who have fallen asleep in Christ have perished. If for this life only we have hoped in Christ, we are of all men the most to be pitied.
>
> But in fact Christ has been raised from the dead, the first fruits of those who have fallen asleep. For as by a man came death, by a man has come also the resurrection of the dead. For as in Adam all die, so in Christ shall all be made alive. But each in his own order: Christ the first fruits, then at his coming those who belong to Christ. Then comes the end when he delivers the kingdom to God the Father after destroying every rule and authority and power. (I Cor. 15.14–25, RSV).

The same thought is put across in Romans 4, and shortly in the opening verses of I Peter: 'we have been born anew to a living hope through the resurrection of Jesus Christ from the dead, and to an inheritance which is imperishable, undefiled, unfading, kept in heaven for you' (1.3–4, RSV).

The Church's mission may be seen as a responsibility to preach the resurrection. Something of this resurrection character of our mission may be hinted in that curious injunction of Christ to his disciples sent to preach his truth that they give no one greeting on the way. This may be a recollection of Elisha's sending out his servant Gehazi to raise the son of the Shunammite to life again: 'Gird up your loins, and take my staff in your hand, and go. If you meet anyone, do not salute him; and if anyone salutes you, do not reply' (II Kings 4.29); the mission of the disciple is to raise men to Christ's new life. We can see how this worked out in the apostolic preaching in the account of the miracle of Peter's almsgiving: 'I give you what I have; in the name of Jesus Christ of Nazareth, walk. And he took him by the right hand and raised him up . . . and all the people saw him walking and leaping and praising God' (Acts 3.6–8, RSV). And Peter takes this chance to tell the people that though they had murdered the Author of life, God has raised him from the dead, and the rulers of the Temple precincts were annoyed precisely because the healing had been used in this way: 'they were annoyed because they were teaching the people and proclaiming in Jesus the resurrection from the dead' (Acts 4.2, RSV). It is evident that Peter had moved from the healing to a proclamation of Christ's resurrection, and then forwards to a testimony of our resurrection 'in Jesus'.

Peter seems always to have understood his apostolic mission in terms of preaching the resurrection. Thus when there is a discussion about who is to fill Judas' place in their group, Peter makes it a necessary qualification that the man chosen should have been with them at the time when the risen Lord was among them, and further than this he defines the apostolic charge in terms of the resurrection mission: 'one of these men must become with us a witness to his resurrection' (Acts 1.22, RSV). This is certainly a very early piece of the tradition since it puts a great value on the apostolic grouping. This was characteristic of the first closed society of Christians but the activities of Philip and Stephen show us the very early emergence of others as leaders and the account of the early Church in Acts is concerned with the apostles only so far as they were at the centre of the missionary activity. Peter and Paul are prominent but the others, despite their apostolic character, are not thought interesting. So a piece of the tradition which puts emphasis on the apostolic group as a fixed and hieratic element in the Church must derive from a very early source indeed, hence the emphasis on the missionary as a witness to the resurrection must have been part of the faith of the very first Christians.

Similarly in the first sermon accounts in Acts Peter is represented as putting the main stress on the resurrection as the redeeming event. The psalms are quoted as speaking of the resurrection and in the present the apostles are to witness to their fulfilment. David, says Peter, 'foresaw and spoke of the resurrection of the Christ, that he was not abandoned to Hades, nor did his flesh see corruption. This Jesus God raised up, and of that we are all witnesses' (Acts 2.31–2, RSV).

To be a Christian, then, is to be a witness to the resurrection of Christ. The event is the proper subject of the proclamation because it works our salvation and brings us to an eternal home.

B. THE FAITHFUL ACCOUNT

The meaning of the resurrection was, of course, understood before the accounts were composed. The narratives we have of the resurrection story are the results of a generation of preaching, worship and meditation. This must be realized before a proper treatment of the narratives can be attempted. The demands we make of the narratives will not be those we might make of eye-witness accounts. We should expect that the facts should be presented within the enriching context of the inspired interpretation of the community. We inherit not simply a history but a history whose meaning is revealed to us.

M. Guitton, a lay auditor at the Council, has recently suggested that the experience of the risen Christ given to the disciples was truly a gift, a grace. He thinks that the appearance of Christ was not susceptible of empirical verification but was simply granted by God to some men of his choice. 'It would seem to me that if Tiberius or Tacitus, if Philo or Pilate or Josephus had happened to be present in that room where Jesus appeared, none of these would have seen anything at all.'

Fr Dulles says that Acts supports this hypothesis of the vision being given by the gift of God. Peter in the house of Cornelius says to the assembled people: 'God raised him up on the third day and made him manifest; not to all the people but to us who were chosen by God as witnesses, who ate and drank with him after he rose from the dead' (Acts 10.40–41).

I do not find Guitton's thesis so unacceptable that it can be immediately ruled out. It certainly brings home in a particularly vivid manner the faithful nature of the Christian experience. So that it would give us a straightforward explanation of the strangeness in Matthew's narrative of the final appearance: 'when they saw him they worshipped him: but some doubted' (Mt. 28.17). On this thesis the oddity here could be explained on the supposition that those who doubted could not see and therefore could not worship. The publication of Guitton's thesis and its support by Dulles brings home, too, the wide freedom of the Catholic apologist today. The nineteenth-century historicist would never have allowed this.

At the same time I am not entirely happy about Guitton's suggestion. Given that the accounts of the resurrection are 'written up', they were written up with a purpose, they are intended to assure men that such a thing occurred and is meaningful. The details of the story may be rather more indicative of the 'intention' than of 'what happened' but this means only that the evangelists believed that through such a narrative a better understanding of 'what happened' is to be gathered than by any other means. So we are left with the empty tomb, the fish bones and the washing up. Peter's speech is not simply a claim to choice and vision but an affirmation, immediately joined to these, of real meals after the resurrection.

If the purpose of Peter's remark and the gospel accounts of Jesus eating is simply to show that he was present to the apostles not only in the sense of his real presence to us in the Eucharist, or in the sense of his commemorative presence in a picture or statue, but in flesh and blood—capable of munching and digesting food—then I am unable to conceive of a body capable of eating and drinking which is not visible to Pilate and Josephus. If these details are to prove anything, whether historically accurate or not, makes no difference here, they must be meant to prove a present physical body.

Peter is speaking not of the visibility of Christ being limited to certain men, but the favour of being present when Christ made one of his post-resurrection appearances as being limited to certain men. Similarly if some saw him they might yet doubt in the sense of not being convinced that he was the same Jesus, or that one ought to worship Jesus. If there were no possibility of seeing and doubting then there would be no possibility of seeing and believing. Whether or no there were fish-bones left in the supper room would depend on whether he ate fish, and all we need to know is that there could have been fish bones because the evangelist knew that he could have eaten fish. This seems to me the reasonable meaning of the narrative.

Be that as it may, the important thing is to notice that the gospel narratives of the resurrection are written with the same intention as the I Corinthians 15 account of the resurrection—that men should believe in the risen Lord and commit themselves to him. And it is noticeable that the two accounts, and the Petrine speech quoted earlier, appeal to the same notion of witnesses as the guarantee of credibility. These things happened and we can believe it because men who were there have testified and their word is true. The formula is the same as in the gospel of John.

Why was a meal taken as the means of putting Christ across in the resurrection narrative?

I think it was selected for two reasons—in addition to the fact that it happened, for so no doubt did other actions of Christ in this period before the final resurrection appearance of the Ascension.

(i) *Liturgical reasons*

It was in the meal of the Eucharist that the early Christians knew they were meeting the risen Christ: 'The bread which we break, is it not a participation in the body of Christ?' (I Cor. 10.6).

(ii) *Old Testament memories*

In the old covenant God made meals with his people. Abraham entertained him at his tent, Abel's fatlings were a meal for God, and David celebrated the coming of the Ark by a feast for all the people. These are but a few of the meals at which God presented himself to his chosen race. They are all, of course, taken up in the manna, which Christ in turn took up as the sign of his presence in the Eucharist.

It is particularly in meals of fish and bread that the risen Lord is manifested. These two come together in many of the meals recorded in the gospels:

(a) the eucharistic language of this passage will be more carefully considered in another section: 'taking the five loaves and two fish he looked up to heaven, and blessed, and broke the loaves and gave them to the disciples to set before the people; and he divided the two fish among them all' (Mk 6.41, RSV).

(b) 'what man of you, if his son asks him for bread, will give him a stone? Or if he asks for a fish, will give him a serpent' (Mt. 7.9, RSV).

(c) 'Have you anything here to eat? They gave him a piece of broiled fish' (Lk. 24.41).

(d) 'They saw a charcoal fire there with fish lying on it and bread . . . they knew it was the Lord' (Jn 21.9; 12).

The resurrection and the eucharistic presence of Christ are one in these passages. For, of course, as we shall see in more detail in later sections, the fish is the primitive sign of Christ, Lord and Saviour, and the bread is the sacrament of his presence.

If the meals are the sign of the risen Lord what is the reality to which they sign? What is the character of the resurrection on which the whole of the Christian faith depends: 'If Christ be not risen our faith is in vain' (I Cor. 15.16).

The resurrection was not seen by anyone. On that at least all the evangelists agree in their account of the Easter event. So the emphasis is placed by the New Testament writers, not on the historical event, this is presumed, but on the continuing results of this event—the Church is the result of Christ's continuing presence with his people. The resurrection appearances are not a series ending with the ascension, they are the beginning of all Christ's presences to his community—the last word recorded of the risen Christ is: 'Behold I am with you always to the close of the age' (Mt. 28.20). So the resurrection is both the promise of our resurrection and the witness of Christ's presence with us now.

This final promise of his presence is carefully positioned in Matthew's gospel since it rounds off the whole of his christology. The risen Lord finally fulfils the Old Testament promise which is proclaimed at the beginning of the gospel. In the first chapter of Matthew there is the story of the dream of Joseph which is so written that we shall advert to the Isaiah prophecy of the child to be born of the young woman: 'All this was so ordained to fulfil the word which the Lord spoke by his prophet: Behold, the virgin shall be with child and shall bear a son, and they shall call him Emmanuel (which means God with us)' (Mt. 1.22). For Matthew the full truth of Jesus as the Emmanuel is not made among us until the resurrection, whenceforward Christ is always with his people. His gospel is constructed to lead us to recognize the various events of Christ's life as steps towards the establishing of the new community within which Jesus, the Lord, is always with us. The resurrection is evidently the central notion of Matthew's christology and therefore of his ecclesiology.

Matthew's gospel is only one example of the general belief of the New Testament communities that the resurrection makes sense of their life in the Church of Christ. We should expect, indeed, that the whole of the gospel narrative of Christ's work would be dominated by a resurrection pattern, that this act should give a shape and a direction to the Christian understanding of all the other acts of Christ. This is in fact the case, and I shall in the next section make an attempt to demonstrate the continuing effect of the resurrection event and the traditions in which it was handed from one Christian community to another on the primitive view of the previous events of Christ's life.

C. THE RESURRECTION APPEARANCES AND THE TRANSFIGURATION

As an example of the way in which the resurrection tradition affected the writing of other parts of the gospel, I shall first rehearse a comparison of the resurrection appearance in the last chapter of John's gospel and the transfiguration account in the synoptic writers.

It is generally agreed that the last chapter of John, like the last verses of the longer ending in Mark, is an addition composed by a different hand from the rest of the gospel, but this does not affect my present discussion since I am using the passage precisely as a piece of community tradition. It may well be that the variant endings of Mark and John derive from the variant liturgical readings of different eucharistic communities. The passage I am concerned with begins: 'Jesus appeared to his disciples again afterwards, at the sea of Tiberias, and this is how he appeared to them . . . ' (Jn 21.1ff.).

(a) The incident concerns Christ, Simon Peter and John, in the presence of James and the other disciples.

(b) It begins with a recognition of Christ as the Lord.

(c) The context is one of a meal at which Christ gives the disciples bread and fish—this we have earlier noticed is eucharistic in symbolism, cf. 6.11.

(d) Christ addresses Peter as 'Simon, son of John'.

(e) Christ three times asks Peter to commit himself to him.

(f) This is followed by a commission to lead the Church,

(g) together with a prophecy that Peter will be crucified; 'the death by which he was to glorify God' was known by the time the gospel was written.
Isaiah 65.2: 'I will stretch out my hands all day to a rebellious people' is taken by Barnabas (12.4) and Justin (I Apology 35) to refer to crucifixion.

(h) All this comes with the command 'Follow me'.

(i) The other disciples may see the Second Coming.

This written account is, of course, the last form of the oral tradition of the incident. That it was current among the community is shown, if demonstration of this kind of thing is necessary, by the author's attempt to prevent a false interpretation having further currency: 'The saying spread abroad among the brethren that this disciple was not to die; yet Jesus did not say to him that he was not to die but "If it is my will that he remain until I come, what is that to you?"' (21.23, RSV). And the story as we now have it has a community sanction, 'we know that his testimony is true'.

What is the point of this story? Why did the community, or the evangelist himself, add it to the already completed gospel with its perfectly shaped account of the resurrected Lord? An answer to this kind of question can only be given in a tentative form, but perhaps the skeleton of the account which has just been made gives some indications of the lines upon which an answer should be given.

The predominant notion in the beginning of the story is the identity of the risen Lord with the Jesus whom the disciples had known before the crucifixion. The recognition is set in an emphatic position: 'It is the Lord', after it has been said that at first the disciples 'did not know that it was Jesus'. It is perhaps significant that the figure is recognized as Lord, he is the one who now rules as the divine Messiah.

Secondly, the disciples do not have to question him, they all knew well that it was the Lord. They know well once they are taking part in the meal which he offers them, and whose elements they have brought him except for the bread. Taking part in the meal brings them to know the Lord. That he himself provides the bread is perhaps an indication of the total giving that is characteristic of the eucharistic Lord.

Thirdly, the story is emphatically directing attention to the setting up of the community, of the establishment of a shepherd as delegate of the one whose sheep we are. The story thus moves from the fact of the risen Lord through his eucharistic meal to the community and its pastoral care for the Christians. This is the least that the incident can be said to mean.

Professor Barrett suggests that the intention of the appendix was to replace the old view of the destiny of the beloved disciple with the new idea that while he would die before the Parousia, he through his written gospel would 'constitute himself the permanent guarantor of the Church's tradition'. This expresses precisely my view of the gospel as a witness to the traditional understanding of the early community, individual as a witness but communal in content and purpose.

The incident of the recognition after the fishing may have been a separate block of oral tradition with no settled place in the narrative of Jesus' acts since it seems to occur again in Luke (5.1–11) at a different position. There the disciples are again given a heavy shoal of fish after toiling uselessly before Christ came. Peter again acknowledges the Lord: 'Depart from me, for I am a sinful man, O Lord', and again there is the commission to lead the Church: 'Do not be afraid, henceforth you will be catching men'; and again the notion of following Christ: 'they left everything and followed him' (Lk. 5.8–11).

The story has been told, evidently, many times, and it would seem that John has used the oral tradition and even its vocabulary here. It can be shown, too, I think, that the influences which shaped this story have shaped others in the gospels.

I shall take first the account of the Transfiguration. The story is set down in Mark's gospel thus:

Jesus went with his disciples into the villages around Caesarea Philippi; and on the way he asked his disciples: Who do men say that I am? . . . then he said to them: Who do you say that I am? Peter answered: Thou art the Christ. And he strictly charged them not to tell anyone about him. And now he began to make it known to them that the Son of Man must be much ill-used and be rejected by the elders and chief priests and scribes and be put to death, and rise again after three days. This he told them openly; whereupon Peter, drawing him to his side reproached him. . . . Back, Satan, he said . . . and he said to them: If any man has a mind to come my way let him renounce self and take up his cross and follow me. . . . Believe me, there are those standing here who will not taste of death before they have seen the kingdom of God present in all its power.

Six days afterwards Jesus took Peter and James and John with him, and led them up to a high mountain where they were alone by themselves, and he was transfigured in their presence . . . and he forbade them to tell anyone of this until the Son of Man had risen from the dead (Mk. 8.27–9.8).

The first seven and a half chapters of Mark's gospel are written to demonstrate 'who Christ is'. Mark presents his evidence in terms of miracles and parables until there is enough for men of goodwill to judge aright. He then places an announcement of 'who Christ is' to conclude the section, an affirmation that he has given the necessary proof. This is what the confession of Peter, 'Thou art the Christ', provides.

The transfiguration is therefore an important structural element in the gospel; it marks the end of the first section and is parallel to the resurrection as marking the end of the second section.

If we now consider the transfiguration narrative beginning with the Caesarea Philippi text in connection with the Johannine description of the resurrection as analysed earlier we find this set of parallels:

(a) Christ, together with Peter and John (and James) with the other apostles.
(b) It begins with a recognition of Christ as the Lord.
(c) Nil.
(d) Nil.
(e) Perhaps 'Back, Satan' refers to Peter doing the work of Satan in suggesting that Christ grab the kingdom without suffering, which is what the *three questions* of Satan add up to.
(f) Nil.
(g) They are told to take up the cross
(h) and to follow Christ.

94

(i) Some of the disciples, it seems, will not die until the Second Coming.

The gap (c)–(f) with only a small hint at (e) would lead one to suppose that there is no dependence on the same oral tradition as is enshrined in John 21, but it is noteworthy that Mark associated this narrative with the resurrection of Christ. The disciples are not to speak of the transfiguration until Christ is risen. If we move on to Matthew's gospel in this connection and take into account that this gospel is ecclesial, it is the only gospel that uses the word 'Church' in an institutionalized sense, and that it is a gospel characterized by much more fulsome description of conversation and events than Mark's, we are led to suppose that these two characteristics reflect the liturgical tradition of the community to which he belonged. Matthew's work probably comes from a Syrian Christian community and his 'additions' are in fact quite old Christian traditions. This helps in understanding the differences of the transfiguration narratives in Mark and Matthew. Mark is writing to produce a vivid account, he writes at a brisk and lively pace. Matthew is producing a liturgically directed narrative and puts in what Mark omits:

> Now Jesus called the disciples and said: I am moved with pity for the multitude; it is three days now since they have come along with me, and they have had nothing to eat. I must not send them away fasting. . . . His disciples said to him: Where could we find loaves enough in a desert to feed such a multitude? Jesus asked them: How many loaves have you? Seven, they answered, and a few small fishes.
>
> Thereupon he bade the multitude sit down on the ground, and he took the seven loaves and the fishes with them, and when he had blessed and broken he gave these to his disciples, and his disciples to the multitude. And they all ate and had enough; and they took up what was left of the broken pieces, seven hampers full. Four thousand men had eaten, not counting the women and children. And so, taking his leave of the multitude, he went aboard the ship, and crossed to the region of Magedan.
>
> Then Jesus came into the neighbourhood of Caesarea Philippi; and there he asked his disciples, What do men say of the Son of Man? . . . Who do you say that I am? Simon Peter answered: Thou art the Christ, the Son of the living God. And Jesus answered him: Blessed art thou, Simon son of Jona; it is not flesh and blood, it is my Father in heaven that has revealed this to thee. And now I tell thee this, Thou art Peter, and it is upon this rock that I will build my church; and the gates of hell

shall not prevail against it; and I will give to thee the keys of the kingdom of heaven; and whatever thou shalt bind on earth shall be bound in heaven; and whatsoever thou shalt loose on earth shall be loosed in heaven (Mt. 15.32–39; 16.13–19).

Matthew's transfiguration narrative breaks down thus:

(a) Christ together with Peter and apostles.
(b) It begins with the recognition of Christ as the Lord.
   Sutcliffe has argued that the 'confession of St Peter' of Christ's divinity here had its original setting in a post-resurrection appearance, which shows how strong the post-resurrection pattern is at this point.
(c) The recognition is led into by a meal given by Christ, a meal of loaves and fishes.
(d) Peter is called 'Simon, son of Jona'.
(e) Nil.
(f) The commission to lead the Church: 'I give to thee the keys of the kingdom. . . .'
(g) The disciple is to take up his cross
(h) and follow Christ
(i) and some will not taste death until the Second Coming.

It seems evident that the transfiguration in the oral tradition of the community has something of the same shape and vocabulary as the resurrection tradition. Some have supposed that the transfiguration, particularly in Mark's structure, is a post-resurrection appearance inserted for pedagogic and literary reasons in a different position in the gospel. It seems to me more likely that the vocabulary and skeletal likenesses derive from Mark's realization that the whole of Christ's career is to be interpreted in resurrection terms.

The transfiguration account is not employed in the gospel in the same way as the resurrection appearances. It is an event with its own significance, however much that significance depends on the resurrection. The primary purpose of the transfiguration is to present the Christ of the Parousia. This certainly was the view of the Fathers. They took the promise of seeing Christ in his parousia glory to be fulfilled in the transfiguration. It is an eschatological event. It tells us also something of our own life with Christ.

We see first of all that Christ is at the centre, the past and present look to him. The past, Moses and Elias, point to Christ and speak of him. The present, Peter, James and John, understand now the significance of the past and present. They do not yet know what to do but they sense that worship is demanded by the nature of the situation. They do not yet possess a liturgy but they wish to erect tabernacles. And our worship is, of course, our going to the Father through the Son. The voice of the Father is heard because we are in the company of the Son. We are made a worshipping community when we realize the transfiguration situation.

The transfiguration may seem a little remote from our lives. It may be as well to take something from the gospel which brings home the resurrection pattern to the Christian. The intention of the gospel writers was that men should come to believe in Christ and have life and have it more abundantly. This abundant life is the life given by the resurrection and it is this life which enables us to rise in Christ.

4. The Miracle Narratives

How is Christ's life given to the Christian? The gospels, which may seem silent at this point, have an eloquence. They are full of stories in which the resurrection pattern is employed to arrange the event so that it strikes home to the reader that he too will rise. The transfiguration shows us Christ as he is and enables us to understand him, to realize who he is; the miracle stories show us Christ working in the community. It may be that unless we have faith we cannot enter into the kingdom, but we must remember that since we have faith we will receive. The miracle stories are paradigms of what we receive.

Let us begin with the miracle narrative of the palsied man who was let down through the roof of the house where Jesus was preaching:

> And now they came to bring a palsied man to him, four of them carrying him at once; and found they could not bring him close to, because of the multitude. So they stripped off the tiles from the roof over the place where Jesus was, and made an opening; then they let down the bed on which the palsied man lay. And Jesus, seeing their faith, said to the palsied man: Son, thy sins are forgiven . . . I tell thee, rise up, take thy bed with thee, and go home. And he rose up at once, and took his bed, and went out in full sight of them; so that all were astonished and gave praise to God (Mk. 2.3–12).

If we produce a skeleton of this narrative we have something like the following:

(a) Four men carry the man on a stretcher—as a man is carried by his friends on a bier.

(b) The man is let down through a hole 'dug out' (Mark's phrase) in the roof. It may be that already the Roman Christians had copied the Jewish Romans and begun hewing out graves for themselves in the catacomb fashion.

(c) The man meets Christ.

(d) Christ forgives his sins.

(e) The man is told 'Rise up'.

(f) He does so and goes home to his friends.

(g) Everyone praises God.

The narrative of the miracle is written in such a way that it teaches the Christian what to hope for after his death and burial. The dead Christian is to meet Christ, have his sins forgiven, and 'rise up' to share with his friends the praise that all give to God.

This is no isolated parallel that might occur by accident. The story of Jairus' daughter is written up in just the same way:

> So they came to the ruler's house, where he found a great stir, and much weeping and lamentation. And he went in and said: What is this stir, this weeping? The child is not dead, she is asleep . . . he sent them all out, and, taking the child's father and mother and his own companions with him, he went in to where the child lay. Then he took hold of the child's hand and said to her: Talitha cumi (which means, Rise up, my girl). And the girl stood up immediately . . . and they were filled with wonder . . . and he laid a strict charge on them to tell no one of this, and ordered that she should be given something to eat (Mk. 5.38–43).

This is analysable thus:

(a) The prayer of her father brings Christ to the girl (notice that the palsied man similarly did nothing and Christ rewards the faith of the man's friends, this perhaps encourages prayer for the dead?).

(b) The child is said to be not dead but asleep.

(c) Christ says to her 'Talitha cumi: Rise up'.

(d) She is handed back to her friends,

(e) who are full of wonder,

(f) and she takes part in a meal.

98

It has sometimes been supposed the denial of death is Mark's way of avoiding a miracle as if he were some kind of Christian proto-rationalist. Really he is employing the common terms of the early Christian community who made a distinction between the death of the pagan and the death of the Christian which was a prelude to resurrection and was termed 'falling asleep'. We can see this usage coming into being in the oral tradition remnant of John 11: 'he said to them: "Our friend Lazarus has fallen asleep, but I go to awake him out of his sleep." The disciples said to him: "Lord, if he has fallen asleep, he will recover." Now Jesus had spoken of his death, but they thought that he meant taking his rest in sleep. Then Jesus told them plainly: "Lazarus is dead"' (11.11–14, RSV). Here the two terms 'asleep' and 'death' are one for the Christian. I shall consider this marvellous story at greater length in the final chapter of this study. The meaning of the death of a Christian is brought out again in the story of Stephen, the man whose death is described in terms which emphasize its entire conformity with the death of Christ. The account concludes with Stephen's imitation of Christ in forgiving his executioners: 'He cried with a loud voice: Lord, do not hold this sin against them. And when he had said this, he fell asleep' (Acts 7.58); and, perhaps surprisingly, in the judgement upon the Christians who have celebrated the Eucharist improperly at Corinth: 'That is why many of you have become weak and ill, and some have fallen asleep' (I Cor. 11.30).

It is not therefore that sinners die and good men sleep, all Christians sleep. Of the witnesses to the resurrection, some five hundred of them, mentioned in I Corinthians, some are alive 'though some have fallen asleep', and this is used by Paul to show the importance of the resurrection of Christ for all Christians: 'For if the dead are not raised, then Christ has not been raised. If Christ has not been raised, your faith is futile and you are still in your sins. Then those also who have fallen asleep in Christ have perished' (I Cor. 15.16).

Of course the longer delayed was the Parousia the more open the early Christians appeared to mockery. They waited for an event which would not happen. That this was so can be seen in the second-century letter of II Peter, where the author comforts the Christians with the reassurance that though 'the fathers' (that is the Apostles and their contemporaries) are dead and time is running on nothing can be seen of Christ coming again: 'scoffers will come in the last days with scoffing, following their own passions and saying: "Where is the promise of his coming? For ever since the fathers fell asleep, all things have continued as they were from the beginning of creation"' (3.3–4, RSV).

The Second Coming is to be a 'new creation' and men will have a new life. The connection between the sleep and the new life is brought out in many New Testament passages: the first letter to the Thessalonians is a typical expression of this belief (4.14.): 'since we believe that Jesus died and rose again, even so, through Jesus, God will bring with him those who have fallen asleep.' And this hope was expressed in the early liturgy as the pericope of responsory in Ephesians 5.14 testifies: 'Awake, O sleeper, and arise from the dead, and Christ shall give you light.' This text will be discussed in another context but it ought to be noted here also.

Perhaps the nearest approach to the Jairus' daughter incident in the early Church record is the incident of the young boy Eutychus at Troas. The lad was tired of listening to Paul's sermon, and as he sat on the window sill he nodded off to sleep and then off the window sill. Since he was on the third storey he was dead when they took him up. But his sleep of death was a preparation for a new life. Eutychus was brought to life by Paul and took part in the Eucharist that was then celebrated. The meal of Jairus' daughter was evidently a sign of the Eucharist and a sign of the banquet that all Christians were to share in the kingdom of Christ's Father.

It is not insignificant that one of the few phrases we have in the Aramaic that Christ spoke is included in this narrative and that this should be the command to rise.

The same distinction between a Christian's understanding of death and other men's is brought out in the story of the epileptic boy which occurs immediately after the transfiguration narrative: 'He lay there like a corpse, so that many declared: He is dead. But Jesus took him by the hand and raised him and he stood up. [Luke adds] He gave him back to his father, and all were filled with wonder' (Mk 9.25 and Lk. 9.43–4).

(a) The boy is like a corpse and 'they said he is dead'.
(b) The father asks for help and faith.
(c) Jesus raises him,

(d) and gives him to his family.

(e) All are filled with wonder.

The community intention behind all these narratives is obvious. The three people are raised because of the prayer of other people, the faith of others even, though this seems strange to us now, and the result of their rising is that more people accept that Christ's work is God's work and join in the worshipping community.

Similar resurrection concepts are present in the story of the lunatic of Gerasa:

This man made his dwelling among the tombs . . . when he saw Jesus from far off, he ran up to him . . . the swineherds fled and told the city and the countryside so they came out to see what had happened; and when they reached Jesus they found the possessed man sitting there, clothed and restored to his wits, and they were overcome with fear . . . and Jesus said to him: Go home to thy friends (Mk. 5.3, 6, 14–15, 19).

(a) The man is among the tombs.

(b) He is freed from the devil's power (which is equivalent to the palsied man being forgiven his sins).

(c) He sits, clothed and restored (like Christians at the resurrection in glory—something similar is promised the apostles who will sit on the twelve thrones, and all this reflects the position of Christ, sitting in glory at the right hand of the Father).

(d) He finds himself with his friends.

And again, the narrative of the widow and her son at Nain shows the same signs of resurrection imagery and patterning:

As he drew near the city gate a dead man was being carried out to his burial; the only son of his mother, and she was a widow . . . and he said, Young man, I say to thee, rise up. And the dead man sat up and spoke; and Jesus gave him back to his mother, and they were all filled with awe, praising God (Lk. 7.11–16).

(a) The boy's body is surrounded by his friends and relations.

(b) He is dead.

(c) He is told by Christ, 'Young man, I tell you to rise up'.

(d) He rises and is given to his mother.

(e) All are filled with awe and glorify God.

101

This is always the pattern of Christ's work. The miracle narratives do not demand the resurrection shaping, they could have been written up without it. The evangelists want to show us that every act of Christ is a witness to the resurrection faith, and every act of Christ leads to our sharing his resurrection. Christ always raises us up, makes us one with him in the praise of his Father and restores us to our friends. It is no accident that one of the first miracles that Mark records is that of the raising up of Simon's mother-in-law. This little miracle story has the pattern of all the longer narratives. 'Now Simon's mother-in-law lay sick with a fever and immediately they told him of her. And he came and took her by the hand and lifted her up, and the fever left her; and she served them' (Mk 1.30–31, RSV).

(a) Jesus is with his friends and the woman's friends.
(b) They tell him of her illness.
(c) He comes to her and lifts her up.
(d) She makes a meal for him and all her friends there.

Perhaps the most startling use of the resurrection language in a miracle story occurs in the third chapter of Mark's gospel when the evangelist is recounting the story of the man with the withered hand who was cured by Jesus on the sabbath. Everyone in the synagogue is watching to see if Jesus will break the sabbath and give them a chance to attack him: 'so he said to the man who had his hand withered: Rise up and come forward. Then he said to them: Which is right, to do good on the sabbath day, or to do harm? To save life, or to make away with it?, (Mk 3.3). The vocabulary of the narrative moves with extraordinary ease towards an alignment of the cure of the hand with the resurrection of the body. Jesus begins by telling the man not that he is to hold out his hand to be seen and cured but that he is to 'rise up'. Then the question asked of the watching Jews is not whether it is right to heal on the sabbath but whether it is right to save 'life'. The man is not dying but Christ sees all his miracles, or at least we can say that Mark sees all Christ's miracles, as signs of his resurrection gift of life to men. The withered hand is the result of the forces of death and disease and sin in the world, its cure is a sign of the resurgence of the forces of life and health and good in the world through the person of Christ and given to us through his resurrection.

We are taught in all these narratives that Christ's life-giving power is made available to us, that his healing is a forgiveness for us, in his resurrection. The deathly power of sin is broken like the seals on the rock of the tomb.

Exactly the same theology of resurrection and forgiveness of sin is to be found in the Epistle of James when the author is talking of the work of Christ among the sick members of the post-resurrection community: 'Prayer offered in faith will restore the sick man, and the Lord will raise him up; if he is guilty of sins, they will be pardoned' (5.15). The activity of Christ among the sick of Galilee is continued in his activity in the prayerful Christian community.

It is evident that here we have come to the pattern of the final resurrection appearance in the first version of John. The risen Lord gives to his community a charge to forgive men's sins. It is with this account of the resurrection of Christ that I shall deal in the next section.

E. THE RESURRECTION AND BELIEF

In the first version of John's gospel the present chapter 20 was designed to present both the fact and the meaning of the resurrection of Christ. It contains the traditions of various appearances of Christ to his disciples and of the proper response that we should make to these testimonies and to the present Lord among us in the eucharistic liturgy. Various strands of christological thought are brought into the pattern of the resurrection, and I will first of all deal with these before going on to treat of the main effects of this narrative.

(i) The account stresses in various ways that the resurrection is the fulfilment of the old scriptural witness. In this it is like the primitive catechesis set out in the first chapters of Acts. John says of the disciples at the empty tomb: 'They had not yet mastered what was written of him, that he was to rise from the dead' (Jn 20.9). The disciples go home but one, Mary, stays at the tomb entrance. She has a sense that it is only at the resurrection scene that meaning for the carrying on of normal life can be found, but of course she cannot understand the happiness. Still weeping, she looked into the tomb. And at once the Old Testament world proclaims itself. The angels are about her, the messengers of God are speaking to her. Then after their heralding work, their evangelism, she sees Jesus, but only vaguely: 'she turned round and saw Jesus standing there, without knowing that it was Jesus' (20.14). She thinks he is a man, an ordinary man, a gardener. It is the new man, the new Adam, who has risen to make the garden of the world again. I think that this Adam reference is deliberate since the detail of the 'gardener' recognition is prominent enough for John to have meant something by it, and the Adam image certainly fits.

Besides the general tone of the Old Testament being fulfilled, and the particular case of Adam, there may also be in the later part of this chapter a reference to the Suffering Servant of Yahweh of Deutero-Isaiah with the insistence of Thomas on the significance of the nails and the wounds as proof of Christ's identity.

(ii) John has a definite view of the ascension of Christ which is a corrective to much later speculation. When Mary greets Christ with the old name of 'Rabboni' he says to her: 'Do not cling to me thus; I have not yet gone up to my Father's side. Return to my brethren, and tell them this; I am going up to him who is my Father and your Father, who is my God and your God' (20.17).

After the appearance to the disciples when Thomas is absent, Jesus comes again and says to Thomas: 'Let me have thy hand; put it into my side' (20.27). The attitude has changed and one can only infer that it is possible to touch the body of Christ because he has by the time of the third appearance recorded in this chapter gone to his Father. The ascension, therefore, is to be thought of as happening between the appearances, between each appearance Christ ascends to his Father. So the ascension as a separate mystery of Christ's redemptive work disappears. The ascension is the last resurrection appearance.

(iii) The account of the second appearance concludes with the commission: 'Receive the Holy Spirit; when you forgive men's sins, they are forgiven, when you hold them bound, they are held bound'(20.22).

I want to leave until later the consideration of what this text means in the life of the Church but evidently it is framed within the context of an ecclesial activity. The text presupposes that it is the intention of Christ to found a community which will continue his work among men.

After these three important points which are briefly indicated in the accounts of the resurrection in John 20, I want to proceed to two further points of the narratives: the necessity of belief in Christ for salvation, and the Eucharist as the continuing presence of Christ in his community.

That the resurrection leads to faith is part of the primitive catechesis and of this there are several evidences in this chapter. When the two disciples run to the empty tomb they go in and see the linen cloths and the napkin for the head: the younger of them 'saw this and learned to believe' (20.8). When Thomas protests against the notion of Christ appearing again in their midst he does not say that there is no such thing as ghosts or that men do not rise from the dead but simply: 'you will never make me believe' (20.25). The only acknowledgement demanded by the risen Lord is belief: 'cease thy doubting and believe' (20.27), and this not on empirical evidence but on the witness of the community: 'Thou hast learned to believe, Thomas, because thou hast seen me. Blessed are those who have not seen, and yet have learned to believe' (20.29). There is therefore a demand upon the community to preach the risen Lord so that men may come to faith in him: 'so much has been written down that you may learn to believe Jesus is the Christ, the Son of God, and so believing find life through his name' (20.31).

John presents the same doctrine as Paul in the First Epistle to the Corinthians. The faith which saves is the resurrection faith, unless there is a resurrection there is no faith, and our community life is in vain.

It is to a believing community which is celebrating his meal that the risen Lord comes. The community is of the faithful. The sense of the community action in the liturgy is never far from the language of this resurrection commentary in John's penultimate chapter. Some eucharistic elements may be set out here:

(a) The first Christians very early changed the great day of the week from the Jewish Sabbath to the commemoration of the first day of the week with its Easter significance. This is part of the notion behind verse 19: 'on the same day, the first day of the week . . . Jesus came and stood in the midst of them'. The phrase 'on the same day' would have been enough to designate the time of the events, John intends to link the event of Easter with the Christian Pasch. Jesus stands in the midst of them as he had promised he would be with his

105

congregation: 'wherever two or three are gathered together in my name, there am I in the midst of them'.

(b) Both in verse 20 and in the third resurrection appearance of the chapter at verse 26, Jesus gives his people the liturgical greeting: 'Peace be upon you'.

(c) All this happens according to some well-credited texts in 'the room in which they had assembled'. The assembly of Christians was almost a technical term for the eucharistic meeting of the Church and is certainly referred to here.

At all points in this narrative we find that John has been thinking of the actual once for all resurrection appearance of Christ, and the continuing presence of Christ in his eucharistic community. He does not think of them separately but as two aspects of the same event. The Lord is as much with him in the eucharistic assembly as he was in the room in which they had assembled on the first Easter evening. He is as much present because seeing is not believing, believing is seeing. John meets the Lord of faith in the Christian assembly. With the influence of this liturgical community on all the New Testament writers I will deal in the next section.

IV

The Liturgical Expression of Christ

1. THE OLD TESTAMENT LITURGY

IN this section I have come to the last of my original three elements in the shaping of the New Testament writings. The prophetic office of the Old Testament led to the event of Christ's resurrection; the resurrection itself leads to the foundation of the new worshipping community. It is within this community that the evangelists lived and wrote. The liturgy is the environment of their meeting with Christ and so inevitably influences their appreciation of Christ among them.

In order that we may have some sense of what the liturgy of the Christian community is, it is necessary to have a notion of what the old liturgy had meant to those Jews who became Christians and who after their excommunication from the synagogue saw in the Christian liturgy the fulfilment and development of their liturgical life in the old covenant. These naturally asked themselves about the significance of the Temple. A similar question exercised the members of the Qumran community. The two groups came to similar conclusions. The Temple is significant in the pattern of revelation as a sign of the future community. In the Manual of Discipline the Dead Sea sect speaks of itself as a 'holy house' or 'sanctuary', and the Christians were told by Paul to understand themselves as the Temple of the Holy Spirit.

I have begun with a general account of the meaning of the Temple in the lives of the Jews, and with the influence which the Temple cult exerted on the formation of the traditions which enshrined the Jews' concept of God's saving work, and have then gone on to say something of the way in which these old liturgical traditions have been shaped by the New Testament community into an expression of Christ's saving work. Since this is a large subject I have, in the main, confined my remarks to references to this process at work in the gospel of John and his treatment of the Tabernacles tradition.

A. THE TEMPLE AS UNIVERSE

Although, as we have seen, the dominant image of the relationship between Israel and Yahweh was that of the Exodus complex, the Hebrews did not suppose that God had acted but once decisively in their history. God is ever with them, ever manifesting his generous love for them. One of the factors which contributed to the triumph of the Temple over all other shrines in the kingdom was that it was connected with the permanent presence of Yahweh at the Ark of the Covenant and not with the intermittent presence of Yahweh at the Tent of Meeting. The Israelites were assured of God's continual presence.

Though the conservative and theocratic elements in the early monarchy were uncertain about the wisdom of the developments that were taking place in the celebration of Yahweh's relation with the people—Nathan opposed the building of the Temple by David because it was against the Tent-tradition, and the northern tribes refused to accept the development from the popular Exodus covenant to the royal Davidic covenant—yet for the men of Judah Yahweh was enthroned in his Temple in Jerusalem through the mediation of the royal covenant. The pedigree of this covenant is written in the prophecy of Nathan: 'The Lord will make you a house. When your days are fulfilled and you lie down with your fathers, I will raise up your offspring after you, who shall come forth from your body, and I will establish his kingdom. He shall build a house for my name, and I will establish the throne of his kingdom for ever' (II Sam. 7.11–13). It is generally agreed among modern exegetes that this prophecy has been subject to two redactions. First it was enlarged from a prophecy personal to David to one which would include his heirs, and then it was further worked upon to make it a prophecy for the whole people. The Temple is the developing sign of what God is doing for his people and is understood afresh from generation to generation.

It is this covenant with David centred on the Temple that the children celebrate when they greet Christ as the 'Son of David' coming to his Temple, and this covenant lies behind much else of the imagery of the entry into Jerusalem, but I want in this section to concentrate on the material sign of God's harmony with the Davidic house. The royal family is allowed to build 'a house for my name', a Temple for God.

The Temple became the place where the Israelite could meet Yahweh in a way that was not open to him anywhere else. The Temple was linked with the Exodus event by the presence of the Ark of the Covenant, and with the Nathan prophecy and covenant by its character as a royal chapel. In the liturgy of the Temple the will of God was worked out in external signs. The prophet Isaiah, for example, represents the sense of theophany which must have been felt by many Hebrew worshippers when he describes his experience in the Temple as the choir sang the 'sanctus' chant: 'I saw the Lord sitting upon a throne, high and lifted up; his train filled the temple. Above him stood the seraphim . . . and one called to another and said: "Holy, holy, holy is the Lord of hosts; the whole earth is full of his glory"' (Is. 6.1–3). The Hebrew acknowledged the presence of God in the liturgical rites of the sanctuary. The Temple became a microcosm of the world, within it the Lord arranged the whole of creation. This is seen very well by the way in which the Genesis creation narrative is written in cultic terms.

The story we have has been constructed from various Semitic elements by the Temple scribes and bears their ecclesiastical imprint. The narrative reflects the priestly conception of the universe as the primordial Temple of God. In the world there is meant to be celebrated a cosmic liturgy, and so the best way to describe the world as it is derives from the liturgical context. The terms of the Creation story are taken from the cult and its rubrics. Everything created is described in terms of an ordered ceremonial. The plants and animals and birds are all to perform 'after their kind' in an ordered pattern of ritual, just as the Levites and priests proclaimed the wonder of God in the formal rubrics 'after their kind' in the sanctuary. The whole of created time is arranged not in the normal (for pagans at least) pattern of sunrise to sunset but in the cultic time when the synagogue and Temple worship began the day with a vigil ceremony rather like a modern breviary's 'First Vespers', so we have in our present creation story 'it was evening and morning the first day', and the general neutrality of the cosmos is refuted by an insistence that it keep the sabbath rest.

The sabbath rest is a good example of the way in which cultic requirements influenced the structure of the story. It seems quite certain that the old myths and legends which the scribes adapted for their own purposes—that is, for the showing of God at work in the world—were arranged in a purely secular fashion round a seven-day creation pattern. By dint of some rather clumsy editorial work—the third and sixth days have two works each, and the making of the firmament is oddly divided between the second and third day— the scribes made their material fit into the already fixed pattern of a religious week of six working days and a seventh day of rest. Thus they happily provided divine approval of a weekly holiday and established the notion of the sabbath as peculiarly belonging to God.

The scribal interest in liturgical performance comes out again in the ritual language of the text which is not, in this case, due to the vagaries of Douay or Knox. The structure of the narrative proceeds by the device of repetition of a series of small phrases of a formal character: 'And God said', 'And it was so', 'And God saw that it was good.' The literary shape of these phrases suggests something of a versicle, response and antiphon pattern. It is not impossible that these phrases were the congregational responses to the formal recitation of the narrative at one of the great festivals of the year in the Temple liturgy. At any rate they are an obvious ritualistic element at work in the story-telling.

Since the priestly writers were concerned with the maintenance of their view of the world they would be anxious to present the function of man as a praising creature. This is precisely what we find in the creation story. The rite of creation is one in which man has the supreme place, he directs the liturgy of the universe. This comes out in the power he exercises over all the beasts. He tells them their names: 'The Lord God formed every beast of the field and every bird of the air, and brought them to the man to see what he would call them; and whatever the man called every living creature, that was its name. The man gave names to all cattle and to the birds of the air and to every beast of the field' (Gen. 2.19). He is a kind of universal master of ceremonies, directing each living creature and naming its place in the cosmic liturgy.

Man is, of course, in the creation narrative, more than some universal M.C., he has his own work of praise to perform. In Ezechiel's picture of the First Man he is shown in the garden wearing a pectoral on which are twelve jewels rather like that worn by the high priests in post-exilic Jerusalem. This shows that the cultic function of the First Man is not peculiar to the Genesis narrative. In Genesis, however, man's sacerdotal function is not stressed so much as another. The Babylonian zigguratic temples, the seven-storey mountains of paganism, had in their innermost shrine a statue of the god. In the great universe, built in seven stages (according to the original legends), God has set out his whole wonder and creative power, and in the centre of things, he has set man to proclaim that: 'God said: "Let us make man in our own image, after our likeness; and let them have dominion over the fish of the sea, and over the birds of the air, and over the cattle, and over all the earth, and over every creeping thing that creeps upon the earth"' (Gen. 1.26).

In this famous passage the divine mission of man is asserted. Man is made in the image of God. We are inclined today to abstract this description of man and to reduce it to some Greek idealism. We speak of man figuring God by his intellectual and spiritual powers. This is not precisely the meaning of the text, instead man is presented as the image of God in the liturgical sense. He is the physical representation of God in the world. The Jews made mock of other men's images of god, Isis and Osiris, Apollo and Athene. Other gods have base metal statues to show them forth, dead gods have dead idols:

> Their idols are silver and gold,
>> the work of men's hands.
> They have mouths, but do not speak;
>> eyes, but do not see.
> They have ears, but do not hear;
>> noses, but do not smell.
> They have hands, but do not feel;
>> feet, but do not walk;
>> and they do not make a sound in their throat.
> Those who make them are like them;
>> so are all who trust in them. (Ps. 115.4–8).

To worship such gods, to accept that divinity is hedged in such statues is to have become less than a man. Only within the true liturgy can the man find himself, only there can he be the image of God. Thus Jeremiah describes the apostates of his time, men of Israel who have gone over to false worship though they have kept the old forms in the Temple: 'Hear this, O foolish and senseless people, who have eyes, but see not, who have ears, but hear not' (Jer. 5.21). Their worship is false so they have become false men, they have accepted foreign values and foreign gods. That those who serve foreign gods and stand as suppliants before their images have become like the gods themselves—mere images, not fully human—is a commonplace of Old Testament thought. They lose a sense of real human values.

Men become like beasts when they glory in their empire and authority. They eat grass as the great king Nebuchadnezzar ate grass, they scratch in the earth as Nebuchadnezzar scratched with his finger-nails as long as birds' talons. They cannot of course become beasts, they can only seem like beasts. Belsen is an attempt to deny reality and cannot in the end win through. It is perhaps significant that the false images of Egyptian gods are hawk- and jackal-headed with human bodies. They symbolize those bestialities which reign when the human image of god refused his place in the cosmic liturgy. And chaos comes on those who refuse their vocation to be men of God. Paul writes of such men in the pagan world of his time: 'Claiming to be wise they became fools, and exchanged the glory of the immortal God for images resembling mortal man or birds or animals or reptiles' (Rom. 1.22-3, RSV), and of the chaos that resulted for them: 'Therefore God gave them up in the lusts of their hearts to impurity . . . to dishonourable passions . . . to a base mind and to improper conduct' (1.24-8, RSV).

Paul himself suggests that it is in the liturgical worship of God in the new community that a true order of things is to be found and moral chaos avoided: 'they exchanged the truth about God for a lie and worshipped and served the creature rather than the Creator, who is blessed for ever. Amen' (1.25, RSV). He is obviously there employing a quotation from the early Christian liturgy as the climax of his paragraph.

Man is made in the image of God. He is not a statue of stones and jewels, he has eyes and he sees, he has legs and he walks, he is alive. He is a fitting representation of the living God in his world. The priestly writer has given dignity and purpose to man without giving way to any dangerous element of anthropocentrism.

After the Fall the cosmic liturgy becomes inarticulate. Nature cannot find a proper voice and God becomes *Deus absconditus*. Man became so self-regarding that he forgot that the wonder that is man is but an image of the wonder of God. The Fall is the result of man worshipping his own capacity and not recognizing his dependence upon God. That is, praise is ended, the liturgy ceases in the cosmos.

This is the predicament of natural theology which we all recognize to be a tentative, hard-won, unsatisfactory procedure, trying to find the words in the things and never quite managing to stand up and sing. This, again, is the predicament of other religious movements, those which have not the direct revelation of God that is possessed by, or rather possesses, the Judaic-Christian people.

All religions have been told something of God, but unless God speaks out men are confined frustratingly in dim half-truths. Sometimes, of course, men refuse to be circumscribed, they make a frontal attack on God, they decide to claim the divine sphere for themselves. This is the meaning of the Babel narrative. Men built a temple to themselves, seeking to invade the heavenly kingdom by a strategic tower. Then they found that they did not possess the proper words, they could not explain things to one another. They had, in fact, more words than they could use. Thus they cheated themselves of a liturgy which would set words and men in order to the praise of God —not until the Word became man could harmony be established.

The revelation given to the Jews is a liturgical revelation, it is communicated through worship. Particularly is it a Temple revelation. Man builds a Temple in Jerusalem so that he may have a ritual activity which will, in however faint a way, imitate the cosmic liturgy that once was and so bring him into some shadowy harmony with God again. The Temple is a substitute for the world of praise that is destroyed. This is an idea which became part of traditional Jewish theology. In his explanation of the meaning of the two rooms of the Temple, the 'holy Place' and the 'Holy of holies', Philo makes much of the notion that the Temple is an image of the universe. And in the Manual of Discipline the Qumran community has linked the sacred liturgy with the activity of Adam before the Fall and has set its hopes on a restoration of the universal cult in the new community of Qumran:

He built for them in Israel a firmly established house the like of which has not existed from ancient times until this day. They that hold fast unto it are [destined] for life eternal, and theirs is the glory of Adam,

113

even as God has sworn unto them by the hand of the prophet Ezechiel, saying: 'The priests and the Levites and the sons of Zadok that kept the charge of my sanctuary when the children of Israel went astray from me, these are they that shall offer unto me fat and blood'.

I take this text from Dr Bertil Gartner's work on *The Temple and the Community in Qumran and the New Testament*, where he uses it in his discussion of the Qumran community's thesis that it was in the community that the new Temple had arisen after the desecration of the Jerusalem Temple by impious priests. To the notion of the community as Temple I shall return later in this work, but at the moment I want only to notice that the 'glory of Adam' is associated in the community literature with the Ezechiel description of the priestly service in an ideal Temple. For this community evidently the new Temple service, in whatever sense they thought of it, was a realization of that service Adam gave in the first days of the world.

At the disruption of life by Adam's offence God announced that the scheme of things would be different, the animal kingdom is set against man, the woman and the man are to know suffering and toil, travail is to be the lot of the child-bearing mother. Paul remembers this when he is writing to the Romans and suggests that the whole of creation is in travail, trying to bring forth the kingdom of God on earth again: 'the creation waits with eager longing for the revealing of the sons of God; for the creation was subject to futility, not of its own will but by the will of him who subjected it in hope; because the creation itself will be set free from its bondage to decay and obtain the glorious liberty of the children of God. We know that the whole of creation has been groaning in travail together until now; and not only the creation, but we ourselves' (Rom. 8.19–23, RSV). That the world suffers because of man's sin is not a thought new in Paul. Jeremiah had understood this long before: 'How long will the land mourn and the grass of every field wither? For the wickedness of those who dwelt in it, the beasts and the birds are swept away because men said: "He will not see our latter end"' (Jer. 12.4).

For the cosmic liturgy to be made again the Man who is sinless must come. The new man must come who will undo the work of Adam. It is the consideration of the world and the nature of God that makes Paul understand Christ as the Second Adam who will make

114

it possible for all to praise his Father properly. For Paul the redemption is the setting right of the cosmic liturgy.

Christ has, in Pauline terms, begun a new creation, he has renewed the human race as the image of God. This new creation is spoken of in terms of the Genesis account of the old creation: 'Put off your old man which belongs to your former way of life and is corrupt through deceitful lusts, and be renewed in the spirit of your minds, and put on the new man created after the likeness of God in true righteousness and holiness' (Eph 4.22–4; cf. Col. 3.9–10). We are to do this because of the work of Christ who both shows us what we are to be and gives us the power to perform it: 'He is the image of the invisible God, the first-born of all creation . . . he is the beginning, the first-born from the dead . . . and through him (God) reconciles to himself all things, whether on earth or in heaven' (Col. 1.15, RSV).

This is the picture which Mark presents in his temptation narrative. Christ the new Adam who brings the human race, animals and angels into harmony, reconciled with his Father. All this is done in the Spirit of God and is done in the context of liturgical expression. The new creation like the old is the setting up of a Temple in the world, making the world one Temple.

It is important to stress the universalist character of the new Temple. It is to be a popular expression. The objection of the conservative opposition to the Davidic Temple was that the revealing presence of God was given originally to a free people and that the consequence of the building of a sanctuary on royal ground by royal decree would be the political dominance of the king and the disappearance of the old theocratic amphictyony. God would cease to be immediately present among his people, his presence would be mediated through the king. Nathan is opposing a religious feudalism. He was right to be concerned. At the same time it was the will of God that there should be a covenant with the Davidic royal house. How are these two to be combined? The period of the monarchy has a history of struggle and tension between the old popular covenant and the royal covenant which was never fully resolved. The destruction of the monarchy released the situation only by putting aside an essential element in the saving history of Israel. At the resurrection Christ rebuilds the Temple in his community. The whole people enjoys the presence of the Lord. At the same time Christ rises to make all men sons of David. To the whole community a kingdom is given: 'You are a chosen race, a royal priesthood, a holy nation, God's own people' (I Pet. 2.9). And to this royal people a vocation is given: 'that you may declare the wonderful deeds of him who called you out of darkness into his marvellous light' (*ibid.*).

The Temple-centred view of the world was given a terrific shock at the Babylonian sack of 586 B.C. The disaster had been expected by those Hebrews who were sensitive to the contemporary political and moral situation. Between the years 597 and 587 Jeremiah and Ezechiel made great efforts to prepare the people for 'the new thing' that Yahweh was about to do. Ezechiel thought of the events of 586 as the result of Yahweh leaving the corrupt city of Jerusalem on the backs of the winged cherubim: 'the glory of the Lord went up from the midst of the city' (Ez. 11.23). No one listened to the prophets. It seemed to the people unthinkable that the Temple covenant could come to nothing and they be left alone.

After the disaster the uppermost thought of the people was to call Yahweh to them again. The Book of Lamentations and the Psalms contain many examples of the appeals to Yahweh made by those who were left behind in Jerusalem and by those who were taken away to Babylon: 'Remember thy congregation, which thou hast gotten of old, which thou hast redeemed to be the tribe of thy heritage. Remember Mount Zion, where thou hast dwelt. Direct thy steps to the perpetual ruins; the enemy has destroyed everything in the sanctuary! Thy foes have roared in the midst of thy holy place' (Ps. 74.2). And Ezechiel envisages a time when Yahweh will come back to his restored sanctuary as the climax of his saving work for the people: 'This is the place of my throne and the place of the soles of my feet, where I will dwell in the midst of the people of Israel for ever' (Ez. 43.7).

On the rebuilding of the Temple after the Exile the earlier cult tradition was subject to a radical rethinking. The new Temple was not, as the first had been, the centre of a powerful and prosperous Israelite state. The significance of the Temple was that of a prophetic sign of the coming reign of God.

This had been foreseen by Jeremiah when he described the new Jerusalem as not requiring a Temple since God would be present in the whole city: 'At that time Jerusalem shall be called the throne of the Lord, and all nations shall gather to it, to the presence of the Lord in Jerusalem' (Jer. 3.17), and by Ezechiel when he prophesied that Jerusalem would be renamed because of the total presence of Yahweh: 'The name of the city henceforth shall be "The Lord is there"' (Ez. 48.35).

We have, therefore, in the Old Testament, two ways of thinking about the Temple in the final community of the Lord: one line of thought looks for a new Temple in which Yahweh will dwell, the other expects that in the new Jerusalem there will be no Temple since the whole city will be filled with the glory of God. That these are not necessarily exclusive notions can be seen from the occurrence of both in the later chapters of Ezechiel.

In the New Testament we can distinguish both lines of thought about the eschatological significance of the Temple. The rebuilding of the Temple in some sense at least seems to have been an idea present in the first community of Palestine. For example, at the 'Council of Jerusalem', James in giving his judgement quotes the passage to this effect in Amos: 'In that day I will raise up the dwelling of David that has fallen' (Amos 9.11). James sees in the Gentiles coming to Christianity a fulfilment of the eschatological pilgrimage of the nations to the Temple. This is the background also to the Pauline language about building the Temple for the Holy Spirit. On the other hand the idea of the new Jerusalem not having any need of a Temple is the dominant one in the Apocalypse. Ezechiel had envisaged a river of life flowing from below the threshold of the Temple making fertile the valley of Arabah, like the lifegiving river of paradise. The Apocalypse has the river of life flowing by the tree of life but not from the Temple threshold. Nor are the pillars of the Temple to be seen, there is no sun and no moon, no signs of God's presence: 'the city has no need of sun or moon to shine upon it, for the glory of God is its light' (21.23). And since God himself is present there is no need for the makeshift liturgy any more: 'I saw no Temple in the city, for its temple is the Lord God the Almighty' (21.22).

B. THE TEMPLE AS SAVING HISTORY

The presence of God in the Temple was not, of course, a static presence. The Hebrews knew that God was ever working in their midst. They expressed this sense of God's presence and of his abiding power in the architectural features of their Temple. We have noted already how the Temple reflected the universe and the vanished

117

cosmic liturgy. The account of the building of the Temple shows how the people thought of themselves as setting up a new universe to bring some hint of the glory of that liturgy among them. The decorative motifs of cherubim, palm trees and open flowers, pomegranates and lily-work, set out in paint and stone the lost garden of God. The Temple frieze is a picture of Eden, everything bright and new, everything in an ordered procession, everything good and giving delight. It is now possible to go on to say something about the way in which the Temple represented the saving work of Yahweh's redemptive action in the history of the People.

The Hebrew taking part in the great processions of the Temple liturgy thought of this cultic action as re-creating the Exodus procession in the desert. The escape from Egypt was of a people led by their God: 'When you went forth, O God, at the head of your people, when you marched across the desert' (Ps. 68.7); then Yahweh was leading them as he did in the Temple procession:

> They see your processions, O God,
>   the procession of my God, my king, to the sanctuary:
> the singers in front, the musicians coming last,
>   between them, maidens sounding their timbrels.
> In festive gatherings bless the Lord;
>   bless God, O you who are Israel's sons.
> There is Benjamin, least of the tribes, at the head,
> Judah's princes, a mighty throng,
> The princes of Zebulon, the princes of Naphtali (Ps. 68.24–7.)

It may even be that the way in which the strange wanderings of the Hebrews in the desert are described derives from the pattern of the pilgrimage procession from station to station. Certainly they are not to be accounted for by economic or military necessities. The back and forward wandering may have been conceived as the equivalent in history to the back and forward processions of the cult within the limited area of the Davidic city. The whole book of Deuteronomy reflects the liturgical sequence of the covenant renewal festival, as Professor von Rad has demonstrated, and is shaped by the pilgrimage form.

The Temple is the continuation of Yahweh's saving act during the Exodus and so provides the pattern for Yahweh's desert dwelling. The details of the Exodus measurements, materials and furnishings of the Tent of Meeting are said to be according to the design of

Yahweh: 'Let them make me a sanctuary that I may dwell in their midst. According to all that I show you concerning the pattern of the tabernacle and of all its furniture, so you shall make it' (Ex. 25.8). The inventory and directions which follow could never have been realized in the desert, and hardly at Gilgal or Shiloh where the Tent was later erected. Only the Temple fulfils the pattern.

It is to be remarked that although the Temple managed to incorporate the Ark and its amphictyonic tradition, the tradition of the Tent of Meeting was able for some time to remain independent. However, the Temple did take over the vocabulary of the Tent. The presence of the Lord manifested at the dedication of the Temple by Solomon is spoken of in Tent terms. The noun *miskan*, tabernacle, derives from the verb *sakan*, to pitch a tent, and the priestly writer uses *sakan* for the presence of Yahweh in the Temple, and another verb, *yasab*, to sit down, for Yahweh's presence in heaven. Yahweh's presence is tented in the Tabernacle and the Temple.

In the new covenant we may descry something of the old pattern. At the Incarnation the Word of God 'pitches his tent' to dwell among us, and at the ascension he 'sits at the right hand' of the Father. His presence among us is in the new Temple of the Christian community.

That the Temple is the sign of God's saving work in history is brought out in many features of the Temple cult and decoration but I will concentrate upon the free-standing pillars in front of the building, and the great 'bronze sea' between them.

(a) *The Two Pillars*

Hiram, the Tyrian craftsman employed by Solomon to decorate his Temple, set up two pillars which the workmen called Jachin and Boaz: 'He set up pillars in the vestibule of the Temple; he set up the pillar on the south and called its name Jachin; and he set up the pillar on the north and called its name Boaz' (I Kings 7.21). Pillars of this kind seem to have been included in the design of many pagan temples roughly contemporary with Solomon's building. They are featured on Sidonian coins representing shrines and they certainly occurred at the shrine of Burj-as-Samali near Tyre and the Temple of Baal-Herakles at Tyre, and the Temple of Aphrodite at Paphos.

In most of these cases it can be shown that the pillars were topped by gratings for braziers and it is probable that atop the two pillars of Solomon's Temple there burnt continually a high flickering sacred fire. It is to be expected that the Hebrew Temple would exhibit the characteristics of pagan shrines because Solomon employed pagan builders and artisans for his project since there were no Hebrew craftsmen with sufficient skill and artistry. The pillars themselves were the work of men from Tyre who knew the Baal-Herakles temple: 'King Solomon sent and brought Hiram from Tyre. He was the son of a widow of the tribe of Naphtali, and his father was a man of Tyre, a worker in bronze; and he was full of wisdom, understanding and skill, for making any work in bronze. He came to King Solomon and did all his work. He cast two pillars of bronze . . . then he made the molten sea' (I Kings 7.13ff.). The two pillars were a dominant part of the edifice. The description given of their measurement and design although now difficult to reconstruct was given in immense detail in I Kings 7. They obviously made a great impression on the scribe who set down the account for the royal archive.

During the day the Jew in the city or in the surrounding country would see, if he looked towards the Temple, the smoke of the fire rising from the pillars, and at night the flame and spark of the fire would glow in the darkness. Whenever the Jew looked to the Temple he saw the light burning as a sign of the presence of God in his Jerusalem sanctuary.

So much did the pillars impress their image upon the people's imagination as signs of the divine presence with them that when the scribes came to write down the story of God's providential care for them in history they could find no other image so suitable as the pillars for affirming the continual presence of God with his people. In the Exodus narrative the people of God know that God is with them by the pillar of cloud by day and the pillar of fire by night: 'the Lord went before them by day in a pillar of cloud to lead them along the way, and by night in a pillar of fire to give them light, that they might travel by day and by night; the pillar of cloud by day and the pillar of fire by night did not depart from before the people' (Ex. 13.21–2).

Again, when the scribes wanted to impress upon their people that the creating God is always present in his universe, and has been present from the beginning, they took the same images of the twin lights, the sun by day and the moon by night. These are not to give light. They are created on the fourth day while light is present from the first word of creation. The sun and the moon are set as signs of God's presence in his universe. They are not called 'sun' and 'moon' in the Genesis text because these were the names of pagan solar deities, and because what was wanted was an emphasis on the consistent signing of God. To keep in mind the pillars of the Temple, which appear from some parts of the Kings account to have been of different heights, they are called the 'greater' and the 'lesser' lights.

The pillars in the Temple precinct, the sun and the moon, and probably the rainbow in the Noah story, all perform the function of signing the presence of God in his world. And Isaiah suggests that such a signing of his presence will continue ever in the heavenly Jerusalem after the Judgement: 'Over Mount Sion, the shrine of his name, there shall be a cloud by day, and a fire by night, veiling his glory' (4.5). All these images come together in the angel described in the Apocalpyse—which is itself, according to Massey Shepherd, a liturgical book—when he comes to swear the will of God: 'him who lives for ever and ever, who created heaven and what is in it, and the sea and what is in it, and the earth and what is in it' (10.6), who is presented as the messenger of God: 'a mighty angel coming down from heaven, wrapped in a cloud, with a rainbow over his head, and his face was like the sun, and his legs like pillars of fire' (10.1).

Of course the apostles became the angels of God, bearing his messages to men as they were instructed by Christ: 'Let your light so shine before men that they may see your good works and give glory to your Father who is in heaven' (Mt. 5.16). The light of the flame they had received at Pentecost was to point to the presence of the Lord among men, as the light of the sun had witnessed to the creator and the light of the Exodus pillars witnessed to the redemptive work of God. The Old Testament understanding was summed up in the pillars of the Temple, the new community has living witnesses as its pillars in the Church: 'James and Cephas and John, who were reputed to be pillars, gave to me and Barnabas the right hand of fellowship' (Gal. 2.9).

(b) *The Divided Waters*

Together with the pillars Jachin and Boaz, Hiram placed in front of the Temple a great bronze bowl full of water. This was set upon the backs of bullocks and presented the Hebrews with a sign of God's strong power.

In the neighbouring Baal culture the triumph of the god was represented by a victory over unruly waters, and in the highly developed mythology of the Babylonians the victory of the good god Marduk over Tiamat, the monstrous goddess of chaotic waters, was represented by a placid artificial sea in the Temple area. Similar pools are attested by several ancient writers. Lucian speaks of the sacred lake of Hierapolis next to the Temple complex. The command of the god over the elements is expressed in his setting a rim round the seeping element of water which once out of control might overwhelm the world. The Flood stories from many cultures, especially those of the Tigris–Euphrates area, testify to this rule of water as a divine attribute.

The Jews inherited these stories and made them their own in the narratives of the Temple. The account of Noah comes at once to mind as an account of God controlling water and being able to save man from water when he wills. But there are elements in the Exodus–Genesis complex of stories which depend on something of the same idea.

The Jews were always terrified and over-awed by water. They were totally unable to manage it. This inability comes out in the description of the building of the Temple by Solomon. There were no Hebrew sailors experienced enough to bring the necessary materials down the coast from Tyre to Palestine, a very short distance, and Tyrian sailors and ships had to be employed. We can see the same timorous attitude in the story of the apostles' fright when the waves began to rise in the lake of Galilee, and in Mark's ennobling that stretch of water as the 'Sea' of Galilee. Above all, perhaps, the Hebrew horror of water comes out in St John's description of the heavenly Jerusalem, where everybody would be happy— no golden sands and paddling for him, simply the blessed relief: 'And there was no more sea' (Rev. 21.1). and the only movement allowed the water is applause at the coming of the Lord: 'Then I heard what seemed . . . like the sound of many waters . . . crying "Hallelujah! For the Lord our God the Almighty reigns!"' (Rev. 19.6, RSV). The power and mastery signified by the edging rim of the bronze dish is to be found in the Exodus narrative. God makes a dry path through water so that his people may cross, then he exerts his control in the contrary manner and sends the water to drown the enemies of his people. The incident of the 'Red Sea' is an interesting example of the way in which an event of which the people have but the haziest tradition can be employed to present a meaning of which they are passionately certain. The Hebrews were in the original narrative pursued across not the Red Sea but through some marshy country (A Reed Sea) near Lake Timsah. The Septuagint writers translated 'yam suph' (sea of reeds) as 'Red Sea' because of the peculiar traps of Hebrew writing. Only someone who had no care for geography and likelihood could have suggested that Moses led his people through such a detour when hurrying from the Egyptians as to go down to the Red Sea on the way to Palestine. The Septuagint version ruins, also, the happy picture of the Israelites jumping from tussock to tussock dry-shod through the marsh, while the Egyptian forces were trapped in the swamp, and became a mass of unmanageable chariots, reins, wheeling horses and men, caught up together in the confusion. The power of God is shown by his control of the water—that is all that concerned the Septuagint writers and the original recorders of the story—the details of where and when and even how this happened were very secondary matters in their estimate.

Israel understood that the people itself had been created by the election manifested in the Exodus and the accompanying covenant promise. The Exodus and the Creation are therefore in many ways thought of as one action, or at least as actions bearing the same impress. The creative act of God is often described in redemptive terms. The legendary material of the goddess Tiamat being sliced in two by Marduk became the basis for the description of God dividing the waters, and this division was conceived as like that at the Reed Sea: 'Was it not thou that didst cut up the primal dragon in pieces, that didst pierce the beast of chaos? Was it not thou that didst dry up the sea, the waters of the great deep; that didst make the depths of the sea a way for the redeemed to pass over?' (Is. 51.9). The Levantine legend is used only as machinery to show the wonders of the God who brought them out of Egypt.

The same concern for demonstrating God's abiding power is at work in the first Genesis account of creation. There is a division of the waters of chaos in much the same imagery as the division of chaotic Tiamat like some flat fish in the Gilgamesh epic. The great difference being that the power of God is further emphasized by omitting any mention of a battle or struggle—chaos does not attempt to resist the divine order. God is not simply able to control the waters, it costs him no effort at all to do so. He has this quiet pool in his Temple court.

The pillars, Jachin and Boaz, and the great 'bronze sea' thus provide a description of what God is doing now among the people, they refer back to his past covenant activity and further back to his creating activity, but they also refer to his present and his future presence and power in the midst of his community. It is evident that the Jewish converts to Christianity would realize that the Temple sign refers forward to Christ. The climactic point of the reference arrives in the gospels with the visit of Jesus to the Temple.

C. JESUS COMES TO THE TEMPLE

In John's gospel the visit of Christ to the Temple is described in terms of a revolution and a demand for faith. The Jews ask Christ for a sign that he has authority to overturn the tables and drive out the money-changers: 'Jesus answered them: "Destroy this temple and in three days I will raise it up." The Jews then said: "It has taken forty-six years to build this temple, and will you raise it up in three days?" But he spoke of the temple of his body. When therefore he was raised from the dead his disciples remembered he had said this.' (Jn 2.19–22, RSV). Jesus takes the Temple as a sign of himself. The great witness of God's presence in Israel finds its fulfilment in the presence of Christ.

The Temple is represented in the New Testament as the context of Jesus' authoritative preaching: 'He was teaching daily in the temple' (Lk. 21.37), and 'early in the morning all the people came to him in the temple to hear him' (Lk. 21.38). And the Temple is declared to be the setting for the first Christian community after the ascension: 'They went back to Jerusalem with great joy, and were continually in the temple blessing God' (Lk. 24.52–3), and like Jesus they were 'daily attending the temple together' (Acts 5.42). It is within the Temple precincts that their first recorded miracle is performed. The man born lame is begging for alms at the Beautiful Gate of the Temple and is cured so that he can join the the Temple service: 'leaping up he stood and walked and entered the Temple with them, walking and leaping and praising God' (Acts

3.8, RSV). In this, as in so many other ways, the community was continuing the messianic activity of Jesus' ministry. The community was Christ in the world.

The messianic expectation is for one who will be so concerned for the Temple that he will say: 'The zeal of thy house has consumed me' (Jn 2.17; cf. Ps. 69.10), and it is this that the community realizes is fulfilled in Jesus' coming to the Temple and sending out the money-changers and the sellers of oxen and sheep and pigeons.

The Temple in which Jesus taught was the third to be built on the site. Solomon's temple, the first building and the one which gave both plan and significance to the succeeding post-exilic and Herodian temples, had been the House of the Lord since the dedication at the Feast of Tabernacles, 952 B.C. Though its successors were not considered so wondrous as the first Temple they were thought to have an identical significance in the Hebrew cult. God dwelt in his tent in the midst of his people. The whole of Israelite society centred on this building, within its courts the worship, commerce and government of the people were carried on.

The actions of Jesus at this nodal point, therefore, may well have a significance that actions elsewhere did not have in the eyes of his contemporaries. It is, in fact, his visit to the Temple which occasions, in the Synoptic traditions at least, the setting out of his design for the new community.

After he has driven out the money-changers and the bird-sellers, the blind and the lame come to him in the Temple and he heals them and the children dance round him singing in the Temple court, 'Hosanna to the Son of David', and the priests are furious and tell Jesus to stop their singing. Jesus replies: 'Have you never read: "Out of the mouths of babes and sucklings thou hast brought perfect praise"?' (Mt. 21.15-16, RSV). This is a quotation from Psalm 8. Whenever Christ refers to an Old Testament passage it is always revealing to look at the context of its original use. This is true in this case, certainly. It has been noted that the Temple was thought of as a microcosm, a tiny universe in which the universal praise of God could be proclaimed after the Fall. The Psalm Jesus quotes is concerned with the praise of God by all the universe. The verses which follow his quotation are these: 'When I look at thy heavens, the work of thy fingers, the moon and the stars which thou hast established; what is man that thou art mindful of him?' (Ps. 8.3–4), and this is followed by a reference to the creation narrative of the naming of the beasts: 'thou hast put all things under his feet, all sheep and oxen, and also the beasts of the field, the birds of the air, and the fish of the sea' (Ps. 8.6–8). All this is framed within the antiphon of the Temple liturgy: 'O Lord, our Lord, how majestic is thy name in all the earth!' (Ps. 8.9).

Christ's reign is seen as universal, all things are put under his feet, the children are acknowledging the Lord's anointed king.

Similarly, the quotation from Isaiah 56: 'My house shall be called a house of prayer', comes from a passage devoted to the welcome of the Gentiles into the Temple courts for the worship of God: 'My house shall be called a house of prayer for all peoples'.

The whole world of stars and beasts, the whole race of Hebrews and Gentiles, these are the kingdom which has been given to Christ.

In the Temple, the central point of the old nationalistic worship, Christ proclaims salvation to the whole world and to all men. This is the relevance of his quoting Jeremiah 7.11 about the 'den of thieves', for the original context is of Yahweh's threat to destroy the Temple in Jerusalem as he had destroyed the shrine at Shiloh because of the faithless and hypocritical worship of the Jews. Yahweh then speaks of the way he has 'sent my servants the prophets day after day' and no one listened. This is the theme of the universalist parable about the wicked vine dressers Christ then tells to the people and the priests gathered round him in the Temple. And the priests realize that the parable is told about their neglect of God's people.

The vine image has a long Old Testament history behind its use in this parable. An account of this will be developed more fully in a consideration of John's use of the image. Here it is enough to note that the vine is Israel and the vineyard owner is the Father who sends his prophets and at last his Son to those who are set to tend the vine —to the priests and scribes who are called to preach the word of God to the people. The vine is to be given to others. The people of God is to include the Gentiles.

The same notion, together with further references to the eucharistic meal and the eschatological banquet, is worked out in the following parable of the king's great supper. The originally invited guests do not bother to come. The Jews neglect God, so others are brought in.

This general opening of the kingdom is the fruit of the resurrection and Jesus goes on to speak of this to the Sadducees. He blames them for their rejection of belief in the resurrection since it shows they have no faith in God's power nor in his promises in the Scriptures. 'You are wrong, because you know neither the scriptures nor the power of God' (Mk 12.24, RSV).

The setting up of the new community, the planting of the new vine, the giving of the new banquet, the resurrection, all tend towards an understanding of the eschatological nature of Christ's work. The Temple in which he speaks is to be renewed by destruction. The disciple came to point out to him the imposing structure of the Temple buildings: 'But he answered him, "You see all these, do you not? Truly, I say to you, there will not be left here one stone upon another, that will not be thrown down"' (Mk 13.2). The Temple is the sign of this world, and the Jewish world is to be destroyed. The sacrilege in the holy place prophesied by David will be the signal for those in Judaea to flee to the mountains; destruction will begin in the Temple and will lead into the glorious coming of the Son of Man as Judge of the world.

Daniélou has pointed out that Apocalypse 7.9–17 envisages the eschatological liturgy as a Feast of Tabernacles. It contains three elements of the ritual of the feast, palm branches in hands, tabernacle for Christ, springs of living water, and he shows that Matthew's prophecy of the final coming of the Christ is set out in terms which point to the last day being a celebration of the Feast of Tabernacles, a time when the Tabernacles psalm (117) is sung again: 'Believe me, you shall not see me from now on, until the time when you will be saying: Blessed in the name of the Lord is he who comes.' It is therefore desirable that something should be said of this feast and its significance to the Jews of Christ's time before proceeding to examine its significance in the gospel narrative.

D. THE FEAST

The Feast of Tabernacles took its origin from a viticultural orgy of the Canaanites. And though it soon became in Israel a totally Yahwist celebration some aspects of the feast even at the time of Christ retained their original traces of the Jebusite El-'Elyon cult. There are in some Old Testament pericopes evidences of the continuation of the pagan motifs in the Jewish celebration. For example the description of the festal city in Psalm 46: 'There is a river, whose streams make glad the city of God, the holy abode of El-'Elyon.'

When the feast was taken over into the Hebrew ritual the agricultural aspects were played down in favour of the celebration of God's redemption of his people from Egypt. The Tabernacles, the booths of branches in which the people lived for the eight days of the feast, became less significant of the harvesting huts and more of the tents of the Exodus. The thirteenth painting in the synagogue of Dura-Europos represents the Israelites in their tents during the desert journey precisely as dwelling in booths of the Tabernacles kind. Again, in Psalm 63, coming to the festival is seen as coming to an oasis in the Exodus journey: 'as in a dry and weary land where no water is, I have looked upon thee in thy sanctuary, beholding thy power and thy glory.'

The Mishnah presents the Feast as an occasion particularly of light and water. The great moment of the celebration was the procession on the evening of the first day when great lights were lit in the Temple court, and a dance of torch-bearers was performed by the rabbis and holy men. There are several accounts in the Hebrew traditional writings which evidence to the way in which the gaiety and lights affected the people. The Mishnah says: 'He who has not seen the rejoicing at the place of the water-drawing has never seen rejoicing in his life', and, 'There was not a court in Jerusalem which was not made bright by the light of the water-drawing.' And an anonymous tanna suggests that 'a woman could sift wheat by the illumination of the place of the water-drawing.'

There may well be a retrospective romanticism about these sayings. The Jews are looking back to a time of happiness and prosperity when they had the great festivity in their city, but the sayings do point to the light and the water as the sources of the happiness and of the great effect these had on the imaginations of generations of Jews.

In the lights, while instruments of 'all kinds without number' played, leaps and jumps and juggling tricks were performed by the rabbis. The Rabbi Simeon b. Gamaliel could, says the Sukkah record, juggle with eight lighted torches in the air, and the Rabbi Levi lamed himself in a peculiarly difficult contortion. The excitement of the spectators was so great that special barriers and galleries had to be erected for the women's protection during the rejoicing.

The whole festivity ended only with the trumpet sounding at cock-crow.

In the prophecy of Zechariah there is a splendid passage written in connection with the Feast of Tabernacles, describing the way in which the people of Jerusalem will be oppressed in their city and also the way in which many nations shall come up to the Feast—perhaps we may understand this, in an accommodated sense, as the rejection of the Jews who would not recognize themselves in the light of Christ, and the welcome of the Gentiles. But, more importantly, Zechariah writes of the day of the Lord, which is the same day as the day of the Feast: 'and in the time of the evening there shall be light. And it shall come to pass that living waters shall go out from Jerusalem. And the Lord shall be king over all the earth. In that day there shall be one Lord, and his name shall be one' (Zech. 14.7–9). Similarly in the vision of the waters in Ezechiel streams pour out from the Temple to all the world.

At this point, of course, the relevence of Jesus' quotation from the Old Testament, 'fountains of living water shall flow from his belly', becomes apparent. He is himself the source of the life-giving Spirit for the whole world. John returns to this image, and its relevance for our sacramental life, in his account of the soldier's act on the death of Christ: 'one of the soldiers opened his side with a spear; and immediately blood and water flowed out' (Jn 19.34). Evidently he is here giving an account of the streams flowing from Christ's body in order that his contemporary Christians, and we following them, should appreciate that from the redeeming work of Christ in his body the Church flow the sacraments of baptism and the Eucharist.

Glasson suggests that John 19.34–5 may refer to the rabbinic tradition found in Shemmoth R. 1222a where Moses is said to have struck the rock twice and the first time it gushed blood, then the second it gushed water.

The connection between the belly of Christ and Jerusalem is to be found in the common rabbinic teaching that Jerusalem was the navel of the world. This idea is found in Ezechiel's description of the Jews as 'the people who were gathered from the nations . . . who dwell at the navel of the world' (Ez. 38.12). So that it is now possible to see how the Feast and the water spring and the navel of the earth all come together in their fruition in Christ. The Feast is of light and water, images of Christ that John has already expounded, and the city of Jerusalem may be said in a real sense to have found its true reality in the person of Christ. The city was the centre of the true religion, in the city was the visible Temple of God and his invisible presence, and now it is not in stones that God dwells but in Christ and through him in his people.

The water of the Feast of Tabernacles was brought in large pitchers from the pool of Siloam and poured out in the Temple as a purifying libation over the altar of burnt offerings. This certainly took place on the first seven days of the Feast and may very well have taken place on the eighth day also since this had become assimilated to the others in historical times. Professor Dodd, in his splendid book *The Interpretation of the Fourth Gospel*, points out that the Feast was associated with prayers for rain, and may have been a survival of a primitive rain-making ceremony, since the festival was celebrated about the time when the first rains of autumn might be expected. He goes on to show what symbolic reference the Jewish commentators found in all this: 'The idea of the satisfaction of the need for water in order to live recurs in rabbinic discussions of the festival and its meaning, and water is made to symbolise various spiritual blessings.'

Professor Dodd refers to the rabbi Joshua ben Levi who wrote in the third century of the waters of Tabernacles being associated with the gift of the Holy Spirit. This is, of course, very like the theology of John's interpretation of the Feast and its meaning. At any rate, as most commentators agree, there is a gain in significance if we hold all this symbolism in view when we consider Jesus' saying: 'If any man is thirsty, let him come to me and drink' (Jn 7.37).

All these references to life and living water reach their fulfilment in the Baptism which Christ gives to his people. When the Israelites lived in the tents or tabernacles during the Exodus event, they had been given water for the journey in the desert from the rock, the rock which is Christ. For Christ now provides his people with water for their journey, he springs up an ever-flowing fountain of redemption. Baptism is a call to follow Christ into the land of his glory. It is significant that the Ezechiel passage about the flowing water of the Temple continues with a description of the lively fish in the streams: 'wherever the river goes every living creature which swarms will live, and there will be very many fish; for this water goes there, that the waters of the sea may become fresh; so everything will live where the river goes' (Ez. 47.9). The image of the waters of the living fish was taken up by the early Christians as an image of baptism—the Christian fish, the members of the race of the ichthus, could only live in the flowing, living water of Baptism which is Christ's element.

Zechariah describes the last great battle and the victory of the Jews over all the enemy nations: 'then every one that survives of all the nations that have come against Jerusalem shall go up year after year to worship the King, the Lord of hosts, and to keep the feast of Tabernacles' (14.16).

The connection of the feast with the giving of water is emphasized in the punishment for those nations who do not come to the Feast: 'there shall be no rain for them' (14.17). The Targum takes care of Egypt, which did not depend on rain for its crops, it will not escape: 'The Nile shall not rise for them.'

A similar setting of triumphant Israel and prostrate enemies surrounds Isaiah's reference to the Feast. He speaks of the Assyrians terror-struck at the voice of the Lord, and the coming of the Messiah at the time of the festival: 'You shall have a song as in the night when a holy feast is kept; and gladness of heart, as when one sets out to the sound of the flute to go to the mountain of the Lord' (Is. 30.29). Isaiah is thinking of the midnight inaugural ceremony of the Feast and of the music of the flute-players as the People of God climbed up from the city to the festivities on the Temple rock.

Another man thinking of the procession and the water-drawing and the feast of lights is the exiled levite who composed the liturgically framed Psalms 42 and 43. These are really one psalm and they speak wholly in terms of the autumnal celebration of the Feast of Tabernacles. Their imagery is taken from water and light and their frame from the processional throng of people to the feast: 'These things I remember as I pour out my soul: how I went in the throng, and led them in procession to the house of God, with glad shouts and songs of thanksgiving, a multitude keeping festival.' He speaks of his thirst for the waters of God and his desire for God is expressed in terms of the waters: 'As a hart longs for flowing streams, so longs my soul for thee, O God. My soul thirsts for God, for the living God', and God's coming to the man is expressed in terms of light and the feast: 'Oh send out thy light and thy truth; let them lead me, let them bring me to thy holy hill and to thy tabernacle.' He hopes for the time when all will be well and he can rest assured: 'At night his song is with me.'

Besides the nightly illumination of the court of the women there was a daily procession of the people who carried the lulab and the ethrog, the bundle of palm branches with myrtle and willow, and the citrous fruit, in their hands and marched round the altar each day; they did this seven times on the seventh day. The origins of this procession are obscure but the Jews of our Lord's time explained them in Exodus terms as a commemoration of the march round Jericho.

We may well have in Psalm 118 a song sung during this procession towards the Temple which was rendered antiphonally by the levites within the Temple and the crowds approaching. Psalm 118 was part of the Hallel sung at all the great festivals (it is probably the hymn referred to in the Johannine Last Supper narrative) but this psalm was especially associated with the cult of the Feast of Tabernacles. The psalm includes the verses which the Mishnah says were sung round the altar: 'Save us, we beseech thee, O Lord. O Lord, we beseech thee, give us success.' 'Save now' or 'Hosanna' was repeated as a cry so often that the palm-branches waved in the procession became known as 'hosannas'. It would seem that in this a rubric has become a nigric and entered the text, since the rhythms of the psalm demand that we should translate 118.27 thus: 'The Lord is God, and he has given us light (Order the festal procession with branches) up to the horns of the altar.'

The festal procession moves towards the altar in the light of the lamps of Tabernacles singing the song and waving the branches. It would seem that the events we celebrate on the II Sunday of Passiontide derive something of their impulse from Tabernacles as well as from Passover. The 'Hosanna' for Christ is exactly the shout that one would expect for the Light of the World and the giver of Living Water.

The liturgical action is seen by the Hebrews as recreating the world of God among his people. We have noted the view of the Temple as a miniature and make-shift universe trying to give something of the universal praise once raised by creation. In the Tabernacles feast it seems that the presence of the Lord was both recalled as at the Exodus and realized as immediate and actual at the time of the celebration. The Hebrew cult represented the saving work of God in the past, and by the liturgical repetition and renewal made that salvation present to the worshipper. The Exodus providence of God is with them once more in the festal cult. The Lord comes to them at the feast.

He comes at the drawing of the water from the Pool of Shiloh which was brought up to the altar and poured out to the sound of the trumpet.

Isaiah describes this water-drawing in terms of God's immediate presence among the people: 'With joy you will draw water from the wells of salvation. And you will say in that day . . . "Shout and sing for joy, O inhabitants of Zion, for great in your midst is the Holy One of Israel"' (12.3–6).

The coming of Yahweh to his liturgical people was shown in the procession of the people coming up to the Temple: 'Thy solemn processions are seen, O God, the processions of my God, my King, into the sanctuary—the singers in front, the minstrels last, between them maidens playing timbrels' (Ps. 68.24). And the people come in the procession in their tribal companies as they thought of themselves travelling in the wilderness. The whole congregation, in tribes and families, goes in solemn procession through the city, from station to station, as the Hebrews had wandered from place to place, not by direct route but along the *via sacra*, the route God had determined in the desert. The people lead Yahweh into his city and his Temple as he had moved towards the promised land. This cultic repetition of the event influenced the final writing of the Exodus story, so that we have now a liturgical interpretation of history. The flight from Egypt is not to be distinguished from the cult procession, they are to be understood in terms of one another: 'O God, when thou didst go forth before thy people, when thou didst go a progress through the wilderness, the earth quaked, the heavens poured down rain at the presence of God; yon Sinai quaked as God went marching' (Ps. 68.7–8).

The Exodus and the Creation are to be understood as part of the one continuous act of God, they are part of the one event recited in the festival rites in the procession to the Temple:

O give thanks to the Lord of lords,
for his steadfast love endures for ever; . . .

> to him who by understanding made the heavens,
>   for his steadfast love endures for ever;
> to him who spread out the earth upon the waters,
>   for his steadfast love endures for ever,
> to him who made the great lights,
>   for his steadfast love endures for ever, . . .
>
> to him who smote the first-born of Egypt,
>   for his steadfast love endures for ever;
> and brought Israel out from among them, . . .
>   for his steadfast love endures for ever; . . .
> to him who divided the Red Sea in sunder,
>   for his steadfast love endures for ever
> and made pass through the midst of it (Ps. 136.3; 5–7; 10–14).

It is within this context of liturgical presentation that John writes his gospel. His understanding of Christ's self-disclosure is handed on to us through the liturgical pattern of water and light.

E. Tabernacles and the Gospel of John

In the gospel of John we are presented with an account of Christ and his work which is so constructed that we learn at least as much about what Christ does here and now among us, as of what he did in Galilee and Jerusalem. John is the evangelist of the Church's recognition of herself, of the self-realization that takes place in the sacraments of Christ, particularly the sacraments of Baptism and the Eucharist.

We have by our participation in these sacraments accepted a commission to preach Christ, 'and him crucified,' as these sacraments are shown as the streams from the side of the crucified Lord. We are to preach him as active among us. Mark and Luke were certainly more than historians, they were writing to make alive to other men the experience that those who knew him in the flesh, in an historical moment, had had of Christ. These evangelists are existential enough but it is evident that their understanding of Christ, their theology, depends heavily upon the actual recorded events of the past being interpreted as past, as once for all, and causative of the present. For John the past and the present are equally expressions of the incarnate Lord. Jesus acts now and we recognize his action now, just as he has acted and was recognized. We may well understand the present in the light of the past, but it is the present that we first wish to understand. Of course the difference between Mark and Luke, on the one hand, and John, on the other, is merely a matter of emphasis. Mark is a theologian and John is an historian. The callings are not mutually exclusive in the Christian gospel.

It would certainly be wrong to suggest that John was generally uninterested in actual events. The man whom Jesus loved is not likely to deal in abstractions. John remembers well enough the sights and sounds and feel of things when he was walking with Jesus. But it is equally certain that the man whom Jesus loved is not likely to think of that love as in the past. The love of Jesus is eternal, and it would be surprising if John did not speak of that love as present to him.

The present love of Jesus is expressed in his Body, the Christian community. This is a truth to be looked at, like most of St John's truths, from two aspects, and these not separately but together. The love of Jesus is expressed both in his creating such a community, and in the love for him which is expressed in the community action, especially in the liturgy. John is writing as a member of a fully ordered community, he is concerned with the community expression of Christ. He is the theologian of the community today as Luke is the theologian of the community's history. John wants to make his readers aware of the constant action of Christ in his sacramental signs. Above all, he wants the Christians to understand what the sacraments are. He is alive to the danger of their becoming simply rituals and commemorations, of their living action being forgotten. So he creates in his gospel a theology of Christ in his signs, of Christ as the sign. The emphasis is laid on Christ as a person whom we encounter, within the sacramental life of the Church.

The work of Bultmann, though it is evidently not acceptable in every aspect, has made it once more a commonplace in theological discussion that there is a great difference between the mere being of things in the physical universe and the consciousness of being and becoming which characterizes the existence of men. We must conserve at every point in our religious thinking the importance of the personal. This is especially the case, if anywhere, in the theology of the sacraments. And it is here that John's personal encounter with Christ is of unique importance to us as we try to take part in such a personal encounter ourselves.

The real actions of Christ in Galilee and Jerusalem are understood by John, not simply as historical actions, but as signs towards us now, and the signs of the sacramental economy are understood by John, not as mere signs, nor even as causative or effective (in the impersonal sense), but as present actions of the Jesus who walked with him by the lakeside and along the dusty streets of Jerusalem.

Nor is John limited in his appreciation of reality past and present, to the dimension of his personal past and present. In both directions of time he reaches out to perfect his own understanding. He comprehends in love the past of his Hebrew people and the future of his Christian people. The main purpose of this present analysis of John's intention when writing his gospel is of his relevance to us, but it would be unbalanced not to proceed by a prologue in terms of the past covenant. John himself says as much in the first words of his gospel which are a deliberate echo of the first words of the Old Testament. The one God acts in all our history, the one Word is present in a creative and redeeming act towards men.

Yahweh is a God of the Covenant. He enters into a personal alignment with a particular people. He is not thought of in terms of cause and effect but in terms of personal intervention in the history of a people. The God who brings men out of a particular bondage in Egypt, and leads them to a particular Promised Land in Canaan. He deals with his men in an always personal manner. The central doctrine of his revelation to the Israelites is the affirmation of how their history is to fare forward: 'I will be your God, and you will be my people' (Ex. 6.7). God is the faithful God, and however much the people prove unfaithful to him the constant theme of the Old Testament is of a God who does not forsake his people, who loves always. History is the history of a personal encounter and the free personal response, sometimes of love, sometimes of apostasy, of the Hebrews to God's offered love. Revelation leads up to a time when the people finally reject their Messiah and turn from their Christ. Revelation leads up to the time when God maintains his faithfulness even to death, even to the death of the Cross. In Christ the faithfulness of God is shown and in Christ the perfect response of man is at last given to the love of God.

Jesus can represent us effectively, however, only if we enter into a personal relationship with him. The God who acts, acts consistently; as he has never in the past demanded an automaton reply from a human being, he does not do so now. We have to accept Christ as our representative before the reality of his redeeming work can be properly applied to us. We must be faithful to our new covenant or else we shall be as irresponsible as the Jews. And our situation is like theirs in all things except this: that we come to the Father through Christ and his work.

John therefore writes his gospel round the sacramental activity of Christ among us in order that we shall understand the necessity for a personal response to the personal invitation offered us in Christ. John knows and feels his kinship with the people who have rejected Christ; he is a Jew. He knows what it means to a Jew to be a member of the people whom God brought out of Egypt, to be a Jew and wait for the promised Messiah, the first coming of the Lord. But he is also a Christian, he understands what it is to be one of the people created in baptism, to be one of those who continually cry, 'Come, Lord Jesus', in expectation of the second coming of the Promised Lord.

It would be pleasant to discover some autobiographical fragment of St John which would present an account of his first visit to Jerusalem for the Feast of Tabernacles as a little boy with his parents. For I think it not improbable that the origins of the gospel shape and tone are to be found in such an experience. John thinks of our Lord in terms of the Feast, Christ is for him the wine of the harvest festival, the water poured out from Jerusalem for the world, the light which shines in the darkness, the bread of the banquet given by God. The images of the Feast dominate his gospel. This is evident in the Prologue which sets the tone of the work. There Christ is described as 'the light' shining 'in the darkness and the darkness could not master it' and he is said to have 'pitched his tent among us' or perhaps 'pitched his tabernacle among us'. It is evident too in the whole design of the work in which images of vines and lights and waters come through again and again. These derive ultimately from the Exodus events but are mediated more immediately through the celebration of the Feast.

Jesus is represented in this gospel as taking up the old image of the vine and its festal celebration. In the sacramental context of the Last Supper Jesus speaks to his priestly community and speaks of his integral personal union with each of them and of each with every other:

> I am the true vine, and it is my Father who tends it. The branch that yields no fruit in me, he cuts away; the branch that does yield fruit he trims clean, so that it may yield more fruit. . . . I am the vine, you are its branches; if a man lives on in me, and I in him, then he will yield abundant fruit; apart from me you can do nothing. If a man does not live on in me, he can only be like the branch that is cast off and withers away; such a branch is picked up and thrown into the fire, to burn there (Jn. 15.1–6).

John here presents Christ as the fulfilment of the Old Testament understanding of God's relation to his people.

Dr A. Guilding has shown that Tabernacles haphtarah include Jeremiah 2.21, 'I planted you a choice vine', and Isaiah 4.6 (RSV, ch. 5:1 ff), 'My beloved had a vineyard', and Hosea 14.7, 'They shall blossom as the vine.' So Christ shows himself as true vine at Tabernacles. She says of the Johannine Supper narrative: 'We have in the Supper Discourse a recapitulation of the cycle of Jewish feasts placed in the historical setting of the last supper . . . the primary allusion is to the vintage of the autumn feast and to the Tabernacles lections which speak of Israel as an empty vine.'

Isaiah had long before presented the love of God for the Hebrew race in terms of the Palestinian countryman's care for his vineyard:

> Let me sing for my beloved
>   a love song concerning his vineyard:
> My beloved had a vineyard
>   on a very fertile hill.
> He digged it and cleared it of stones,
>   and planted it with choice vines;
> He built a watchtower in the midst of it,
>   and hewed out a wine vat in it;
> and he looked for it to yield grapes,
>   but it yielded wild grapes.
> And now, O inhabitants of Jerusalem
>   and men of Judah,
> judge, I pray you, between me
>   and my vineyard (Is. 5.1–3).

The master of the vine has been cheated somehow, the Lord has been rejected by the Jews, they are a faithless people: 'the vineyard of the Lord of hosts is the house of Israel, and the men of Judah are his pleasant planting; and he looked for justice, but behold, bloodshed; for righteousness, but behold, a cry!' (Is. 5.7).

However many the times that God has worked for his people, they so many times have refused his redemption, they have allied themselves with false nations and their falser gods, they have demanded luxury and refused the bread of the Lord and the wine of the Lord. The same image of the vine is used in the book of Jeremiah, when he is speaking of the apostasy of the people: 'Many shepherds have destroyed my vineyard, they have trampled down my portion, they have made my pleasant portion a desolate wilderness . . . they shall be ashamed when the time comes to gather the fruit because of the fierce anger of the Lord' (Jer. 12.10). And the people knew that they had played the Lord false, and knew that their misery derived from their apostasy, not simply as punishment, but as the inevitable and inherent consequence of irresponsibility and rejection of the personal call of Yahweh. The same image for Yahweh's punishing Israel is employed in Ezechiel: 'Like the wood of the vine . . . which I have given to the fire for fuel, so will I give up the inhabitants of Jerusalem' (15.6). So they cried to Yahweh to come again, to renew their vocation, to look after the vine: 'Turn again, O God of hosts! Look down from heaven, and see; have regard for this vine, the stock which thy right hand planted . . . Restore us, O Lord God of hosts! let thy face shine, that we may be saved' (Ps. 80.14, 19).

John remembers all this imagery of the vine and the personal relationship between Yahweh and his people that it presented. And he understands it as a Christian. He sees that the Old Testament speaks to us of Christ. Christ is the true vine. In the old covenant there was the sign but not the fullness of reality. In Christ we have the reality which is signified. He *is* the vine.

The fixed difference between Yahweh and the people, a difference which was not removed by the covenant—indeed the necessity of the covenant arose only as a recognition of this difference—is integral to the Old Testament sign. Because of the difference the sign could only be a sign. In the new kingdom the people and God, the vineyard and the vine-dresser, are one in Christ who is the vine himself. The incarnational truth of Christ demands as its complement the existence of a fleshly community which will express the divine—the Church exists because of our oneness with God in the incarnation. John is not concerned primarily, however, with the fulfilment of the Old Testament understanding of God in the person of Christ. He is much concerned with our present position. The vine is we now.

139

At the Last Supper Matthew records our Lord saying: 'I tell you this, I shall not drink of this fruit of the vine again, until I drink it with you, new wine, in the kingdom of my Father' (26.29).

At the crucifixion John records that Christ did drink a bitter and decayed wine: and at the same time announced that his work was completed: 'Jesus drank the vinegar, and said, It is achieved. Then he bowed his head and yielded up his spirit' (19.30). The vinegar is drunk away from his friends, it is not drunk with them, not a community action, but after the resurrection we find Christ again taking part in meals with his disciples, and in our own paschal time we eat the bread and drink the wine of the Lord. Only like the vine, the wine has become, not simply a sign of his presence, but himself present. He is with us as wine in the kingdom. We have now the eternal banquet, we share now the Eucharist of the Lord. What was sign and hint and prophecy among the Hebrews, what was reality when they were with Christ in Jerusalem, is become one, and we have the reality under the sign, and the sign is the reality. John's understanding of the past of the Hebrews, and of his own present, gives him an understanding of our present. And his pattern is completed in the image of the Apocalyptic angel who gathers the grapes from the world's vineyard, when the clusters are ripe. For the Eucharist banquet is eschatological, we eat and drink towards the time when we shall eat and drink for ever in Christ.

John's use of the vine image is, thus, directed towards a realization by the Christian community of what community means for Christians. He is teaching precisely the same doctrine as that which Paul puts across to his converts in terms of a body and its members. In many ways the Pauline image, since it is more human, is more adaptable, can be used to illustrate many different things about our relation with Christ, but in one matter the image of John is better framed. The Johannine image of a vine with its branches is perfectly expressive of our total dependence on Christ, without him we can do nothing; without the sap rising in the trunk-stem of the vine the branches and wistrels would die and fall away useless. The living Spirit of Christ must rise in our lives before we can perform one Christian act, our Christian actions are the actions of Christ: they have the value that all Christ's actions have: 'I am all at once what Christ is, since he was what I am, and this Jack, joke, poor potsherd, patch, matchwood, immortal diamond, is immortal diamond.'

Every Christian act, so far as it is Christian, that is, done by a baptized man responsibly, is a sacramental act. The leaf of the vine is as much vine as the trunk of the whole plant, and we are each of us Christ when we are baptized into Christ and act in him. The doctrine of the Body of Christ, therefore, demands an explanation in terms of Christ, of our entry into the community and our activity within the community, of our baptism and our Eucharist and our preaching of the gospel. It is of these three main aspects of the community's activity that John writes.

All this is a development of the original vine impulse of the Feast of the Tabernacles. John has taken the old indication and understood that it points to the Christ and the Church.

In the Hebrew celebration of the vine feast not much of the viticultural aspect survived to the time of Christ; John developed a small and historical hint. There was much for him to develop and it was more evidently set out for him in the contemporary Hebrew liturgy in the images of *light* and *water*. John's gospel is in some ways a meditation on the meaning of these elements in the new Feast which is Christ. The stories of Nicodemus and the woman at the well of the Samaritans are springboards for the explanation of what light and water now mean to the Christian, and they lead up to the presentation of Christ himself in the Temple during the Feast.

There was a man called Nicodemus, a Pharisee, who came to see Jesus by night. A man who came out of the blackness, who was afraid and hesitating, but who dimly perceived that if he came to Christ he would find light and truth. And he was told that he must be baptized into light, that he would come out of the darkness of sin, out of the grave of self, into the light of God. And that this light is to be had only in the person of Christ and acceptance of him as the only Light of the World: 'Rejection lies in this, that when the light came into the world men preferred darkness to the light; preferred it, because their doings were evil. Anyone who acts shamefully hates the light, will not come into the light, for fear his doings will be found out. Whereas the man whose life is true comes to the light, so that his deeds may be seen for what they are, deeds done in God' (Jn 3.19–21).

When St Mark spoke of Christ and of our seeing in his light, he was mainly concerned with our coming to see who Christ is, to seeing him transfigured for ever in the presence of his Father. There is certainly something of this in St John's thought also. But the main emphasis in John's writing is that Christ shines out and is evident, he does not have to be sought, he is not obscure. He is to be seen. He presents the divine life to us. He is to be a sign to us, the sign of the cross lifted up to show us what the love of God is. At the end of his ministry Philip asks him to let them see, and Christ replies: 'What, Philip, here am I, who have been all this time in your company; hast thou not learned to recognize me yet?' (Jn 14.9). And when John is summarizing his own experience of Christ it is in words of sight and wonder: 'we have seen his glory, glory such as belongs to the Father's only-begotten Son' (Jn 1.14).

For John the great Christian endeavour is not to find out about Christ, not to see him—that is obvious enough; what John conceives as the Christian task is seeing ourselves as Christ sees us. We have to be ready to face up to the truth about ourselves as it looks in the light of Christ. The light of Christ is thought of as a searching light which shows us up suddenly in its beam; we must resist the temptation to conceal ourselves in our own shadow, to skulk in the corners of pride and sin, to turn our backs and ignore the light. It is possible to reject him, to misconceive what the light is for: 'the light shines in the darkness, and the darkness was not able to comprehend it' (Jn 1.5). Sin can neither overcome nor understand the light of Christ. It is only those who act in the light who can bear the light.

If we do not respond to the light, if we leave it behind us, then we are already judged. We have by our own action refused the proffered love, and since we are personal responsible beings God does not force our love: 'God so loved the world that he gave up his only-begotten Son, so that those who believe in him may not perish, but have eternal life. When God sent his Son into the world it was not to reject the world, but so that the world might find salvation through him. For the man who believes in him there is no rejection; the man who does not believe is already rejected' (Jn 3.16–18).

We judge ourselves and condemn ourselves, when we refuse Christ. We judge ourselves when we refuse the fellowship of the faithful in the liturgy. This is what Paul means when he writes to the Corinthians: 'A man must examine himself first, and then eat of that bread and drink of that cup; he is eating and drinking damnation to himself if he eats and drinks unworthily, not recognizing the Lord's body for what it is' (I Cor. 11.28–9). The Body of the Lord here, in almost

Johannine fashion, means both the eucharistic Body and the ecclesial Body of Christ. The whole context is designed to stress the oneness between our liturgical community action and our life in Christ.

There is no self-knowledge apart from Christ. The only mirror that shews us what we must be and what we are now is Christ. Nicodemus learns who he is by learning to recognize who Christ is.

The same self lesson is brought out in the incident that John records immediately after the visit of Nicodemus. It is a parallel and complement that John next tells the story of the Samaritan woman coming to the well of Jacob for water and finding Jesus sitting on the well-wall. The woman is forced to know herself, to acknowledge what sort of person she has become through her profligate way of life: 'Jesus said to her, Go home, fetch your husband and come back here. I have no husband, answered the woman. Jesus told her, True enough thou hast no husband. Thou hast had five husbands, but the man who is with thee now is no husband of thine; thou hast told the truth over this' (Jn 4.16–18). And the woman went back to her people, and acknowledged that she had come to know herself in the presence of the Hebrew stranger; she said to them: 'He told me all my life's story' (4.29). In the conversation with Christ she had been forced to speak the truth about herself because she had been in the presence of truth and recognized it for truth. This is the baptismal situation. The water that she wishes to have from Christ, the water which will be eternally hers, is given at baptism, given to those who proclaim Christ as the truth, who answer the questions about him with a faithful 'I believe'.

The sign of her reception of Christ is that she is aware of what has happened and can announce it to her people. She recognizes the truth about herself and therefore can preach the truth of Christ to others: 'Many of the Samaritans from that city came to believe in him through the woman's testimony' (4.39). The woman has recognized, as John intends that we shall recognize, that the consequence of self-knowledge is the acceptance of Christ, and the consequence of such an acceptance is the vocation to preach Christ to other men. The vocation to preach comes in the sacrament of water, a sacrament that once given makes demands for a life-time of service, and gives an eternity of reward: 'The man who drinks the water I give him will not know thirst any more. The water I give him will be a spring of water within him, that flows continually to bring him everlasting life. Then, Sir, said the woman, give me water such as that, so that I may never be thirsty ' (4.13–15).

John recounts this incident *for us*. The woman is obviously not baptized at this point, but later in his gospel John shows what the fountain of water really is: Christ acts in the sacraments as he is now, not as he was walking in Jerusalem, nor as he was suffering on the cross, but as he is now risen and glorified, continually sending us his spirit who befriends us:

> On the last and greatest day of the feast Jesus stood there and cried aloud, If any man is thirsty, let him come to me, and drink; yes, if a man believes in me, as the scriptures say, fountains of living water shall flow from his belly. He was speaking here of the Spirit which was to be received by those who learned to believe in him; the Spirit which had not been given to men because Jesus had not yet been raised to glory (7.37–9).

During the Feast also Christ stood in the city and cried out to the people of Jerusalem: 'I am the light of the world, he who follows me can never walk in darkness—he will possess the light which is life' (8.12). The sign has become reality. Christ is the light. The pillar of fire was simply a sign of God's presence, Christ is both sign and signified.

He is also the bringer of light to men and the light to whom men are to witness.

There is a wonderful account of how one man bore witness to the work that Christ had done in him by the pool of Siloam, the pool of purification. Jesus was walking out of the Temple and he saw a blind man and determined to bring him into the light: 'As long as I am in the world, I am the world's light. With that he spat on the ground and made clay of the spittle; then he spread the clay on the man's eyes and said to him, Go and wash in the pool of Siloam. So he went and washed there and came back with his sight restored, (9.5–7). At once the cured man is called to bear witness to the Lord. He is summoned by the Pharisees. And they questioned him and wanted to find some easy natural explanation for his sudden sight. They then make further inquiries and he remains to help them with their inquiries as they question his parents. It evidently took some courage to speak of Christ to the inquisitors: 'They questioned them: Is this your son, who, you say, was born blind? How comes it, then, that he is now able to see? His parents answered them, We can tell you that this is our son, and he was born blind; we cannot tell how he is able to see now; we have no means of knowing who opened his eyes' (9.19–21). So the Pharisees are driven to accept the reality of the cure but do not accept it as a sign of the Lord. The cured man, however, knows what is happening to him: 'They said, This man to our knowledge is a sinner. Sinner or not, said the other, all I know is that once I was blind and now I see' (9.24–5).

In their blindness they turn their backs on the reality, they move backwards to a safer time, to a sign of the Lord rather than the face of the Lord: 'Keep his discipleship to yourself, we are the disciples of Moses' (9.28). They will not listen to the cured man any more, they thrust him out. They remain themselves in interior darkness. To the man who has witnessed to him and recognized him as the Lord, Jesus says that he has come 'that those who are blind may see and those who see shall become blind' (9.39).

The Pharisees judge themselves and retreat into unreality and darkness of sin. The faithful man comes into the light. Dr Guilding remarks in this connection:

> In John 9.24 the Pharisees address the man healed of blindness with the very words of Isaiah 66.5, bidding him 'Give glory to God'. . . . The man born blind makes his confession of Christ, and thereupon in fulfilment of Isaiah's prophecy, he is cast out of the synagogue for Jesus' sake. The Isaiah passage was read at the feast of Tabernacles as a haphtarah of Leviticus 12.

The faithful man comes from the celebration of the Feast of Tabernacles into the lively light of the resurrection: 'if thou hast faith thou wilt see God in glory' (Jn 11.40).

It is to be noted that the account of the man born blind has been so written that John's readers may apply it at once to their own situation. The man thrust out of the synagogue is John's contemporary. It seems unlikely that disciples of Jesus were denied a part in the synagogue worship during his lifetime; we can see in Acts how at first they took an active part in the synagogue service. After the destruction of Jerusalem in A.D. 70 the Christians spoke of the catastrophe as a punishment on the unbelieving Jews. The Pharisees then became violently anti-Christian. They rejected the Septuagint —the Greek version of Scripture used by the Christians—and made it impossible for Christians to remain in the synagogue by the introduction of the 'Heretical Benediction' into the Shemoneh Esreh prayer. Thus the Jews of Jabneh after A.D. 70, rather than the contemporaries of Jesus, are spoken of in this part of the account.

F. TABERNACLES AND II CORINTHIANS 5

The gospel of John is certainly not the only New Testament writing to derive an impulse from the celebration of the Jewish Tabernacles Feast. It would be too lengthy a business here to examine all the passages which seem to be at least partially dependent upon the Tabernacles pattern, so I will take only one example, and that one which at the same time brings out the meaning of Christ's act for us.

In II Corinthians chapter 5, Paul is making a short description in imaginative terms of the Christian life. He does this within the language of Tabernacles: 'Once this earthly tent-dwelling of ours has come to an end, God, we are sure, has a solid building waiting for us, a dwelling not made with hands, that will last eternally in heaven' (5.1). Here the reference is not directly, although obviously it is ultimately, to the tent-dwellings of the Exodus, but to the tabernacles of the Feast. The Greek verb employed is much more a word of dismantling a booth of Tabernacles than of striking a tent, as Professor Manson says in an article in the *Journal of Theological Studies* (1945). And the intention of Paul is to stress the eschatological kingdom which we inherit: 'it is for this that we sigh, longing for the shelter of that home which heaven will give us . . . we booth-dwellers here go sighing and heavy-hearted' (5.2).

We are not to suppose that the expectation of the coming heaven is all that we have. Paul, like John, connects the Tabernacles imagery with the giving of life, and life of the Spirit: 'our mortal nature must be swallowed up in life. For this, nothing else, God was preparing us, when he gave us the foretaste of his Spirit' (5.4).

The feast of the travelling Israelites in exile before they reached their homeland gives Paul a set of images for the Christian life: 'we recognize that our spirits are exiled from the Lord's presence . . . and have a mind rather to be exiled from the body and at home with the Lord; to that end, at home or in exile, our ambition is to win his favour' (5.6, 8–9).

The chapter continues with a consideration of the coming judgement which will decide whether or no we are to enter the homeland. This, too, is a Exodus theme. The prophecy of Zechariah in connection with this Feast is entirely concerned with the coming of the Messiah and the establishment of the Kingdom of God, and there seems to have been a tradition among the Jews that the Messiah would actually come to them in the month Tisri, in which month Tabernacles falls.

In the Tabernacles imagery as it was interpreted by the rabbinic authors, the Lulab and the Ethrog which the festival pilgrims carried in the Jerusalem processions signified the people's thanks to God for his promise that the world would be new created in the Messianic kingdom. This is brought out in the festal psalm (102) in which the people celebrate the forgiveness and the creating activity of God and acknowledge that God has looked favourably upon them, 'that men may declare in Zion the name of the Lord, and in Jerusalem his praise, when peoples gather together, and kingdoms, to worship the Lord' (vv. 21–22).

In the day of the new creation, as Psalm 27, which is connected with the Feast, suggests, the tabernacle tent will preserve the people of God from the wrath: 'He will hide me in his shelter in the day of trouble; he will conceal me under the cover of his tent' (v. 5).

Paul, therefore, is still within the framework of Tabernacles when he refers to the coming of Christ as Judge of the world: 'All of us have a scrutiny to undergo before Christ's judgement-seat, for each to reap what he has earned in this mortal life, good or ill, according to his deeds' (5.10).

He continues immediately with a further Tabernacles theme which we have already noticed in John's account of Jesus' visit to the Temple during the Feast, that of the giving of life. Paul links this more immediately with the crucifixion: 'Christ died for us all, so that being alive should no longer mean living with our own life, but with his life who died for us and has risen again' (5.15). This life is exactly what Paul means by the 'new creation' desired by the Jews. The new life of Christ is the total fulfilment of the eschatology of the old Tabernacles hope: 'when a man has become a new creature in Christ, his old life has disappeared, everything has become new about him' (5.17).

The giving of life, the new creation, and the coming of the kingdom —all the images of the Tabernacles celebration—are all one in Christ.

147

2. THE NEW TESTAMENT LITURGY

In the previous section I have attempted to describe some of the ways in which the Old Testament liturgical celebration was related to the Old Testament narrative. The liturgical celebration greatly influenced the shape of the accounts of the events, and at the same time it was the events which were celebrated in the liturgy. The event and the account continually interacted until each could be talked about in terms of the other. The Temple festival of Tabernacles and the present narrative of the Exodus cannot be considered separately, they belong together as manifestations of the Hebrew people's sense of God's redemptive work among them. In turn the Hebrew realization of God expressed in the feast and the narrative greatly influenced the shape of the Christian liturgy and the methods of the Christian writers. The Exodus celebration in Tabernacles is both one of the directing influences in the gospel narrative and one of the influences in the eucharistic liturgy. There is no dividing off any one particular influence from the rest. The necessary isolation of any one in a description of the whole complex of ideas and images and rites cannot be regarded with anything but regret.

I want to go on now to a consideration of the early Christian liturgy as an expression of the faith of the community in Christ. I shall at the end of this section consider in more detail two sacramental activities of the early community, but I want to begin with a general consideration of the sacramental principles which gave rise to our seven sacraments. The famous passage in I Peter which declares the Christian people to be a priestly nation, and the parallel verse in the Apocalypse which says that by the work of Christ we are made 'a royal race of priests to serve God, his Father' (1.6), suggests that like the Pharisees, as Professor Jeremias has long ago shown, and like the members of the Qumran community, as Dr Gartner has recently shown, the early Christians demanded of members of their community a level of sanctification equivalent to that demanded of the priests who served in the Jerusalem Temple. If the Christian is a priest in what Temple does he serve?

At the cleansing of the Temple in both the Synoptic and Johannine narratives Jesus makes statements which constitute a claim to be the Temple of the new society, and in John's gospel the claim is emphasized by a glossarial note bringing out the meaning in case the reader missed it: 'The temple he was speaking of was his own body' (2.21). Although at the time the disciples seem not to have understood the kind of claim that Jesus was making, John records that after the resurrection the saying was seen to make such a claim and that this was a fulfilment of the old covenant scriptures: 'when he had risen from the dead his disciples remembered his saying this, and learned to believe in the scriptures, and in the words Jesus had spoken' (2.22).

That Jesus himself referred to his disciples as a priesthood seems certain from the account in Matthew's gospel of the incident of their plucking the ears of corn on the sabbath which caused so much scandal to the Pharisees. Jesus' reply to their criticisms is to say that the priests of the old Temple were always allowed to perform their service on the sabbath and it was not counted as a technical breach of the sabbath regulations: 'have you not read in the law that the priests violate the sabbath rest in the temple, and none blames them?' (12.5). So in the new order of things the disciples are seen as priests. Christ has become the new Temple and each member of the community is to share in the service of God 'in Christ Jesus'.

That the whole community is to be regarded as a priestly order serving in the new Temple of Christ may be the theological and liturgical explanation, as distinct from the economic explanation, of the 'primitive communism' recorded in Acts: 'All the faithful held together, and shared all they had, selling their possessions and their means of livelihood, so as to distribute to all, as each had need' (2.44), and: 'None of them was destitute; all those who owned farms or houses used to sell them, and bring the price of what they had sold to lay it at the apostles' feet, so that each could have what share of it he needed. There was a Levite called Joseph, a Cypriot by birth, to whom the apostles gave the fresh name of Barnabas, which means, the man of encouragement; he had an estate which he sold, and brought the purchase money to lay it at the apostles' feet' (4.34-7).

The priests of the Temple shared the income of the Temple amongst themselves—hence their vigorous defence of the merchants who rented stalls in the Temple courts. The new community may have understood that it was required to share its material goods because it was a priestly community sharing the service of the Lord. It may well be that the sin of Ananias and Sapphira, with whose punishment we shall be concerned later, was not simply that they intended to gain a reputation for generosity while retaining their own wealth but that their refusal to share all they had with the other members of the community was a refusal to join with the others in the priestly service of God symbolized by this sharing of property.

The way in which the community dealt with these two sinners exhibits the community as thinking of itself empowered to judge cases just as the old priesthood exercised a judicial function in the old society. That such a function was regarded as the proper office of a priest even after the sacerdotal society had fallen into desuetude can be seen in Ezechiel's description of the priesthood in the new Temple looked for by the Jews during the Exile: 'In a controversy they shall act as judges, and they shall judge it according to my judgements. They shall keep my laws and my statutes in all my appointed feasts and they shall keep my sabbaths holy' (44.24). We shall see in the penultimate section how the early Christians considered Jesus as founding a judicial society in the very act of founding a worshipping society of priests.

The exercise of a judicial function, like the sharing of material goods, is a side-effect of the central truth of the existence of the Christian community as a Temple community. On the great principle that what happens to Christ happens to his community, and what is characteristic of Christ is characteristic of his community—a principle which we saw at work most obviously in the use of the Exodus imagery in the New Testament—as Christ is the new Temple so his community is the Temple. In the community God dwells as he had dwelt in the old Temple. This is given the clearest expression in Paul's second letter to the Corinthians: 'You are the temple of the living God; God has told us so: I will live and move among them, and be their God, and they shall be my people' (II Cor. 6.16), which in its turn depends on a gathering of Old Testament quotations concerned with God's dwelling in his sanctuary among the chosen people, Exodus 25.8; 29.45 and Leviticus 26.12. Paul thinks of the Shekinah of God dwelling in the new community as it had dwelt in the desert community and the temple community. The idea that God would come to dwell again in the midst of a community rather than in a temple 'made by men's hands' is not found only in the New Testament writings. It is a hope current among the members of the Qumran community and in that community which produced the Book of Jubilees.

Since Christ is the new Temple the whole Christian community is the new Temple. Since the whole Christian community, taken together, is the new Temple then in the actualization of the community of Christ which takes place in the eucharistic celebration the local community at Ephesus or Corinth is the Temple. Thus Paul writes to the local church of Corinth: 'Do you not understand that you are God's temple, and that God's Spirit has his dwelling in you? If anybody desecrates the temple of God, God will bring him to ruin. It is a holy thing, this temple of God which is nothing other than yourselves' (I Cor. 3.16).

The Shekinah is present in the local gathering of the Church. The Spirit dwells in the group round the Eucharist and makes their celebration a sign of the coming kingdom and of the kingdom come for the members of the community. That is why the new community as a whole has to obey the demands for holiness which were previously made on the priests of the Temple. To offer service in a blemished condition physically was forbidden to the old priesthood, to come to the Eucharist in sin is forbidden to the new priesthood. We are to be 'a holy people' because we serve in 'the holy place' which is the whole community.

The performance of the cult by the whole community in its every activity is described by Paul in his letter to the Ephesians: 'United in the same Spirit we have access through him to the Father. You are no longer exiles then, or aliens; the saints are your fellow citizens, you belong to the house of God' (2.18). In the old Temple the liturgy had been confined to a small group of hereditary priests at the centre with circles of varying degrees of participation about them, Israelite men, women and strangers. Gentile strangers, even pilgrims or proselytes like the Ethiopian converted by Philip the deacon, were not able to approach anywhere near the central complex of the Temple. There was a wall with thirteen entrances set up as a boundary between the area where any worshipper or sightseeing tourist might stand and the area reserved for members of the Jewish community. Two of the notices warning Gentiles not to pass through the gaps in the wall have been discovered by archaeologists which announce: 'No stranger is permitted to enter the enclosure or the precincts of the holy place. If any man is discovered violating this rule his death will be his own responsibility.' This dividing wall has no place in the new Temple which is for all men and in which all men are to penetrate to the centre. As Paul declares to the Ephesians: '[Christ] has made the two nations one, breaking down the wall that was a barrier between us' (2.15).

In this Temple everyone has 'access in the Spirit to the Father' while in the old ritual only the High Priest, and then only once a year on the Day of Atonement, went into the Holy of Holies. But in the new Temple community we are all priests in the 'house of God' which, as the author of I Timothy says (3.15), 'is the Church', and in which everyone is to offer sacrifice: 'Brethren, I appeal to you by God's mercies to offer up your bodies as a living sacrifice, consecrated to God and worthy of his acceptance; that is the worship due from you' (Rom. 12.1).

The sacrifice of the new Temple is, therefore, not simply a limited cultic ceremony, it is the whole effort of the Christian life to be holy as the Temple service demands, it is the continual activity of charity. As the author of the letter to the Hebrews puts the case: 'we must offer to God a continual sacrifice of praise, the tribute of lips that give thanks to his name. Meanwhile you must remember to do good to others and give alms; God takes pleasure in such sacrifice as this' (Heb. 13.15–16).

All this is, as Hebrews says, 'through Christ'. There is no Christian sacrifice apart from Christ, there is no Temple apart from him. This is emphasized in the letter to the Ephesians: 'Apostles and prophets are the foundation on which you were built, and the chief corner-stone of it is Jesus Christ himself. In him the whole fabric is bound together, as it grows into a temple, dedicated to the Lord; in him you too are being built in with the rest, so that God may find in you a dwelling place for his Spirit' (2.20–22).

The imagery of the chief stone and of the other stones is used again in I Peter to bring out the view that the Christian is a Christian so far as he is another Christ doing the actions of Christ. In this epistle Christ is described as the 'living stone' and the Christians are told that they must be 'living stones' built on Christ. They are to be just like him in their service in the new Temple.

We can now see that the image of the Temple is used in three connections by which it relates to Christ, to the Church, and to the Christian. The image is used of the person of Christ in the gospel and then of the community which is Christ's body, and of the activity of the individual member of this body, in the epistles. The liturgy of the new Temple, therefore, is Christ's act of worship of his Father done within the community context of the Church by the Christian. The sacraments of the new liturgical covenant, therefore, are properly called Christ's actions, and the Church's actions, and the actions of the individual Christian. In the next section I shall point out how the sacraments are to be understood as the Christian's Christ-like activity.

(1) THE SACRAMENTS OF CHRIST

Just as the old liturgy expressed in signs the events of the old redemption of Israel from Egypt, so the new liturgy expresses in signs the new work of God in Christ redeeming his people. The signs are essentially commemorative of the events. The commemoration essentially makes the events present for the worshippers.

We can appreciate this capacity for making present the past event in our own sacraments if we consider them in an order which is not common in the theological manuals. If we take the sacraments in the order of Baptism, Confirmation, Penance, Anointing of the Sick, Eucharist, Holy Order and Marriage, and then arrange them in three pairs and one other thus:

(a) Baptism and Confirmation,
(b) Penance and Anointing of the Sick,
(c) Eucharist and Holy Order,
(d) Marriage,

it is possible to understand the sacraments more clearly as active reflections of Christ's life and work in the past and in the present. The groupings correspond to the gospel pattern of Christ's activity.

(a) Baptism and Confirmation at the beginning of our Christian life correspond to the Baptism of Christ by John in the Jordan.
(b) Penance, the forgiving of sins, and Anointing of the Sick correspond to the ministry of Jesus in Galilee and Judaea during which he went about forgiving sin and restoring men to health.
(c) Eucharist and Holy Order derive from the activity of Christ at the Last Supper.

(d) Marriage, as I shall make clearer in a moment, both sums up the Christian participation in Christ's ministry and is the sign of his continued activity among us after the resurrection.

A scheme such as this, which takes the origin of the sacraments from the life of Christ, needs perhaps a rather lengthier defence than I can suitably provide here, but it has at least some immediate advantages. Not the least of these is that the problem of divine institution of the sacraments is made much easier of solution. It has ever been a difficulty among Catholic theologians to reconcile the dogmatic truth that Christ immediately and directly instituted the seven sacraments with the paucity of evidence for such an institution in history. We certainly cannot seek in New Testament texts for words of explicit institution of each of the sacraments by Christ. If we had resort to such measures there would be a long pause in the consideration of Confirmation, Matrimony, Holy Order and Anointing of the Sick, at least, among the sacraments we now celebrate. Some theologians have therefore had resort to the expedient of suggesting that the sacraments were instituted by Christ explicitly during the period of the Paschal appearances and so passed into the tradition of the community. Such an institution is, of course, very possible but in the absence of any direct proof this explanation has the aspect of ingenuity. It has recently come to be realized that in fact we do not need an explicit verbal institution of each sacrament separately by Christ. We have simply to understand that in instituting the Church Christ was instituting a community with a particular nature expressible in particular actions. As Professor Karl Rahner remarks in his paper on *The Church as the Church of the Sacraments*, the Church 'can recognize that certain acts flowing from her nature are fundamentally and unconditionally the accomplishment of that nature and so are what we call sacraments.'

The Church is only to be expressed in these ways because only these ways have their origin in the nature of the Church. We do not therefore have to seek individual texts explicitly ordaining certain rites, we have only to seek the sacramental principle of the Church's nature and to show how these rites in various ways express this one nature. The nature of the Church is a complex matter which can be speedily summed up as the sign of Christ's redeeming presence in the world, or more shortly still, Christ in the world. We have therefore, in order to explain the existence of the sacraments, to show that they are expressions of Christ in the world.

At this point we come to the great distinction to be made between the Old Testament liturgy and the New Testament liturgy. The Old Testament liturgy expressed God in the world and influenced the narratives of Hebrew history which were trying to put across the notion of God always in the world. The New Testament liturgy derives from the history of God in the world and reflects the continuing presence of God in the world. For the Old Testament experience the liturgical celebration was prior to the history, for the New Testament community the event of Christ was prior to the liturgical celebration. Instead, therefore, of the liturgy shaping the history, history now shapes the liturgy.

The sacraments, therefore, as the prime actions of our new liturgy, are only to be understood on the basis of their presentation of Christ acting now as he has always acted. The life of Christ tells us the meaning of his actions among us.

Such a view of the sacraments will explain several problems of New Testament descriptions and allusions to the sacraments. For example, in the theology of Confirmation a great deal of worry has been caused by the conflicting evidence of the New Testament accounts in Acts as to whether confirmation was a separate sacrament or simply part of the one baptismal initiation rite. Confirmation seems to have been administered in the primitive community in Samaria but not in that of Jerusalem. The difficulty of distinguishing these two sacraments in the life of the Church derives from the difficulty of distinguishing them in the life of Christ. At the Baptism of Christ by John in the Jordan we have a twofold event: Christ is baptized with water as a sign of his community with the sinful people who needed the baptism of repentance for sin, and the Holy Spirit of God descends upon him. Christ is baptized with water and the Holy Spirit. John is explicit in his demand that the Christian must also undergo the same baptism: 'Believe me, no man can enter into the kingdom of God unless birth comes to him from water, and from the Holy Spirit' (3.5).

The parallel is exact. What is different is that we have now given a temporal expression to the two events of baptism in water and the giving of the Holy Spirit. The community has realized that the complex experience of belonging to the kingdom can best be expressed by emphasizing the dual aspect of forgiveness of sin and the reception of the Spirit. Of course it is always possible for the Christian to experience both aspects in the single baptismal reality; the Holy Spirit is given in every sacramental action of the Church. We have to remember that the several sacraments are several because of our limiting receptivity, not because of God's limited giving. Confirmation is not essential as far as the individual is concerned. But for the fullness of Christ's experience to be the Christian's experience Confirmation is required. So now in the Western rite we attempt to make the reception of Confirmation more accessible by granting the administration to parish priests and chaplains of different institutions like hospitals and prisons. This brings our understanding into the world of practice in a way similar to that of the Eastern rites which administer Confirmation to infants at the same time as Baptism. The essential point is that we should understand that Confirmation makes it possible for us to be more like Christ since it brings us more fully into the pattern of his life and work. In this it is exactly like all the other sacraments.

That Baptism and Confirmation were one event in Christ's life made it difficult for the early Christians to be definite about there being one or two rites. The principle that all sacraments reflect the life and work of Christ in our lives produced the difficulty here. On no other theory can the difficulty of distinguishing the two rites be accounted for; it would not arise on any other pattern than that of the events of Christ's experience.

Similarly it may well be that the difficulty of distinguishing in the New Testament records between the office of the episcopate and that of the priesthood derives from their union in the act of Christ at the Last Supper. All the ministries of the Church derive from the function of the minister at the Eucharist. The bishop is early enough in the history of the Church realized to be the one who always presides, whether he is actually present at the celebration physically or whether it is done through his wish by another who has not the fullness of the priesthood but is capable of leading the celebration as the deputed minister. In the Last Supper Christ was both president and consecrator. This was the case also in the very first communities presided over by the apostles themselves. But very early there had to be instituted a separation of presidence and celebration. We can see this in the New Testament where the function and status of

Timothy and Titus, the young bishops, is really that of parish priests
in the communities set up by Paul, the travelling bishop. In time the
multiplication of small communities led to the present distinction of
episcopate, priesthood and diaconate in the one sacrament, which
was not rigidly adopted in the first years. The one act of Christ
instituted the full sacramental activity of the ministry. Within the
community the sacrament was manifested by different ministers.
Probably the links between baptism and confirmation, and between
episcopate and priestly order, are obvious enough. They should
prepare the Christian to expect that such a linkage may exist elsewhere in the sacramental economy. I think that such a linkage is to
be descried in the administration of Penance in general and its
particular performance in the Anointing of the Sick. Like the previous
two couplings, I derive this from the activity of Christ among the
members of his first group of disciples in Galilee.

The ministry of Christ among his contemporaries is described by
Peter as the time when Jesus 'went about doing good, and curing all
those who were under the devil's tyranny'. It seemed to the first
community that what distinguished Christ was the struggle against
the presence of evil in the world, against sin and its attendant
sickness. The illness of the world was intimately connected with sin;
if sin could be defeated then sickness would be eradicated. There was
therefore an intimate connection between the forgiveness of sin and
the recovery of health. This is brought out in the story of the para-
lytic. Christ says to the murmuring Pharisees: 'Which command is
more lightly given, to say to the palsied man: Thy sins are forgiven,
or to say: Rise up, take thy bed with thee, and walk?' (Mk 2.9).
And he demonstrates the defeat of sin by his forgiving power through
the cure of the palsied man: 'And now, to convince you that the
Son of Man has authority to forgive sins while he is on earth (here
he spoke to the palsied man): I tell thee, rise up, take thy bed with
thee, and go home' (Mk 2.10–11).

On the principle we have seen at work earlier we should expect
that the Christian community would realize that if it were to do the
work of Christ in the world it would have sacramental forgiveness of
sin and curing of the sick, and that in order that the double aspect of the
work should be understood in the community, it would express
the work in two activities. This is precisely what we do find. Since
the forgiveness of sin is the primary feature of the work of Christ

in this particular ministry and the curing of sickness a subsidiary effect—and this must have become readily recognizable as the power of miracle-working grew less active in the community after the apostolic age—we would expect that the primary sacrament would be of Penance and the particular case of it be concerned with the sick. This also is precisely what we find. The pattern of Christ's activity is worked out in the sacramental pattern of the rites. We can see the growth of this rite from the personal activity of Christ immediately in the story of the palsied man, through the personal work of Christ mediately in the work of the missionary apostles: 'So they went out and preached, bidding men repent; they cast out many devils, and many who were sick they anointed with oil, and healed them' (Mk 6.12–13).

The priorities are plain enough here. The apostles preach repentance for sin, the men must be ready to accept the forgiveness of Christ, then they rescue the men from the power of the devil, and as examples of their general struggle against sin they particularize the defeat of sickness. The defeat of sickness by the apostles is in direct line with the exorcisms performed by Christ and has the same intention: to show men that evil is conquered in Christ. We can see the same line of thought in the community of James in the early Church. The president of the community writes to the whole Christian Church about their one struggle against sin in the world, and then particularizes the case of the sick of the community: 'Is one of you sick? Let him send for the presbyters of the Church, and let them pray over him, anointing him with oil in the Lord's name. Prayer offered in faith will restore the sick man, and the Lord will give him relief; if he is guilty of sins, they will be pardoned' (James 5.14–15).

Here James is suggesting that the community perform the action of Christ. The demand for faith is always part of the miracle narrative, or at least almost always; the forgiveness of sins is certainly always part of the miracle action of Christ. There is here, therefore, a direct link with the healing miracles of Christ and his exorcisms in Galilee and Judaea. The two sacraments of Penance and Anointing bring into our lives the mission of Christ, just as the Baptism and Confirmation we have received bring into our lives the vocation of Christ.

The connection between the Eucharist and the sacrament of Order which is directed to the eucharistic celebration is evident, and I will not labour this matter here. In the next section I will use the sacrament of the Eucharist as the example to demonstrate how the vital action of Christ in community now is related to the past and the future by the sacramental sign, for the relation to the life of Christ does not exhaust, of course, the significance of the sacramental economy, it simply provides the first principle in the consideration of the complex of sacramental theology. The Eucharist, deriving as it does from the celebration by Christ of the old covenant, being itself the sign of the new covenant, and looking forward to the eschatological victory of the Lord, is a particularly clear example of the way in which all the sacraments reach out in every dimension of our being as the means of our becoming members of Christ more fully.

The Eucharist is not alone, of course, in its reference to the last day. Baptism, at the beginning of the sacramental life, is the promise of the eschatological kingdom, fulfilling the general Hebrew expectation of the water of life at the last times. The urgency with which men of all classes and occupations came out to be baptized by John shows how ready they were to take this as a sign of the coming judgement. But more especially the Christian kingdom is presented in the sacrament of Marriage. What we have now through the risen Lord is signified in the sacrament of man and wife. This is the plain teaching of Paul:

> Wives must obey their husbands as they would obey the Lord. The man is the head to which the woman's body is united, just as Christ is the head of the Church, he, the Saviour on whom the safety of his body depends; and women must owe obedience at all points to their husbands, as the Church does to Christ. You who are husbands must shew love to your wives, as Christ shewed love to the Church when he gave himself up on its behalf . . . that is why a man will leave his father and mother and will cling to his wife, and the two will become one flesh. Yes, those words are a high mystery, and I am applying them here to Christ and his Church (Eph. 5.22–32).

Paul is telling the Ephesians that the words which are used in the Genesis narrative of husband and wife are signs of the relation of Christ and the Church, and that the relation of husband and wife is a sacrament because it presents to the world the work of Christ in his Church now. Marriage is the sign of the kingdom present. Similarly in Revelation marriage is a figure of the relation of Christ and his Church: 'I saw the holy city, new Jerusalem, coming down out of heaven from God, prepared as a bride adorned for her husband' (21–2).

We can see how dominant was the marriage image in early Christian considerations of the eschatological kingdom already present among them by reference to the gospel narrative of Jesus' parables where the wedding-feast is seen as the inauguration of the kingdom, parables like that of the Wise and Foolish Virgins, or that of the men who turn down the King's invitation to the marriage feast of his son, or by glancing at John the Baptist's description of himself as one of the Shoshbim, the friends of the Bridegroom, sharing in the joy of the coming wedding, or by looking at Jesus' own description of the disciples' feasting: 'Can you expect the men of the bridegroom's company to go fasting, while the bridegroom is with them?' (Mk 2.19). Marriage is one of the most favoured images in the gospels when the kingdom is to be described.

This marriage imagery derives, as one would expect, from the Old Testament concept of God's relation to his people. Jewish commentators spoke of Jacob's weary courting and the Song of Solomon as expressions of God's wooing of man. Isaiah speaks of the coming Messianic age as the time when 'as a bridegroom rejoices over a bride, so shall your God rejoice over you' (Is. 62.5), while of the present age Isaiah, Ezechiel, Jeremiah and Hosea all agree that the people are like a wife playing the harlot, unfaithful to Yahweh and running after other baals. There is a pun here on 'baal' which can mean either 'god' or 'husband'. The prophets, like John later, take advantage of an ambiguity in order to assert both meanings at once. Idolatry is adultery.

This imagery derives its basic impetus from the notion that the covenant of Sinai is a marriage between Yahweh and Israel; this is a theme which occurs in several of the prophetic writings, thus Ezechiel says: 'I plighted my troth to you and entered into a covenant with you, says the Lord God, and you became mine' (16.8), and even as early as the composition of the Book of Judges disobedience to the commandments is called 'playing the harlot to other gods' because of the Sinai covenant being thought of in marriage terms.

It is, of course, in the writing of Hosea that the marriage imagery comes to occupy the primary position in the theology of the covenant-interpretation. Hosea thinks of his wife Gomer's unfaithfulness as a working out in his own personal life of the public unfaithfulness of

Israel to Yahweh, and he realizes that all that the deserted husband waits for is the return of the wife in order that they may establish a home of peace and harmony and love again. The kingdom of God becomes for him present in the marriage fulfilment of the covenant with the whole of creation:

> In that day, says the Lord, you will call me, 'My husband', and no longer will you call me, 'My Baal'.
>
> For I will remove the names of the Baals from her mouth, and they shall be mentioned by name no more. And I will make for you a covenant on that day with the beasts of the field, the birds of the air, and the creeping things of the ground. . . . And I will betroth you to me for ever; I will betroth you to me in righteousness and in justice, in steadfast love, and in mercy.
>
> I will betroth you to me in faithfulness; and you shall know the Lord (2.16 ff.).

Hosea is thinking of the coming day of the Lord as a time when the original covenant between man and God in the paradise garden will be present in the world again, so that all the animals are in harmony with man again. And he is thinking of this covenant in extremely physical terms of sexual activity. The coming together of man and woman was spoken of in Hosea's time and later as the man and woman having knowledge of one another. It is this intimate knowledge that Israel will have of Yahweh.

It is this intimate relation between husband and wife which is seen by Paul to be the nearest that we can come on earth to the figuring of the intimate relation of Christ and his Church. Paul summons to mind the whole prophetic handling of the covenant theme and chooses from the many images that there are in the Old Testament for Yahweh's covenant relation with Israel that which is of marriage. Marriage has become for Paul the sign of the new covenant; it is the high mystery because it is the covenant working itself out in the life of the Christian community.

In the new covenant world sacramental Marriage is the sign of the total union of the risen Lord and his community, it is the sign of the environment and context within which the life of the Christian begins and matures until Christ and his Christians are fully one.

We can see, therefore, that the sacraments present us with a pattern of Christ's activity which covers, as it were, the whole range of his work. Baptism, Confirmation, Penance and Anointing of the Sick show us that his Galilean ministry is still active among us; the Eucharist and Holy Order show us that the Last Supper bridge between the Old Testament and Jesus' ministry in the past and the eschatological Kingdom in the future is still among us; Marriage shows us that the risen Lord is indissolubly united with his Church. The sacraments arise out of the instituting work of Christ among his people and are for ever signs of that continuing work.

In the next section I want to examine one of these signs to show something of the way in which the signification is put across in the sacraments.

(2) THE EUCHARISTIC SIGN

The Eucharist is the sacrament upon which the others pivot. It is the central sign of Christ among us to which the other sacraments direct themselves or from which they derive. It is this which gives significance to the whole structure of the Church; if there were no Eucharist there would be no Church, in any sense of the word which we can now recognize. This sacrament therefore, gives us the language in which we may discuss the other sacraments. I do not intend to treat here of the actual celebration of the Eucharist as a rite in the early Church (I have said something of the relation of the Eucharist celebration to the Hebrew Passover already, and those who are interested in further historical discussion will find a plenitude of recent work on the library shelves; a good way to begin might be to refer to 'Jungmann' in the catalogue), but rather to say something of the paradigm-character of the Eucharist in sacramental discussions.

The centrality of the Eucharist is, of course, one of the main notions of that sacramental theology which employs a mediaeval metaphysics based on Aristotle, but it seems to me possible that, for the notions I wish to bring to the fore in this discussion, probably a metaphysics more committed to process is demanded. It may be that Whitehead's description of reality would serve well in this matter. However that may be, some metaphysics does seem to be required if we are to have a useful apprehension of Christ's present work since we have to be able to say something meaningful about 'presence', and about how time past is related to the One whom we affirm is with us now and for ever. The Eucharist raises immediately questions about this relation.

I want in this section to consider some ways in which the Eucharist involves the Old Testament past and the eschatological future with the present celebration of the community.

I will take as my starting-point the actual elements of bread and wine that are traditionally the material of the rite. The choice of bread and wine by Christ is doubtless a development of the ordinary meals he had with his disciples, but also it is a significant reminder of the first Jew's meal with a Gentile. In the old story of Melchizedek, the priest-king of Salem who brought out bread and wine to Abram after the defeat of the kings, we have a hint of the sharing of Jew and Gentile in the worship-meal of the Lord.

The author of Hebrews certainly saw in the Last Supper a pointer back to this incident and thought of Christ as being 'a high priest for ever after the order of Melchizedek', fulfilling the prophecy of Psalm 110: 'The Lord has sworn and will not change his mind, "You are a priest for ever, after the order of Melchizedek" ' (v. 4). Hebrews contains an elaborate similitude between Christ and this king. Melchizedek is, says the writer, evidently greater than the Jews' father, Abraham, since Melchizedek blesses Abraham, and he is not part of the Old Law system, he stands without, superior and sacerdotal: 'He is first, by translation of his name, king of righteousness, and then he is also king of Salem, that is king of peace. He is without father or mother or genealogy, and has neither beginning of days nor end of life, but resembling the Son of God he continues a priest for ever' (Heb. 7.2–3). And Père Daniélou comments on this that Christ is seen as the fulfilment of the covenant with Noah, with all men and 'of all the sacrifices which in all religions and all times men have offered to God, which he takes up and transubstantiates in his own sacrifice.'

The Eucharist takes up the whole past history of men because the Eucharist is Christ and in his person this history becomes meaningful. Christ is the eternal Wisdom of God (I Cor. 1.24), and now, as in the Old Testament book of Proverbs, Wisdom calls to men: 'Come, eat of my bread and drink of the wine I have mixed. Leave ignorance and live, and walk in the way of insight' (Prov. 9.5–6). The only language we have to show how Christ relates the past to himself is the language of his ministry in Galilee, Judaea and Jerusalem; we discover 'insight' to the meaning of all other events through the acts of Jesus.

Earlier I spent some time relating the Eucharist to the Passover, but the present shape of the Eucharist is not simply a fulfilment of Hebrew Passover meals. It has recently been suggested by a Methodist theologian, J. J. Vincent, that in the past Christian commentators have concentrated far too much on the Last Supper as the paradigm for the Christian Eucharist, and that a more developed understanding of the Eucharist should take into account all the meals that Christ had with his disciples. It is evident that the post-resurrection meals recorded in the gospels are meant to be taken as pointers to the meaning of the Christian meal. This is particularly the case with the meal at Emmaus where we may well have a technical term for the Eucharist in the phrase 'the breaking of bread', which is used again in Acts to describe certain meals that Paul took with his friends. But Vincent's argument is meant to take into account the pre-resurrection meals of Christ and the people.

He suggests that we ought particularly to take the feeding of the four thousand and the five thousand into consideration when speaking of the present Eucharist. These miracles of multiplication of loaves and fishes (both of which are signs of Christ) might be taken as evidence that the Eucharist we share is not a meal for those only who have committed themselves to Christ and who are seen by their Christian lives to be worthy to share the meal, but that we should give the Eucharist to all those who would share it; rogues and vagabonds and sinners are not to be excommunicated but fed. At least we can agree with Vincent's suggestion that we take into account the pre-resurrection meals when we consider our own Eucharist, as far as recognizing these meals as signs of the Eucharist.

Certainly the pre-resurrection meals are written up by the evangelists with the eucharistic service in mind. This is easy of demonstration. The feeding of the four thousand in Mark's gospel, for example, is described in terms which derive from the Last Supper and the primitive eucharistic service. This comes out in the description of Christ's actions at the miracle which correspond exactly to the actions of Christ at the Last Supper and to the actions of the President in the eucharistic assembly: 'He took the seven loaves, and having given thanks, he broke them and gave them to his disciples' (Mk 8.6, RSV). The miracle of the five thousand being fed is related in John's gospel in similar terms.

The account of the feeding of the five thousand in Mark's gospel does not have the eucharistic 'gave thanks', but does have a phrase peculiar to this narrative: 'he looked up to heaven', which was incorporated into the Last Supper narrative in the eucharistic liturgy and remains there to this day. The community which formed the traditional account of this miracle evidently saw its eucharistic significance. From this the future eschatological significance opens out.

The Jews saw in the feeding miracles a sign of the imminent coming of the Messiah because it had always been part of their expectation that the manna event would happen again. The eschatological significance of the manna-Eucharist is emphasized in the second chapter of the Apocalypse, where it is seen as a gift of God in the kingdom: 'I will give hidden manna' (2.17), and John's account of one of these miracles combines the past and the present and the future gifts in a curious and effective manner: 'Your fathers *ate* the manna in the wilderness and died . . . he who *eats* my flesh and drinks my blood has eternal life, and I *will* raise him up at the last day' (6.49, 54).

In the eucharistic meal we receive the eschatological 'bread of heaven' that was promised in Psalm 78: 'He commanded the skies above, and opened the doors of heaven; and he rained down upon them manna to eat, and gave them the grain of heaven. Men ate of the bread of the angels; he sent them food in abundance' (vv. 23–5). This is the bread that was expected by the Jewish apocalyptic writers. This is the sign of the last things. Thus in the Apocalpyse of Baruch which was written at about the same time as the gospel of John, the last days are described as the manna-times: 'It shall come to pass at that self-same time that the treasury of manna shall again descend from on high, and they will eat of it in those years because they have come to the consummation of time'. Jesus accepts the manna as a sign of his 'real bread from heaven' and the New Testament authors see in this the sign of the coming heaven at the end of time.

The messianic age for which the Old Testament prepared the Jews has come about in the eucharistic community. We are the people, Paul tells his assembly at Corinth, 'in whom history has reached its fulfilment' (I Cor. 10.11). We are at the climax of things. The Eucharist is the last thing. We have now simply to celebrate the act of Christ 'until he come', and in all things we must be at the ready for the meaning of our history to be manifest in the glorified and gloryfying Lord. He has sounded the last trump, we have to hold the note. In the past God chose out a nation, a group which could be distinguished by social and historical characteristics, before the covenant was made; God chose one group from other groups of the same kind: 'You only have I known of all the families of the earth' (Amos 3.2). And the sign of salvation was exactly the same as the sign of nationality. So there grew up a confidence among the Jews that it was by nationality that they were assured of salvation. This is what John the Baptist attacked: 'And think not to say within yourselves: We have Abraham as our father; for I tell you that God is able to raise up children of Abraham from these stones' (Mt. 3.9).

This complacent assurance through nationality and not through service of God is explicitly rejected by Christ: 'I tell you that there are many who will come from the east and from the west, and will take their places in the kingdom of God with Abraham and Isaac and Jacob, while that kingdom's own sons are cast into the darkness without' (Mt. 8.11). God's covenant is no longer recognizable by the criteria of nationality.

The eschatological banquet brings a judgement upon Israel. And the disciples of Christ are set up as judges of the old People of God: 'As my Father has allotted a kingdom to me, so I allot you a place to eat and drink at my table in my kingdom; you shall sit on twelve thrones judging the twelve tribes of Israel' (Lk. 22–29).

It is for the new People of God that the blessings of the last days are prepared: 'And now the angel said to me: Write thus: Blessed are those who are bidden to the Lamb's wedding-feast' (Apoc. 19.9); it is for them that the apocalyptic notions of the Jews are brought to fruition: the apocalypse of Isaiah speaks of a time when 'the Lord of hosts shall make unto all people in this mountain a feast of fat things, a feast of wine' (Is. 25.6); and IV Esdras describes the coming of the new people into the city of God: 'Build the city and prepare the banquet', and in Enoch men are promised an eternal banquet with the Son of Man: 'they will take their places at his table for ever and ever'. All these visionary ideas, which were familiar to Christ and to the early Christians, are brought to bear upon the understanding of the Eucharist as the bread of the new covenant.

This covenant is the eschatological covenant foreseen by Jeremiah and Ezechiel. Ezechiel describes its constitution thus: 'I will make a covenant of peace with them; it shall be an everlasting covenant with them: and I will bless them, and multiply them, and will set my sanctuary in the midst of them: and I will be their God, and they shall be my people' (Ex. 37.26–7). The new covenant, like the old, will be with a people and will be signed by the presence of God, but unlike the first covenant it will be set up for ever. It is, as Jeremiah says, 'a new covenant', 'not like that covenant I made' with Israel in the Exodus, for this covenant was broken by the Jews. It is a new covenant for ever and not tied to the boundaries of nationalism which is being set up. It is altogether more glorious, as Paul writes in his second letter to the Corinthians: 'what once seemed resplendent seems by comparison resplendent no longer, so much does the greater splendour outshine it. What passed away passed in a flash of glory; what remains, remains instead in a blaze of glory' (II Cor. 3.10). It is altogether free of nationalism: 'No more Jew or Gentile . . . if you belong to Christ then you are indeed Abraham's children: the promised inheritance is yours' (Gal. 3.28).

All this is fulfilled within the eucharistic community which sets up a people of an everlasting covenant that is unlimited with regard to race and nationality, giving unto God an universal praise.

It is possible, of course, for the Eucharist to bring down judgement on the Christians who share it, as Paul suggests to the Corinthians about their agape. The agape feast of fellowship was in early times the context of the Eucharist. The family of Christians met together for a party within which the sacred meal was celebrated. This derived probably from the family Passover setting of the Last Supper, and the comradely breakfast of fish on the shore of Lake Tiberias, but for the men whom Jude addressed and the Corinthians this became an abuse and a scandal. Paul berated the Corinthians about this: 'When you meet together, it is not the Lord's supper that you eat. For in eating, each one goes ahead with his own meal, and one is hungry and another is drunk' (I Cor. 11.20, RSV). The rich have brought their hampers and care nothing that they guzzle and carouse while the poor go hungry and have to wait for the community Eucharist until the drunken orgy is over. These men had forgotten the eschatological element of the Christian understanding of the community and its meal. So Paul warns them of what they were risking: 'Anyone who eats and drinks without discerning the body eats and drinks judgement upon himself' (11.29, RSV).

Paul here means us to take 'body' as referring both to the reality of Christ as the eucharistic species and, probably primarily, to the reality of Christ in his body the Christian community. This is a recurring theme in the Pauline writings. In the previous chapter of I Corinthians he had been discussing the way in which we meet Christ in the Eucharist and this leads immediately into a description of the way we meet each other: 'The bread which we break, is it not a participation in the body of Christ? Because there is one bread, we who are many are one body, for we all partake of the one bread' (10.16, RSV). All meals commit one to those who share the same table. All sacred meals commit one to the god in whose honour they are celebrated; this is true of Israelites of the old covenant and pagans of the demon-cults, as well as of Christians with Christians and Christ. To ignore the fellow Christian is to ignore the presence of Christ and to bring down judgement. He points dramatically to a proof of this: 'That is why many of you are weak and ill, and some have died' (11.30, RSV). The only way to avoid eschatological consequences of an abuse of the Eucharist is to celebrate worthily and to consider the members of the community: 'If we judged ourselves truly, we should not be judged' (I Cor. 11.31).

When he speaks of the illness and death of Christians as a condemnation for sin, Paul is employing the concept of realized eschatology, of a present judgement always attending on our actions and which in itself is a process rather than a final event. This realized present eschatological judgement, like every present act of Christ, is redemptive.

We have to hold in balance both the present and the eschatological event to come. The first community 'partook of food with joy' and knew that Christ was with them, but at the same time the typical eucharistic prayer of that community is, 'Come, Lord Jesus'. We see this dichotomy being held carefully in balance in the account of the Last Supper in John's gospel. The words of Christ among his people are again and again of his coming again to them: 'I go to prepare a place for you, and when I go and prepare a place for you, I will come again and will take you to myself' (14.3, RSV); and, 'I will not leave you desolate, I will come to you' (14.18, RSV); and 'I go away, and I will come to you' (14.28, RSV).

John is emphatic in his description of the disciples at this moment. They do not understand what is happening about them. They cannot hold together the notions of presence and coming. He is equally

168

emphatic in putting across to the reader that it is precisely this presence and coming which must be held together if we are to have a proper understanding of the Eucharist. For the disciples it was the sense of coming that seemed odd, they knew he was here with them. For later communities it is the real presence of Christ among them which is difficult to realize.

There is something of this eschatological feeling in all the meals that Christ takes with his disciples, and it would be an odd Eucharist that did not have a sense of the past manna as giving a reference to the sign of the future glorification. But the Eucharist is not simply concerned with the past of the Israelite people and the future of the nations, it is concerned vitally with the present Christ. This actuality is stressed in the accounts of Christ's meals with his disciples after the resurrection. In Matthew the Galilean appearances are prophesied in terms of presence, 'There they will see me' (28.10), and fulfilled for ever in those terms: 'I am with you always' (28.20).

In Mark, according to the longer ending, which at least has the authority of primitive belief whatever its manuscript tradition, Jesus comes to the eleven at their meal. In Luke Jesus takes part in a meal described in eucharistic terms and is realized to be present to his disciples at Emmaus: 'When he was at table with them, he took the bread and blessed and broke it, and gave it to them. And their eyes were opened and they recognized him' (24.30, RSV), and the disciples hasten to affirm his presence at the meal: 'They told . . . how he was known to them in the breaking of bread' (24.35). Christ coming among the disciples asks: 'Have you anything here to eat? . . . and he took it and ate before them' (24.41).

John's gospel also has a long ending which is concerned with the presence of Christ with the apostles. At the breakfast on the shore of the Lake of Tiberias the disciple whom Jesus loved exclaims to Peter: 'It is the Lord' (21.7), and for the rest, 'They knew it was the Lord' (21.12), and they have their meal: 'Jesus came and took the bread and gave it to them' (21.13).

The Apocalypse too writes of the disciple's meal with his Lord: 'If any one hears my voice and opens the door I will come into him and eat with him and he with me' (3.20)—where the description is of discipleship now and a meal now rather than of the future eschatological banquet. We can all share the post-resurrection presence of Christ because we can all be his witnesses, his faithful disciples.

We have the same claim as the apostles as Peter makes it in the Cornelius story: '[we] were chosen by God as witnesses, who ate and drank with him after he rose from the dead' (Acts 10.41).

In our present Eucharist, therefore, we have to hold together the real presence of the whole of our human history. The manna sign points forward to the last banquet but it can only do this because of the reality of Christ's presence now. The traditional description of the Eucharist as sign, reality and promise is thus precisely the New Testament description and doctrine.

The whole of the New Testament description of our sacraments depends from a realization that the same Jesus who went about doing good is active in the sacramental rite of his community. Later Christian history affords us many examples of men who found this realization too difficult, but it is the New Testament belief.

There may also be indications in the New Testament of men who refused to believe in the reality of the presence of the Lord in the Eucharist species. Higgins in his treatment of the *Lord's Supper in the New Testament* suggests that we may discern the Judaic refusal to commit oneself to the eucharistic body of Christ in the ending of the narrative of the discussion in the synagogue in Capharnaum in John 6. It would seem that some convert Jews lapsed from the Christian community faith because they could not accept the eucharistic doctrine of the Church, and their defection after once following Christ is shown at the end of the eucharistic narrative in John. In response to the Johannine emphasis on the identity of the Christ of flesh and the Christ of the eucharistic species: 'My flesh is food indeed, and my blood is drink indeed. He who eats my flesh and drinks my blood abides in me, and I in him' (6.56), the Jews disputed among themselves: 'How can this man give us his flesh to eat?' (6.52), and many when they heard it, said: 'This is a hard saying: who can listen to it?' (6.60). John is thinking of his own community when he writes his account: 'After this many of his disciples drew back and no longer went about with him' (6.66).

John is aware of the demand for faith and of the necessity of cleaving to Christ. This is the meaning of the dialogue between Christ and the believer which immediately follows the account of the apostasy of the Jewish disciples: 'Jesus said to the twelve: "Will you also go away?" Simon Peter answered him: "Lord, to whom shall we go? You have the words of eternal life, and we have believed, and have come to know that you are the Holy One of God"' (6.67–69, RSV).

The believer does not comprehend and explain the Eucharist, he simply knows that he must keep faith in Christ, there is no one else.

The paradigm of the Eucharist teaches, therefore, that a sacrament is the meeting-place of the realities of all times. This is not to say that time no longer matters. On the contrary. The life of Jesus teaches us that time and place are necessary if we would understand divine activity. We celebrate in our time and place in order that all other times and places may be present in their true significance, and, though the ritual must change historically, we can only talk of the divine in our own historical situation and sacrament by using the terms provided in the history of Jesus under Pontius Pilate.

(3) The Performance of the Sign

In this section I want to say something of the way in which the first Christian community put its understanding of Christ into the practice of the sacramental rite. I have taken as my examples two rites which are well documented in the New Testament, though not, from the nature of these writings, documented in a direct manner: Baptism and the sacramental Binding and Loosing. As introductions to these rites I have made a brief mention of the way in which the New Testament community's interpretation of Christ within the prophetic context of the Old Testament has influenced the shape that the liturgy took in the practice of the community. The Old Testament provides reference points which make it possible to study the community's mind in celebrating Christ in precisely this and not other ways. After these introductions from the Old Testament theology of the first community I have set about trying to establish how the rite was performed in the first period of the Church's history and what this performance entailed in terms of meaning for them. The performance of the rite presents us with the faith of the community; there is not, in any ordered Christian community, a distinction between liturgy and theology.

We meet the New Testament community through its words and deeds. If we can achieve some understanding of the New Testament community's words and deeds in celebration of Christ we may expect to find that we have grown in understanding of our own participation in these same sacraments.

A. BAPTISM

(i) *Christ's Baptism, the Heir and the Kingdom*

If we would understand something of the New Testament doctrine of Baptism we must begin with some consideration of the baptism of Christ by John in the Jordan. The narrative of this event is written up in the gospels in order that the baptism of the Christian should be properly understood in the community.

The account has as its climax the descent of the Holy Spirit upon Christ and the voice from heaven saying: 'Thou art my beloved Son, this day I have begotten thee' (Lk. 3.22). There are obvious difficulties here for the Christian reader, the most puzzling being the proclamation by the Father that he has only this day begotten the eternal Son. The difficulty is enough to account for the early variant reading of 'in thee I am well pleased'. However, any fears that Luke is unaware of the pre-existence of the Son are quite beside the point here. Luke is attempting to teach something about Christ by the use of an Old Testament concept. He is attempting to teach his readers that Christ is the long-awaited messianic King, and he is employing a quotation from the psalms of the coronation ceremony of the Old Testament kings.

In the ritual of coronation the Davidic king was declared to be the Son of Yahweh, ruling as his heir in the kingdom: 'I will tell of the decree of the Lord: He said to me: "You are my son, this day I have begotten you. Ask of me, and I will make the nations your heritage and the ends of the earth your possession."' (Ps. 2.7). The Hebrews had taken into their ritual the pattern of Egyptian royal ceremonial. Thus Amon-Re of Karnak says to the Pharaoh Hatshepsut: 'I am thy beloved father, I will establish thy dignity as the Lord of the Two Lands', and similar sayings in which gods adopt the Pharaohs can be found in other royal inscriptions. The Hebrews did not, of course, think of the divine sonship of the Pharaoh in the mythological terms customary among the Egyptians which suggested that the god was the physical begetter of the heir. In Judah the king became the son of Yahweh because of the promise contained in Nathan's prophecy that the line of David would last for ever within

172

God's good pleasure. Each newly enthroned king was in himself the renewal of the Davidic covenant with Yahweh. It is probable that we should understand the famous passage in Isaiah: 'For to us a child is born, to us a son is given' (Is. 9.6), as the song of Yahweh who is pleased that the messianic kingdom is continued in the Davidic line, rather than as the song of the people at the physical birth of a prince. Yahweh adopts the new king as a promise of the Messiah. When the Messiah comes, he is the only true Son of God.

Professor Daube suggests that a sentence in the Midrashic exposition of Deuteronomy 26.5 ff preserved in the Haggadah service for Passover eve envisages the possibility of a woman conceiving by God. On Deuteronomy 26.7b: 'He saw our affliction and our distress', the Midrash says: 'This means the abstention from sexual intercourse, as it is written (Ex. 2.25), "And God saw the children of Israel, and God knew their condition"'. The Midrash is employing the sexual sense of *know*. Daube thinks this indication of a woman bearing a divine son survived the Jewish purge of texts likely to assist Christian apologetic because it is always difficult to alter liturgical texts. It seems also that the Qumran community thought of the Messiah as the divine Son. A. D. Nock in *Gnomon* 32 suggests that besides that already printed there is unpublished evidence 'for the use of royal ideology, stating the Messiah's relation to God in terms of sonship'.

It is to be expected, therefore, that when the Messiah does come, God will proclaim him in words which will at once be understood as announcing the beginning of his filial reign.

The Baptism of Christ in the Jordan is the beginning of a line of events which declare Christ to be the new heir to the kingdom of God. After the preliminary heralding of the royal titles by the angel at the annunciation, which is adapted from the Judah coronation rite, and the final proclamation at the Baptism, Christ is seen entering his kingdom at the beginning of Holy Week. The Entry into Jerusalem continues the explanation, in royal terms, of the meaning of Christian baptism since it asserts that Christ is the fulfilment of the Davidic promise by presenting him as the new Son of David.

At the end of the Davidic court history the problem of the succession and the fulfilment of the Nathan prophecy, which has always been a dominant motive of the story of David, comes to the fore.

There is a bitter struggle in David's court between the supporters of Adonijah and those of Solomon, the king's two surviving sons. In the end Adonijah seems to have won massive support for his candidacy but Solomon is the chosen son of David. The king ordered Nathan the prophet and Zadok the priest to take the young Solomon outside the city and anoint him in a small village shrine and then to bring him back accomplished king. This is done. The young Solomon is brought back riding the king's own royal ass and the crowds applaud him as he enters his city of Jerusalem all unknown to Adonijah.

The evangelists understood that in his Entry into Jerusalem Jesus was fulfilling the royal messianic entry of Solomon. Jesus had been anointed outside the city by Mary at Bethany and had been brought into Jerusalem to the plaudits of the crowds all unknown to his enemies the official priests. Jesus had been welcomed as the 'Son of David'. His baptismal kingship had been acknowledged.

But, of course, the evangelists also understood that the fulfilment of the baptismal promise had not occurred at the Entry into Jerusalem. This too remained but a sign. It is only after his resurrection that Christ is called the Lord of all. As the great baptismal hymn, that Paul included in his letter to the Philippians, and which we shall look at later in this section from another point of view, puts Christ's triumph, '[he] became obedient unto death, even death on the cross. Therefore God has highly exalted him and bestowed on him a name which is above every name' (Phil. 2.8).

This, again, borrows from the royal coronation ritual of Judah. At the enthronement the king was given a new name by Yahweh. David had been told: 'I will make for you a great name, like the name of the great ones of the earth' (II Sam. 7.9); and as he lay dying the courtiers came to David and congratulated him on the accession of his son: 'Your God make the name of Solomon more famous than yours, and make his throne greater than your throne' (I Kings 1.47); and there is some evidence that until his accession Solomon was called Jedidiah (II Sam. 12.25); and of the messianic ruler proclaimed by Isaiah the prophet says: 'his name will be called "Wonderful Counsellor, Mighty God, Everlasting Father, Prince of Peace"' (Is. 9.6).

Paul makes it plain that it is in the resurrection that Christ is declared at last to be the Son and Heir of God: 'He raised Christ

174

from the dead, and bade him sit on his right hand above the heavens, high above all princedoms and powers and virtues and dominations, and every name that is known, not in this world only, but in the world to come' (Eph. 1.20–21).

At the resurrection, then, we have the full meaning of the baptism. Christ's baptism was directed towards his glorification at the right hand of the Father. So also we must understand that our baptism is directed to our sharing in the glory of Christ. The meaning of our baptism is our possession of the kingdom.

That it is by baptism that we enter the messianic kingdom is shown by many passages in the New Testament. John the Baptist himself describes the baptism that Christ will give in terms that refer to the proclamation of the kingdom: 'He will baptize you with the Holy Spirit, and with fire. He holds the winnowing-fan ready, to sweep his threshing-floor clean; he will gather the wheat into his barn, but the chaff he will consume with fire' (Mt. 3.12). John's words are an echo of 'The Lord shall cleanse ... by a spirit of burning' (Is. 4.4b), and 'You shall make the hills like chaff, you shall winnow them' (Is. 41.15), and 'He is like a refiner's fire' (Mal. 3.2), which are all concerned with the coming of the Lord to take possession of the world and inaugurate his kingdom. It is evident that similar ideas lie behind the account of the wind and fire of Pentecost.

In the passage just cited from the Epistle to the Ephesians, Paul continues by remarking that 'the whole Church is joined' to the ruling Christ. The triumph of Christ is our triumph in him as his body. This is elaborated in royal messianic terms in the Epistle to the Romans where Paul writes of the gift of the Spirit: 'Those who follow the leading of God's Spirit are all God's sons' (Rom. 8.14). This is evidently connected with the account of the giving of the Spirit at the baptism of Christ and of the Spirit leading Christ in the Temptation narrative which follows immediately afterwards. What happens to Christ must happen to the Christian. Paul continues that we have been given 'the Spirit of adoption, which makes us cry out, Abba, Father. The Spirit himself thus assures our spirit that we are children of God; and if we are his children, then we are his heirs too; heirs of God, sharing the inheritance of Christ' (Rom. 8.16).

Just as Christ has been proclaimed at his baptism as the Son of the Father and the new king of Israel, and of all men, so we are chosen as sons by God, we are proclaimed heirs of the Davidic covenant and of the new covenant in Christ; 'only we must share his sufferings' (Rom. 8.17), we must accept the Passion that was begun at the Entry into Jerusalem, 'if we are to share his glory' (8.17) at the resurrection. The pattern of Baptism, Entry and Resurrection Glory which we distinguish in Christ's kingdom is the pattern set for us as well and gives God's meaning to our baptism.

(ii) *The Servant of the Lord*

Although it seems more likely to me that the baptismal narrative originally presented the voice of the Father saying: 'Thou art my beloved Son; this day I have begotten thee', and that this difficult saying was transmuted to 'Thou art my beloved Son; in thee I am well pleased', the transmutation is itself so old that many editions take it to be the original version, and so interesting in its theological implications for the meaning of Christian baptism, that it is worth pausing a moment to examine something of its tenour.

The pericope is obviously dependent upon the text in Isaiah which opens the first of the Songs of the Suffering Servant: 'Behold my servant, whom I support, my chosen, on whom my favour rests' (Is. 42.1). The Suffering Servant was understood by both Hebrew and Christian writers to be a pre-figuration of the Messiah, and we have already noticed in the account of Philip's conversation with the Ethiopian eunuch that the Isaiah description of the Servant of Yahweh had a prominent place among the passages selected from the Old Testament for Christian apologetic: 'The passage of Scripture which he was reading was this: He was led away like a sheep to be slaughtered; like a lamb that is dumb before its shearer, he would not open his mouth. He was brought low and all his rights taken away' (Acts 8.32). The eunuch turned to Philip and asked him of whom the prophet spoke, 'then Philip began to speak, and preached to him about Jesus, taking this passage as his theme'.

There developed a christology of the Servant which influenced most of the writers of the New Testament and was used by them to put across the central concept of Christ's vicarious suffering for the sins of the world. The Acts incident is at the beginning of this process, at the end is the later evidence of I Peter:

> He suffered for our sakes, and left you his own example; you were to follow in his footsteps. He did no wrong, no treachery was found on

his lips; he was ill spoken of, and spoke no evil in return, suffered and did not threaten vengeance, gave himself up into the hands of injustice. So, on the cross, his own body took the weight of our sins; we were to become dead to our sins, and live for holiness; it was his wounds that healed you (2.21–4).

It is significant that the passage in I Peter is not simply a description of what Christ has done. It is also a description of what the Christian must do. It is part of the meaning of the baptismal narrative that we are to take its reference to ourselves and follow the lead of Christ the Servant.

In order to appreciate the way in which we are to follow Christ in our baptism we have to take into account both the Old Testament description of the Servant, and the New Testament account of Christ's action in fulfilment of this.

The Song in Isaiah continues: 'I have endowed him with my spirit, he shall reveal my law to the nations' (42.1). The Servant is to be guided by the Spirit of God in the revelation of God to the Gentiles. The nearest equivalent to this in the Old Testament is the story of the bewilderment of the Assyrian deportees who had been placed in Samaria and did not know how to worship the God of the place, they did not know God's 'law'. The land rose against them and lions prowled and devoured them and they were afraid because they did not know the way to worship God and bring peace to their homes: 'Then the king of Assyria commanded: "Send to them one of the priests who was carried away from that place, and let him go and live there and teach them the law of the god of the land"' (II Kings 17.27). So an Israelite priest who had been deported from Samaria was sent to instruct the new inhabitants how to worship God. The Servant is to teach the nations, the Gentiles, how to worship God. He has a missionary vocation to preach to men.

We can see in Christ's life how the guidance of the Spirit is immediately present after the Baptism: 'he was led by the Spirit into the wilderness' (Mk 1.12); the vocation of the Servant is to be tempted and to be afflicted and to continue proclaiming the gospel: 'And Jesus came back into Galilee with the power of the Spirit upon him; word of him went round through all the neighbouring country, and he began to preach in their synagogues' (Lk. 4.14). He preaches to the poor, the people who traditionally do not know the law of God, the way in which he is to be worshipped. Jeremiah remarks that the poor cannot be expected to know the message of God: 'Then I said: "These are only the poor, they have no sense; for they do not know the way of the Lord, the law of their God"' (Jer. 5.4), and Isaiah speaks of the messianic age as one in which first of all the poor will have the gospel message preached to them and then the world will be a place of miracles; he represents the Messiah as saying of himself: 'The Spirit of the Lord God is upon me, because the Lord has anointed me to bring good tidings to the afflicted; he has sent me to bind up the brokenhearted, to proclaim liberty to the captives, and the opening of the prison to those who are bound' (Is. 61.1).

It is precisely this passage which Jesus chooses as the beginning of his preaching in the synagogue of Nazareth. 'The book given to him was the book of the prophet Isaiah; so he opened it and found the place' where this description was set down. And when he had read it aloud to the people in the synagogue, he began his preaching saying: 'This scripture which I have read in your hearing is today fulfilled' (Lk. 4.21).

Baptism is, therefore, a vocation to preach the coming of the kingdom in Christ, a vocation to engage in the struggle to build up the kingdom among men. Christ goes out after this to exorcize the unclean spirits. The first Christians understood the significance of all this for their own vocation. Peter at the house of Cornelius the Gentile speaks of Christ's baptism as the 'beginning of the story' of our salvation: 'about Jesus of Nazareth, how God anointed him with the Holy Spirit and with power, so that he went about doing good, and curing all those who were under the devil's tyranny, with God at his side' (Acts 10.38), and he goes on to say that the baptism we have received leads to a missionary vocation: 'We are witnesses of all he did in the country of the Jews, and in Jerusalem . . . and he gave us a commission to preach to the people' (10.39, 42), and he understands this vocation as within the context of the fulfilment of the Old Testament: 'All the prophets bear him testimony' (10.43), particularly it is the fulfilment of the Servant who bore the sins of many: 'that everyone who has faith in him is to find remission of sins through his name' (10.43).

To be baptized is to have a vocation to preach Christ's gospel, and this gospel is to be understood as the fulfilment of the promises of God to the people of the first covenant.

(iii) *Christian Baptism*

The baptism of Christ, therefore, is presented by the evangelists as the proclamation of his status as the divine Son of God and the new king of the world, and as the demand for the fulfilment of his work as the suffering saviour. This is a pattern in harmony with the whole of the New Testament understanding of Christ and the Christian. Whoever has a status thereby has a function.

Christ refuses to allow his disciples to call him the Messiah until he has fulfilled the work of the Messiah, and so also for us, we are not to be called Christians until we have done the work of Christians. Baptism announces what we are *and* what we are to do. It gives us a new life in the sense in which we talk of parents giving life to their children, *and* in the sense in which we talk of a man who changes his job as 'starting a new life'. By our anointing we are declared the adopted sons of God, by the giving of the Spirit we are enlivened to take a new part in the work of the community.

Baptism gives us the new life of the Spirit: 'They asked Peter and his fellow apostles: Brethren, what must we do? Peter said to them: Repent and be baptized, every one of you, in the name of Jesus Christ, to have your sins forgiven; then you will receive the gift of the Holy Spirit' (Acts. 2.37). If we share in the Spirit of God it is because we share in Christ. As Paul told the Romans: 'You must consider yourselves dead to sin and alive to God; we were taken up *into Christ Jesus* by baptism' (6.3).

That baptism is not to be thought of primarily as a status-giving rite, but as a call to work which will not be easy, is made clear in the narrative of the attempt by the mother of the sons of Zebedee to claim a place of honour for each of her sons. Christ will not give them a status but he offers them a share in his baptism: 'Have you the strength to drink of the cup I am to drink of, to be baptized with the baptism I am to be baptized with? They said to him: We have. And Jesus told them: You shall indeed drink of the cup I am to drink of, and be baptized with the baptism I am to be baptized with; but a place on my right hand or on my left is not mine to give you; it is for those for whom it has been destined' (Mk. 10.38–40).

So much is baptism a call to suffering that Christ uses it as a synonym for his passion and death. And it is to be noticed that the suffering of Christ is to be the suffering of the disciple. The identity

179

of Christ and the Christian is again asserted, and it is an identity in action. The Christian is to perform what Christ has done. This is at least part of what we mean when we say that baptism makes us one in Christ.

This is at least partly what Paul meant when he said: 'I live, no not "I live" but "Christ lives in me"' (Gal. 2.20).

(iv) *The Shape of the Liturgy of Baptism*

Although the peculiarly Christian understanding of baptism is of the giving of a new life, it would be wrong to exclude the notion of a washing clean from sin. It certainly appears that the New Testament community sometimes understood baptism in such terms. The story of Naaman the Syrian or the ten lepers is concerned with the cleansing from sin of which leprosy was a sign. The notion of baptismal washing effecting a redemption from sin is of course a recurring idea of the Old Testament. Professor Lampe in *The Seal of the Spirit* has gathered many passages to this effect. Thus Isaiah 1.16 and Jeremiah 4.14 urge the people to cleanse themselves of sin, and God himself promises to wash them in Ezechiel 47.1, and Zechariah 13.1.

The typology of the New Testament concerned with baptism is generally, however, that of the Judgement of Sin. Thus the Deluge typology of I and II Peter is related to the baptism of John as an escape from the coming doom. The Deluge changes to fire and was used in Enoch 46 and 47 as a coming judgement and this seems akin to John's idea of Christ judging by fire.

The eschatological significance of the Red Sea passage which Paul in I Corinthians likens to a baptism of the Hebrews is brought out in the picture of Revelations 15 where the saints sing the Exodus Song of Moses. And baptism is itself the present eschaton in II Corinthians 5: 'The old has passed away, behold the new has come.' We join the community which watches for the Last Day.

I want in this section to say something of what can be deduced from the New Testament about the shape of the primitive baptismal liturgy.

It is obvious from the nature of the event that baptism would be given to the catechumenate only when they had received instruction in the faith. This is seen in Acts quite plainly on several occasions. Thus in the story of the Ethiopian eunuch who is instructed by Philip the Deacon in the meaning of a Suffering Servant passage in Isaiah.

Professor Daube shows that when Philip asks the Ethiopian eunuch whether he 'grasped' what he was reading he used a technical rabbinic term for understanding Scripture and this is made plain by the following phrase: 'Then Philip opened his mouth and beginning at the same text preached unto him Jesus' (Acts 8.35). Daube shows that in rabbinic language 'to open one's mouth' means 'to lecture on Scripture' and refers to Philip's beginning from a text, the direction in the Mishnah for the Exodus-recital on Passover eve: 'one should begin with the disgrace and end with the glory, and expound from the verse in Deuteronomy, "A Syrian ready to perish was my father".'

It would seem too that the apostolic food-decree of the Council in Acts 15 may either have been used as an instructional outline or may itself have been influenced by a baptismal instruction already in use. The decree's text runs thus: 'You are to abstain from what has been sacrificed to idols and from blood and from what is strangled.' That it was regarded as an important fixed point in the tradition of the Jewish Christian community can be judged by the repetition in Acts 21: 'They should abstain from what has been sacrificed to idols and from blood and from what has been strangled'. Certainly it has a great likeness to some baptismal instructions. Thus the *Clementine Homilies* present a baptismal catechesis given to the Syrians in much the same terms: 'Pray to Him; abstain from the table of devils; do not taste dead flesh; do not touch blood; purify yourselves by washings; and rest in one word—let each man be minded to do to his neighbour those good things he wishes for himself' (VII, 4). And similar things occur in Didache VI, 3 and perhaps Hemmerdinger's fragments of Book III of Irenaeus.

In his small book on Baptism in the New Testament Oscar Cullmann suggests that something of the primitive liturgy of baptism may be discovered from an examination of the New Testament text. He sets out several texts from Acts, Matthew and Mark which share a particular terminology and all speak of baptism and suggests that the term comes from the baptismal rite. The term is of preventing or hindering:

And the eunuch said: See here is water. What doth *hinder* me to be baptized? (Acts 8.37).

Peter said: Can any man *forbid* water, that these should not be baptized? (Acts 10.47).

Let the children come to me, do not *hinder* them; for to such belongs the kingdom of God (Lk. 18.16).

The situation, Cullmann shows, is always one of a man seeking baptism, of a question being asked as to whether there was any impediment to his being welcomed into the community. From the first of course pagans who had not committed themselves to Christ were excluded, and their children with them, but together with these we find early in Church history exclusions operating against members of certain professions who had to swear oaths to the pagan gods, such as soldiers in the Roman army, or whose way of life was by definition immoral, like that of the actors in Roman comedies. Cullmann supposes, therefore, that the primitive baptismal rite in all communities—since the variety of sources shows the universality of the procedure—which one would have supposed anyway without investigation since it is an obvious precaution—contained a question as to whether anything hindered the baptism of the candidate. This is strictly parallel to the present practice of banns for marriage.

We can, I think, find out from the New Testament something further about the primitive ceremony once the question had been answered and the candidate was ready to be baptized.

There is in the letter of Paul to the Ephesians a quotation from an early hymn from the Christian liturgy which seems to come from a baptismal liturgy. Paul presents it as a verse to be explained: 'It is the light that rebukes such things and shews them up for what they are; only light shews up. That is the meaning of the words: Awake, thou that sleepest, and arise from the dead, and Christ will give thee light' (Eph. 5.13). Baptism was first of all called 'enlightenment' and was, of course, considered to be a passage from death to life, a resurrection shared with Christ. Hence we ought to tie up the previous resurrection miracles with baptism. Jairus' daughter, the widow's son at Nain and the rest of them are signs of the effect of baptism which communicates the life of the risen Lord to his people.

The baptismal hymn to which Paul refers was, I think, in the mind of the redactor in the Acts account of the rescue of Peter from Herod's prison by an angel: 'Peter was sleeping with two chains upon him. . . . Suddenly an angel of the Lord stood over him and a light shone in his cell. . . . Quick, he said, rise up' (Acts 12.7).

Peter had been in prison, awaiting death, he is brought back to light and life and liberty. He is told to rise up. The chains fall off his hands. The event is very like the event of baptism. I think that this was seen by the redactor of the Acts story, perhaps it was the insight of Luke which so shaped the story that he received. At any rate the story is told in just the imagery that is present in the Ephesians hymn. The quotation that Paul cites might almost be the speech of the angel to Peter.

It may be, therefore, that after the question 'What hinders?' came the baptismal hymn about the relation of the ceremony to the communication of the resurrection life and then the baptism itself. The candidate stripped himself naked and was helped by the ministers.

We have perhaps an echo of this in the strange remark of John before the baptism of Christ: 'I baptize you with water, but he who is mightier than I is coming, the thong of whose sandals I am not worthy to untie' (Mk 1.7, RSV). The variant in Matthew: 'I am not worthy even to carry his shoes for him' (3.11), is more easily understood within the context of the baptismal ceremony, as a description of someone holding the clothes while the candidate was immersed, than it is in the circumstances of the Baptist's situation. Unless perhaps he had organized things so expertly that men were detailed to look after his candidates at the Jordan. If this were the case then it would not mean that John was expecting to baptize Jesus, all the evidence points away from this, but simply that he was employing an image taken from the immediate experience of his hearers as they watched the baptisms.

The baptism itself seems from the very beginning to have been by the descent of the candidate into a large pool or pit of water. The pit of water is spoken of in connection with Christ's baptism at the descent of the Spirit: 'He came up out of the water,' and this is related to the destruction of the old Tiamat and Leviathan by the early Christian commentators, perhaps with the words of the prophet Micah in mind: 'Thou wilt cast all our sins into the depths of the sea' (7.19).

Christ's baptism and the chaotic waters come together in the *Testament of Asher*: 'When the Most High shall visit the earth, coming Himself as a man among men, eating and drinking and in peace breaking the head of the dragon by means of water,' which refers to Psalm 74.13, and in the later Cyril of Jerusalem, *Catechetical Lectures* III, 11: 'Since therefore it was necessary to break the heads of the dragon in pieces, He went down and bound the strong one in the waters'; and A. Benoit comments on Ignatius of Antioch (Ephesians XVIII, 2): 'We find in Ignatius the first formulation of an idea which was to remain current in later times, and the roots of which go back to Jewish cosmology: the baptism of Christ purifies the waters infested with demons.' There is evidence in the Pseudo-Clementines and Justin that from an early period baptism was thought of in exorcism terms and that one of the requirements of the candidate was that of prayer and fasting. It may be that in the exorcism story of Matthew 17.21 we have an indication of this practice in an early Jewish Christian community.

There are many indications that Living Water, that is, running water, was generally required, probably because of Christ's likening himself to living water. Thus the *Didache* has: 'If thou hast not living water, then baptize in other water' (VII,3); and the Odes of Solomon XXX, 1: 'Fill ye waters for yourselves from the living fountain of the Lord'.

The Ethiopian eunuch, once he has asked: 'What is to prevent my being baptized?' and been told: 'If you believe with all your heart, you may' (Acts 8.37, RSV), and he has confessed: 'I believe that Jesus Christ is the Son of God' (8.37, RSV), goes down with Philip 'into the water' and Philip baptizes him.

We have here several interesting indications of the primitive baptismal ceremony. Some manuscripts of Acts do not have the demand for belief and the confession of faith. It may be that the original did not contain this verse. But it is significant that those who edited Acts saw in this baptismal situation a proper setting for such a demand and confession. It would seem that the editors inserted these elements because they thought them necessary for a baptismal account. They thought this, of course, because such elements existed in the baptismal ceremony they were acquainted with in their community. We may well, therefore, have a direct quotation from a primitive liturgy in this verse. If, however, the verse is original and belongs to the account, we have equally a demonstration that from the first the baptismal liturgy contained such a demand and confession of faith. Either way we have another indication of the liturgy of the first century. Later the confession of faith became longer and more detailed. I shall point out some of the developments in New Testament times in the next section. Today the recitation of the Creed is the climax of the development from the primitive confession: 'I believe that Jesus Christ is the Son of God.'

After the confession of faith the baptismal descent into the water. The water was usually thought of in the early Church not as a means of washing away a stain but as a grave from which the baptized man rose to a new life. As the author of I Peter says: 'Baptism . . . now saves you, not as a removal of dirt from the body, but as an appeal to God for a clear conscience, through the resurrection of Jesus Christ' (3.21, RSV). And Paul speaks of this resurrection from the grave in the event of baptism in Romans: 'We were buried therefore with him by baptism into death, so that as Christ was raised from the dead by the glory of the Father, we too might walk in newness of life' (Rom. 6.5, RSV); and Colossians: 'You were buried with him in baptism, in which you were also raised with him through faith in the working of God, who raised him from the dead' (2.12, RSV).

We must remember that the texts cited from Pauline letters are mainly concerned with the body of Christians, they are not letters to individuals nor are they directed to the instruction of individuals. The man who is baptized is baptized into Christ, and his community is Christ for him: 'we are all baptized into one body' (I Cor. 12.13).

Baptism is a social sacrament, it is given to the community so that men may be added to the community, only by a perverse individualism could a Christian suppose that it was a private act of his personal committal to Christ and not the concern of others. We recognize this today when despite the practice of baptisms at times other than the assembly of Christians for the Eucharist we go on adding the names to the parish baptismal register so that there is a public record of the baptism. Baptism is given, as St Thomas pointed out long ago, towards the Eucharist of the whole Body of Christ and therefore must be seen as a corporate act of the community of Christ.

While the ceremony is continuing we should remember that the congregation is praying for the candidates. We can see something of this in the account in Acts of the community prayer by the Jerusalem Church for those Samaritans to whom Peter and John were sent, and indirectly we can see the practice of community prayer for the candidate in the stories in the gospels of healing miracles performed at the request of men other than the one to be

185

cured—the four friends of the palsied man, or the commander of the sick servant, come at once to mind in this connection.

After the question, the confession of faith and the immersion in the grave waters the naked Christian rises out of the water. He has to be clothed. This is exactly what happens to Peter in the situation in his prison. The angel knocks off his chains and then instructs him to get ready: 'The angel said to him: "Dress yourself and put on your sandals." And he did so. And he said to him: "Wrap your mantle around you and follow me." And he went out and followed him' (Acts 12.8, RSV). I think that this account is linked with the baptismal clothing of the newly baptized Christian. Certainly this notion of baptism as a clothing is one of the most frequent ideas of the New Testament. Thus Paul writes to the Galatians: 'As many of you as were baptized into Christ have put on Christ' (3.27, RSV), and to the Romans he speaks of the Christian responsibility in just the terms used in the Peter story and the baptismal liturgy: 'It is full time now for you to wake from sleep . . . the night is far gone and the day is at hand. Let us then cast off the works of darkness and put on the armour of light . . . put on the Lord Jesus Christ' (Rom. 13.11, RSV). The images of awakening into light and putting on Christ as a garment are all present in that short passage.

The letter to the Ephesians has a more detailed and involved usage of the image of clothing. The conversion to Christianity from paganism is described in terms of undressing and dressing in new robes, just as the new Christians put on a new robe in the ceremony: 'Put off your old nature which belongs to your former manner of life and is corrupt through deceitful lusts, and be renewed in the spirit of your minds, and put on the new nature' (Eph. 4.22, RSV); and this is developed later into a full-scale description of the clothing of a Christian: 'Stand therefore, having girded your loins with truth, and having put on the breastplate of righteousness, and having shod your feet with the shoes of the gospel of peace' (Eph. 6.14, RSV). Paul might almost be speaking to the newly baptized as he was dressed in the ceremony. Just as I Peter, which is thought by many to be a baptismal liturgy, contains the instruction: 'Clothe yourselves, all of you, with humility towards one another' (5.5, RSV).

Further evidence for the use of the baptismal clothing imagery in the early Church is contained in the descriptions of Christian life in the Odes of Solomon:

XI, 9–10   I stripped off (folly) and cast it from me; and the Lord renewed me with his raiment.

XV, 8   I have put on incorruption through his name: and have put off corruption by his grace.

XXI, 2   I put off darkness and clothed myself with light.

XXV, 8   I was clothed with the covering of thy good Spirit, and thou didst remove from me my raiment of skins (cf. Gen. 3.21).

It may be also that the picture in the parable of the welcome given to the penitent prodigal is an image of the coming of baptism to the sinner who 'was dead and is alive', was 'lost and is found': 'Bring quickly the best robe, and put it on him; and put a ring on his hand, and shoes on his feet' (Lk. 15.22). The welcoming father dresses his son in the new robe, just as the new Christian is dressed after the baptismal waters and before he comes into the community and shares in the meal. Anyone who was not wearing the robe would be excluded from the meal since he would be at once recognizable as neither an established member of the community nor a newly baptized member. He would be recognized as an enemy intruder up to no good. This seems to me the proper interpretation of the man who came to the king's great supper without a wedding garment and offered no explanation of his lack. The eucharistic meal which followed the baptism is only for those who have been new-dressed in Christ. But with this meal I intend to deal in the next section and therefore leave this speculation here.

It may be that the later custom of signing the newly baptized and clothed man with the Cross is to be found in our New Testament texts. Thus in II Corinthians 1.22: 'he has put his seal upon us', and in Ephesians 1.13: 'you were sealed with the promised Holy Spirit', and St Cyprian refers to Apocalypse 7.4 in this connection. Père Daniélou, in *Bible and Liturgy*, pages 64–5, suggests that Paul's remarks in Gal. 6.14–15 are concerned with the baptismal signing with the Cross.

The baptismal ceremony, then, began with a question of the candidate's suitability, went on with a hymn explaining the new life and light that was being given, and with a descent of the catechumen into the grave of water and concluded with the dressing of the man who put on Christ. Within this general pattern there might, of course, be variations from community to community. It would be anachronistic to suppose that the various communities thought themselves bound to a universal form of service. The early Church had a sense of the importance of the truth of Christ and of the manifold ways in which this one truth might be expressed.

It cannot even be said with certainty that the whole Church used one form for the actual baptism, since some of the accounts in Acts suggest that the communities that the redactors of the material were acquainted with used the form 'I baptize you in the name of Jesus' (Acts 8.16, 19.5 and I Corinthians 6.11), while of course the community from which we have received Matthew's gospel used the trinitarian formula universally required at the present time in the Church: 'Go therefore and make disciples of all nations, baptizing them in the name of the Father and of the Son and of the Holy Spirit' (Mt. 28.19, RSV).

What must certainly have varied from community to community was the confession of faith employed by the candidate. Christ's action can be explained in various ways and these have to be adapted to the conditions of the community. Though there was in Christ neither Jew nor Greek, free man nor slave, it was nevertheless the case that converts from paganism needed to be instructed in a way different from that for a convert from Judaism. So we would expect that the New Testament, which reflects the activities of the whole early Church and not simply those of one community, would contain remnants and hints of varied credal statements. This is in fact the case, and with these credal confessions I shall now concern myself.

(v) *Some Baptismal Creeds*

The original use of the creed was not primarily as part of the eucharistic assembly but as part of the confession of faith in the baptismal introduction of a man to the Christian community. The creed was an affirmation of belief in harmony with the community. The creed was a declaration of faith required before admission to the new life of Christ's people.

I want in this section to take a few New Testament passages that reflect fragmentarily the early liturgy of baptism. There are in the New Testament writings, particularly the letters of Paul, patches of writing which demonstrate by their style and vocabulary that they depend from liturgical ceremony. There are what J. N. D. Kelly called 'creed-like slogans and tags' and 'longer passages which, while still fluid in their phrasing, betray by their content, rhythm and general pattern, as well as by their content, that they derive from community tradition rather than from the writer's untrammelled invention'. Some of these liturgical fragments take us back to the original Pentecostal decade. Thus Bishop Robinson writes in his *Twelve New Testament Studies* of a liturgical formula he has demonstrated in I Corinthians 16:

> The fact that Paul can quote a formula with which he can assume, without explanation, that his audience is familiar, indicates that fixed eucharistic forms were in use in Corinth within twenty-five years of the Resurrection. The fact that the formula includes a word that must have established itself beyond possibility of translation before the rise of Gentile Christianity takes us a great deal further back still.

Such protruding passages allow the modern reader to understand something of the primitive relation between Scripture and the liturgical tradition. I want to consider three of these in the epistles of Paul as examples of the way in which the living tradition of the community helped to shape the fixed form of the scriptural witness.

(a) *I Corinthians 15.3–5*, RSV:

> I delivered to you as of first importance what I also received, that
> Christ died for our sins
> in accordance with the scriptures,
> that he was buried,
> that he was raised on the third day
> in accordance with the scriptures,
> and that he appeared to Cephas, then to the twelve.

This little passage is introduced by Paul as a tradition which he has received and which he must hand on to his community. The style is not that of Paul's ordinary usage. For example, he rarely speaks of 'sins' in the plural in such a context. This usage occurs only, I think, in formal passages of this kind. Apart from vocabulary and stylistic differences from the setting in which we find the passage, it is possible even in translation to discover here a christological formula which brings together a total view of the work of Jesus. It is not simply a casual fragment, a piece of tradition without shape or intention. It is not an oddment such as might be scooped up from the sands of the desert or unearthed in the bottom of a jar in some Arabian cave. It is a shaped and coherent entity. It is centred, or rather elipsed, on two points of interpretation of the death of Christ. Christ died 'for our sins' and 'according to the scriptures'. The two emphases, taken together, give us evidence of its milieu. It is patent that the origin of this particular credal statement is to be found amongst a Christian community which was mainly composed of converts from Judaism—perhaps it derives from Antiochian or even Jerusalem Christian circles, or from the milieu of a synagogue convert congregation in Asia Minor—Lystra or Derbe—at any rate it can be shown to derive from Jewish Christian origins.

Two things characterized the Jews of Christ's time—and perhaps of every time. They had a sense of sin and a sense of God working out his will in history. Their scriptures began with an account of man as sinful and went on to show how at various times God had intervened in the course of history to reveal his attitude towards men's actions, convicting them of sin. The structure of their scriptures was of a law given to avoid sin, a history of sinful kings, and a prophetic literature which in various ways demanded the return of man to the ways of God. The old covenant expresses itself perfectly in Peter's unhappy recognition: 'Depart from me, for I am a sinful man.' Of course Scripture is not simply about sin as the responsibility and plight of man, Scripture is also concerned with God as saving man from the consequences of his sin. There is nothing in Hebrew literature which is comparable to the Hesiodic despair after the golden age of the Garden, nor even of the Platonic cyclic revolutions of prosperity, chaos and effort, rather there is a faith in the covenant Lord who saves.

As Luis Alonso Schökel has demonstrated, the recurring theme of Scripture is set out in this pattern:

(a) God gives benefits to man.
(b) God imposes a precept.
(c) Man rebels.
(d) God punishes.
(e) God reconciles man to himself.

This is patent in the general structure of salvation history and in the individual incidents which go to make up this history. Thus the general history of the Jews is of the granting of a covenant by

God and the demand that they should serve him: 'I will be your God and you shall be my people'; the consequent rebellion of the people who turn to other gods and their punishment by God until redemption is offered through Moses initially and then fully through Christ. In particular we can see the schema at work in the Fall narrative:

(a) Adam is created and given a garden of trees and animals.
(b) A command is given that he is not to eat the fruit of one tree.
(c) He disobeys the command.
(d) He loses the garden and its happiness.
(e) A promise is made that a redeemer will come for men.

Together with the sinfulness of man the Jews understood the providential character of God. He ordered all things and without him nothing happened. The Scriptures are the records of God's plan working out in history as year succeeds year. The world is understood as the world of God's purpose. The Scriptures reveal his work and only those things which can establish a claim to be in accord with his work and its pattern are worth considering.

Certain events, notably of course the Exodus, seemed to the Jews to be revelatory of God's salvific will. To the Christian Jew these events lead up to God's revelation in Christ. Paul shows the Jews that the work of Christ is within the pattern, it is 'according to the Scriptures'.

Beyond this it is also true that the Jewish religion, and our own Christianity following on from this, is highly materialistic. Materialism is even today supposed to be part of the Jewish character, both in the sense of demanding empirical evidence and in the sense of being keen on money-making. The Jews of the diaspora had followed the markets, they knew the feel of a coin in their palms, and the necessity of testing the scales oneself. A sharp watch had always to be maintained against deceit and sharp-practice. This is always the case, as the prophet Amos once remarked:

> Hear this, you who trample upon the needy,
>   and bring the poor of the land to an end,
> saying: 'When will the new moon be over,
>   that we may sell grain?
> And the sabbath,
>   that we may offer wheat for sale,

> that we may make the ephah small and the shekel great,
>   and deal deceitfully with false balances,
> that we may buy the poor for silver,
>   and the needy for a pair of sandals
> and sell the refuse of the wheat?' (Amos 8.4–6).

So, appealing to Jewish minds, the Corinthians passage moves from sin and the Scriptures to an assurance that there is good material evidence that Christ has risen—he was seen by Peter and then by the twelve. The structure of the passage is therefore:

(a) we have freedom from sin
(b) in accord with God's plan
(c) and this is attested by witnesses.

The same pattern is at work in the Transfiguration passage of II Peter, where the event of Christ in glory is shown to be in accord with the Scriptures: 'We have the prophetic word made more sure' (1.19); and 'no prophecy ever came by the impulse of man, but men moved by the Holy Spirit spoke from God' (1.21); and guaranteed by sensible witness: 'we were eye-witnesses of his majesty' (1.16); and 'we heard this voice borne from heaven, for we were with him' (1.18).

It is not inconceivable that such a presentation of Christ might well be employed now amongst our contemporaries whose sense of sin peoples the consulting rooms of psychiatrists, whose rootlessness sends them out to purchase more and more accounts of archaeological digs, and whose weariness of propaganda sets the eye-witness at a premium.

However that may be, it is evident that the Jewish liturgical background has evolved an affirmation of Christ and his work 'understandable of the people', an affirmation which Paul therefore uses to put Christ across. It is not possible to place precisely the original setting of this credal affirmation but it certainly has all the marks of a baptismal affirmation within a Jewish community. Perhaps it sprang up in that community of Corinthian Christians to whom Paul was writing, perhaps they had already imported it from another community, or perhaps Paul was making something new for them in his recollection of another community's baptismal service.

(b) *I Timothy 3.16*

> He was manifested in the flesh,
>   vindicated in the Spirit,

seen by angels,
preached among the nations,
believed on in the world,
taken up in glory (RSV).

Here forces quite different from those which operated to produce the Corinthian credal statement are at work. This is a statement which describes Christ in terms understood of a different community. We might in later times have called this 'another christology'.

In the previous credal hymn referred to, the preoccupation was with actions in history—man's sin and God's providence—the scheme of things was temporal and linear. In this piece of writing the dominant images are spatial—everything is set in place, whether of this world among the nations, or in another world of glory.

In answer to the question, 'What has Christ done?', this community has spoken of his work in cosmological terms. Christ has moved from one sphere to the next, he has used his divine power to cut through the chasmic division of heaven and earth. The work of Christ is in terms of descent and ascent:

(a) Christ has become man.
(b) He has shown himself to work in the Spirit of God.
(c) He has been preached among the Gentiles.
(d) Men all over the world have faith in him.
(e) He has ascended into heaven.

This scheme seems to be interrupted by the angels who occur either too late or too soon in the pattern, they should either have been watching at the incarnation or rejoicing at the ascension. So it seems to the modern reader. I do not think that the community which developed this credal statement would have looked at the matter in this way.

We generally use the term 'angel' for a good being; though we sometimes speak of a 'bad angel' we have to add the adjective in order to differentiate such a being from what is commonly meant by an 'angel'. This usage is unlike that of the primitive community of Christians. These early Christians knew the enemy angels of gnostic and hellenistic belief. The angels were, as Schlier has recently written, highly important in the scheme of things expressed in the primitive liturgy. They occur for instance as defeated beings in the baptismal liturgy of I Peter 3.18 ff which speaks of the risen Christ 'who has gone into heaven and is at the right hand of God with angels, authorities and powers subject to him'; they work against men with a mastery of the world as weapon in these dark days: 'We are not contending against flesh and blood, but against principalities, against the powers, against the world rulers of this present darkness, against the spiritual hosts of wickedness in the heavenly places'; they fly in the lower air and influence the lives of men until Christ puts them down under his feet at the triumph of the parousia. We are not to fear them, simply to realize that they are there working against us: 'I am sure that neither death, nor life, nor angels, nor principalities nor things present, nor things to come, nor powers, nor height, nor depth, nor anything else in all creation will be able to separate us from the love of God in Christ Jesus our Lord.'

These may prevent Paul several times from visiting the Thessalonia community but they cannot win out in the end. Christ has won the victory over the wicked angels for us. Christ has driven away the terror of the hellenistic world. His ministry is seen by the community which developed this little credal form as being a defeat of all satanic powers, the miracles of healing turn away legions of devils. So the effect on the angels comes properly between Christ as the one led by the Spirit into the desert temptations and as the one who is proclaimed victorious by the preaching of the Church among the nations.

We may see further indications of the hellenist background of this credal statement in the spatial imagery used to convey the work of Christ.

In the heyday of Greek science when mathematics had been developed to grand proportions, the world had been described in happy mechanist terms. Men had attempted to make a model of the universe, to discover the laws of its physical motion, the structure of its design. The Greek scientists had flexed themselves and joyfully demonstrated how the universe worked. This confidence in science as a means of providing explanations was of course a misunderstanding of the descriptive function of mathematics and it could last only while the science was engaged in discovery. Once the initial creative zest was finished and the world was looked at as it had become a terror struck at the hellenistic mind. The hellenistic Greeks, unlike their ancestors in the spring-like flourish of Aristotelian empiricism and logic, were not at all sure that human reason could rule the world. Quite the contrary, they supposed that the world ruled them. The machinery so far described by the scientists was such that it could not be contained by descriptions, the vast complex would govern the doings of men in its midst. They had recourse not to science but to emotional tranquillizers in the shape of myths, some of them very old, others invented to deal with the crisis. They indulged in the notion of angels pushing spheres and making music because angels, demonic powers, were more easily dealt with than a machine of ineluctable forces. The next stage was to create a pseudo-science of magic and emotion called astrology which would somehow set the doings of the angels in a coherent and manageable pattern.

The Greeks lapsed into a superstitious frame of thought. Supposing the stars to rule them by occult conjunctions and supposing further that evil angels set the stars in unfavourable positions, they became a prey to a magic ritual which all the time demonstrated its futility as a means of shaping life. They were in a desperate condition.

Christ relieved their Greek agony as he had relieved the torment of the Jewish convert. Christ crashed a way through the spheres for himself—the ascension became a triumphant progress through the universe. This progress through the broken machinery of the scientific discovery and through the broken power of the angelic powers is such that we can follow. By Christ's power we can take our position in a glory which is above the spheres. We are to be in our seventh heaven.

Christ is presented in this credal statement in Gentile terms. There is a concentration of his divinity. He brings freedom from the machinery of the devil. This freedom is expressed in the hellenistic liturgy. Paul accepts this as a proper description of Christ's redemptive work. He incorporates this formula because it is an expression of the true christology in a manner which will be understood by the community with whom he is communicating. The liturgical formula shows him how their minds work and he intends to work within the boundaries of their understanding. He realizes what he is called to be, 'All things to all men', as long as he is also the apostle of Jesus Christ.

(c) *Philippians 2.5–11*

Sometimes the liturgical text quoted by Paul is more than a small fragment. Sometimes he chances upon a piece of highly developed

195

theological writing in the cult of a Christian community and this gives him a guide for his thinking on some important aspect of his christology. Such a case of a sophisticated liturgical credal statement is to be found in the letter to the Philippians:

> Have this mind among yourselves, which you have in Christ Jesus, who, though he was in the form of God
>> did not count equality with God a thing to be grasped,
>> but emptied himself,
>> taking the form of a servant,
>> being born in the likeness of men.
>> And being found in human form he humbled himself
>> and became obedient unto death,
>> even death on the cross.
>> Therefore God has highly exalted him
>> and bestowed on him the name which is above every name,
>> that at the name of Jesus every knee should bow,
>> in heaven
>> and on earth
>> and under the earth,
>> and every tongue confess that Jesus Christ is Lord,
>> to the glory of God the Father (RSV)

After the Hallel at the Passover eve meal there came the recitation of 'the blessing of the song', one example of which begins: 'The breath of every living being shall bless thy name', which, as Daube says, shows striking affinities with the glorification of Jesus in Philippians.

There is here evidently a Hebrew christology which is originally dependent upon the suffering servant theology of Isaiah but which has been universalized by the community which brought it into the liturgy.

The shape of the credal statement in Philippians is taken from the fourth Servant Song in Deutero-Isaiah, in which, after the famous description of the tortured servant, which is employed by the primitive Christian communities in the construction of the passion narratives we have incorporated into our present gospels and which, we have already noted, was employed in the primitive Jerusalem apologetic, the song ends with a count of the nations which will be given to the servant as a reward for his acceptance of the suffering. The connection between the innocent suffering and glory is spoken of in casual terms:

> He was wounded for our transgressions,
> he was bruised for our iniquities;
> upon him was the chastisement that made us whole,
> and with his stripes we are healed (Is. 53.5);

and:

> Therefore I will give him the many for his portion
> and the numberless shall be his spoil,
> because he poured out his soul to death
> and was numbered with the transgressors (Is. 53.12).

Since it is necessary for any understanding of Christ, and for an understanding of this celebration of his work in particular, that the Suffering Servant passages are known I shall elaborate on their content and meaning.

According to Mowinckel, Isaiah 53, from which the fourth Song comes, is 'in its form a dirge with tunes from the penitential psalm', and according to Engnell it is conceivably 'a liturgy' in which various verses are assigned to various speakers in the service. Certainly it would be odd to deny the liturgical frame within which the songs are composed.

It would also be odd to deny that Christ adopted the Suffering Servant imagery as properly descriptive of his work. This was especially true, of course, of the crucifixion when he appears as the Servant in his dereliction:

> No form has he nor stateliness,
> nor yet appearance nor attractiveness;
> so disfigured his appearance that he scarce seems human,
> nor is his form like that of the sons of men (Is. 53.2).

The Son of Man so empties himself that even the sons of men do not recognize him as one of themselves:

> Despised and forsaken of men,
> a man of sorrows and acquainted with grief,
> as one from whom men avert their gaze
> he was despised and we regarded him not.
> Yet ours were the sicknesses he carried,
> and ours the pains he bore (Is. 53.3)

The suffering servant theology is behind much of Paul's writing. Thus he writes in his letter to the Romans that 'God put forward his Son' as an expiation by his blood for our sins, and 'gave him up for us all', and it may be that the first credal statement I have dealt with, when it speaks of 'according to the scriptures' that 'Christ died for our sins' has in mind this passage of the Scriptures.

Paul finds in this passage an epitome of soteriology. The causal connection between the willing, obedient acceptance of suffering and the final glory seems to him to be at work both in the exemplary and effective work of Christ and in our true imitation of Christ. He writes in the passage of the Philippian letter which immediately follows the servant passage about Christ, a prescription for the Christian: 'Therefore, my beloved, as you have always obeyed, so now, not only as in my presence but in my absence, work out your own salvation with fear and trembling' (Phil. 2.12, RSV).

The obedience of the Christian leads to salvation. The same thought is worked out in the letter to the Hebrews. The obedience of Christ led to his perfect enjoyment of glory and our obedience will lead to our enjoyment of salvation: 'Although he was a Son, he learned obedience through what he suffered; and being made perfect he became the source of eternal salvation to all who obey him' (Heb. 5.8, RSV).

The letter to the Hebrews also has a passage which employs the same causal terminology as the Isaiah passage and the Philippians credal statement: 'Jesus [was] crowned with glory and honour because of the suffering of death' (Heb. 2.9, RSV).

The christology of this credal statement, therefore, has certain Hebrew characteristics derived from the use of the Suffering Servant imagery, but it would be rash to suppose on this ground alone that it came from a predominantly Jewish community of the Church. The Servant suffers not simply so that he should receive glory from every nation—which would have been in line with a Hebrew conviction that all the Gentiles were destined to serve their Hebrew Messiah—but from the universe of heaven and hell also, so that a narrow nationalist approach will not do in the interpretation of this passage. And even if it were possible to say that the old Jewish notion was of a Messiah to whom everything would be subject, it yet remains to explain how it is that every tongue will be able to acknowledge Jesus as the Lord. To confess Jesus Christ as the Lord means to join in the full worship of him as God, it implies the breaking down of all the cultic divisions between Jew and Gentile. It was never part of the Jewish view that a nationalist Messiah would give a share in the cult to the goim, that they should be brought into the people of god.

There is therefore an element of universalism in this credal statement which is unlikely to come from a purely Hebrew community of Christians. Perhaps by the time such a sophisticated piece of writing was produced, Paul had enough influence to settle the old quarrels of Judaizers and Gentile converts in at least the Philippian community that he loved more than any other.

B. BINDING AND LOOSING

(i) *He that spared not even his own Son*

Among the rabbinic commentators on Genesis there was, at least by the time of Paul, a developed theology of the incident in which Abraham bound his only son, Isaac, on an altar as an intended sacrifice to Yahweh. This theology was further developed in both Jewish and Christian communities in the first centuries of the Christian era. We are not concerned with the developments in Hebrew thought, but the handling of the incident in the Pauline writings and the way in which this was elaborated in patristic work are of interest in the discussion of the Christian sacraments and in particular the theology of the Christian 'binding and loosing'.

As early as Origen it had been seen that in his Epistle to the Romans Paul was thinking of the binding of Isaac when he was writing of the sacrifice of Christ, when he remarked that God 'spared not even his own Son', echoing the angel's words in the Abraham story which commend the patriarch because 'you have not spared your son, your only son'. In the Genesis narrative the offering of Isaac opens out a new era for the tribe of Abraham and a renewal of the great covenant promise: 'I will bless you, and I will multiply your descendants as the stars of heaven and as the sand which is on the sea-shore . . . and by your descendants shall all the nations of the earth bless themselves' (22.17).

Of greater significance in the understanding of the Isaac story in the first Christian community is the reference in the Epistle to the Hebrews: 'Abraham shewed faith, when he was put to the test, by offering up Isaac. He was ready to offer up an only son, this man who had made the promises his own, and received the assurance, It is through Isaac that thy posterity shall be traced. God, he argued, had the power to restore his son even from the dead; and indeed in a hidden sense, he did so recover him' (Heb. 11.17).

The binding of Isaac is thus a type, in the early Christian community, of the sacrifice of Christ, but it is a type which is not precisely square with the event. Isaac, after all, was not sacrificed. He was bound and then loosed. So in a sense the ram in the thicket was the actual type. This is covered up in much of the Hebrew theology of the incident and the rabbis talk as if Isaac was in fact sacrificed. But in the Christian community it seems more to the point to employ Isaac as a type of the redeemed Christian who has been bound in sin and is released by the coming of Christ as a substitute victim.

In his magnificent book *Sacramentum Futuri*, Daniélou has collected many evidences of the way in which the early patristic writers spoke of this event, and on the point of Christ as the substitute for the sinful man he quotes Zeno of Verona: 'As with Isaac, it was one who was offered and another who was sacrificed, so in the Passion of Christ what had sinned in Adam is freed in Christ'; and John Chrysostom: 'A lamb was offered for Isaac, and a spiritual lamb was offered for the world. The reality had been depicted beforehand in type. Consider, I beg you, to what extent everything had been told in advance. In both instances we have an only son; in both instances one who is greatly loved. The first was offered as a victim by his father, and so was the latter offered by the Father. The type carries us a long way, but how much further does the reality go.'

It is not surprising, then, that the redemptive activity of Christ by which his sacrifice is an atonement for our sin should be spoken of in precisely the terms of 'binding and loosing'. By the Christian community's activity of binding and loosing in fulfilment of Christ's injunction, men's sins are forgiven. The work of Christ is applied to us through the binding and loosing within the community. The language of the Isaac incident has become the language of the redemption. By even this cursory examination of the terminology and its background it is possible to understand that in the office of binding and loosing the community was making present to the sinful member the saving work of Christ's sacrifice and resurrection.

It also seems likely that the office of binding and loosing derives something of its form from the court usage in the Israelite monarchy. Thus Isaiah (22.19–23) speaks of the installation of Eliakim as

Royal Steward in these terms: 'I will place on his shoulder the key of the house of David; he shall open and none shall shut; and he shall shut and none shall open.' This is very like the famous description of Peter's function in Matthew, and is quoted in Revelation (3.7) is a similar connection.

In the next section I shall try to reconstruct some elements of the rite by which the early Christians applied this saving work to the man who had by sin ceased to enjoy the full life of the community.

(ii) *The Shape of the Liturgy of Binding and Loosing*

In the First Epistle to Timothy Paul describes a group of sinners and names two of their number: 'By rejecting conscience, certain persons have made shipwreck of their faith, among them Hymenaeus and Alexander, whom I have delivered to Satan that they may learn not to blaspheme' (1.19, RSV). I am not here concerned with what is implied by 'rejecting one's conscience' or with the matter in which the group 'made shipwreck of their faith'. I want to make some effort to understand what Paul meant by the phrase, 'I have delivered to Satan'. This is obviously difficult for it is strange to think of the Apostle handing any Christian, however recalcitrant, over to Satan's power. And even if this were conceivable as a warning to the rest of the community that they had better beware such shipwreck, it is difficult to understand how, except in a modern colloquial sense, such a handing over could be said to 'teach them' anything.

Obviously the Apostle must be speaking of some temporary situation from which the two offenders are meant to emerge as better Christians. There is nothing to show what happened to these two in particular but more information may I think be gathered from various New Testament traditions set down in the gospels and epistles about this handing over to Satan and its remedial powers. In particular something may be learnt of the general practice from the handing over to Satan of a member of the Corinthian Christian community.

Though Paul very often referred to the early communities as assemblies of 'saints' it was rather the efficacy of baptism and his hopes for them of which he spoke than the actual conduct of the people. At times things did not go at all well in the community. We see some sign of this in the story of the incestuous Corinthian. Paul wrote to the Christians of Corinth: 'It is actually reported that there is immorality among you, and of a kind that is not even found among pagans; for a man is living with his father's wife. ... Let him who has done this be removed from among you' (I Cor. 5.1, RSV). He tells them how to deal with the offender: 'When you are assembled, and my spirit is present, with the power of our Lord Jesus, you are to deliver this man to Satan for the destruction of the flesh, that his spirit may be saved in the day of the Lord Jesus' (5.4, RSV).

Two points here seem to be of immediate interest: (i) that the incestuous man is committing a sin 'not even found among pagans', and (ii) that the man is handed over to Satan 'for the destruction of the flesh'.

(i) It is certainly true that Hippolytus rebuffed Phaedra in a similar situation, but it seems strange that Paul should suppose that there was no incestuous relationship of this kind in the pagan world when he was so convinced of its immorality on other counts. He describes the abuses of the Gentile world in very fierce terms in the first chapter of Romans: 'God gave them up in the lust of their hearts to impurity, to the dishonouring of their bodies among themselves because they exchanged the truth about God for a lie' (1.24, RSV). We may perhaps set this vehemence down to apostolic rhetoric, though this is always dangerous in Pauline studies, the saint very often proves to have meant just what he said.

In this case, however, there is some evidence in the New Testament itself that such immorality was known by the Christians to be practised by the pagans.

In Mark's gospel there is a version of our Lord's saying about divorce which allows no exception: 'Whoever divorces his wife and marries another, commits adultery against her; and if she divorces her husband and marries another, she commits adultery' (10.11, RSV). It would seem that this is the original version of the saying. Luke has it also. But Matthew has a different version which includes an excepting clause: 'everyone who divorces his wife, except on the ground of fornication, makes her an adulteress; and whoever marries a divorced woman commits adultery' (Mt. 5.32).

As it stands the Matthew text does not make sense in our translation since it at least requires that some word be substituted for 'fornication' which is not a married person's sin. It could be the general 'impurity' but this would be so general that it would allow divorce on almost any provocation. This would make Christ the follower of Rabbi Hillel who ruled that a burnt dinner or the loss of a wife's attractiveness was a shameful thing enough for the Deuteronomic divorce law to come into effect.

I think that here we have an example of the evangelist taking into account the contemporary situation in the Christian community and glossing the words of Christ so that his present will should be understood. Matthew is dealing here with the situation dealt with by the 'Council of Jerusalem' which sent forth a decree that no Gentile convert should eat the food offered to idols, non-kosher meat, and that they should abstain from '*porneia*'. '*Porneia*' is the word used in Matthew, Acts and significantly and helpfully in I Corinthians where it means quite precisely, 'incest'.

What has happened, I think, in the community is that an incestuous pair have appealed to the Marcan form of the no-divorce saying as a way of continuing their fictional marriage. Matthew is saying that Christ, when he spoke of no divorce, was speaking of real marriages, not those which took place within the forbidden degrees of kinship in Jewish or Gentile Law. Christ was not defending the imitation bond of unreal relationships. It is to be noted that Matthew's text in concerned that the man shall see all is well with himself, while Mark's text is concerned with both man and woman. The exception clause and the dominance of male concerns both point to a situation very like that in Corinth if not precisely that case.

(ii) What does Paul mean by 'the destruction of the flesh'? It is certainly possible that he thinks of sins as being punished by disease and even death, and this not in connection with sexual immoralities or gluttony but in the context of liturgy and sacrament. He writes to the Corinthians in the same letter as he speaks of the incestuous man that their celebration of the Eucharist has brought illness upon them: 'For any one who eats and drinks without discerning the body eats and drinks judgment upon himself. That is why many of you are weak and ill, and some have died' (I Cor. 11.29–30). And again it does appear that the author of the epistle of James supposed that the proper reception of the prayerful anointing of the sick would give health by God's grace. There is nothing Cartesian about the New Testament writers.

At the same time it does seem that handing a man over to Satan for the destruction of the flesh implies something more than seeing in the disease that attacks a man the hand of a just God. The community, on this interpretation, would be actually told to see that the man became ill, to go about things so that another Christian was attacked by Satan. This seems to me a real difficulty. It is doubly so when this is done, as it was also in the case of the delinquents referred to in I Timothy, in order that good may come of it: 'that his spirit may be saved in the day of the Lord Jesus' (I Cor. 5.5). Nor will the popular concept of 'excommunication' precisely fit this case, not by itself at least, since the purpose is not to oust the man from grace in the bell, book and candle manner—all is done precisely in order to save. Nor will it do to interpret the passage in terms of an excommunication, which means simply 'be forbidden the use of the family car', as an American theologian once paraphrased a bishop who had endeavoured to forbid his people to go in for beauty contests. The whole context is one of positive Christian action towards the sinner.

If we would discover the intention of the 'handing over' we would do well to seek it in the liturgical structure of the service, on the classical principle of *lex orandi, lex credendi*. What form did this take? It is not possible to make definite descriptions of course, the liturgy has not come down to us directly in set form, but I think that the New Testament does offer some indications of the nature of this assembly activity.

We must first look for instance in the New Testament when a community judgement is presented. Such instances are not frequent but suggestively enough one occurs immediately after the reference in I Corinthians to the incestuous criminal:

> Is it not those inside the church whom you are to judge? ... When one of you has a grievance against a brother, does he dare go to law before the unrighteous instead of the saints? Do you not know that the saints will judge the world? And if the world is to be judged by you, are you incompetent to try trivial cases? Do you not know that we are to judge angels? How much more, matters pertaining to this life. If then you have such cases, why do you lay them before those who are least esteemed by the church? (I Cor. 5.12; 6.1–4, RSV).

This passage would seem to depend on the tradition conveyed in Matthew's gospel of the matter of disputes:

> If your brother sins against you, go and tell him his fault, between you

and him alone. If he listens to you, you have gained your brother. But if he does not listen, take one or two others along with you, that every word may be confirmed by the evidence of two or three witnesses. If he refuses to listen to them, tell it to the church; and if he refuses to listen even to the church, let him be to you as a Gentile and a tax collector. (Mt. 18.15–17 RSV).

The corresponding passage in Luke 17 does not have the reference to the meeting of the church as a judging assembly. It is evident that here and in the divorce issue Matthew respresents a developed form of the tradition, developed to deal with the situations within the community of the first-generation Christians. This is the only place in the Synoptic tradition where the word 'church' is used in the sense of a legislative body. But it would be wrong to make too much of this. Certainly the assembly has authority; this is shown by the verse immediately following: 'Truly, I say to you, whatever you bind on earth shall be bound in heaven, and whatever you loose on earth shall be loosed in heaven' (Mt. 18.18, RSV). But this is related at once to the liturgical assembly within which the Lord is himself present. It is not a legislature that has been set up but a company of Christ and his friends: 'For where two or three are gathered in my name, there am I in the midst of them' (Mt. 18.20, RSV).

That no judicial context is envisaged is further shown by the question and answer which immediately follows this description of the Christian community: 'Then Peter came up and said to him, "Lord, how often shall my brother sin against me, and I forgive him? As many as seven times?" Jesus said to him, "I do not say to you seven times, but seventy times seven"' (Mt. 18.21–2, RSV). The Jewish exemplary forgiveness of seven times is too juridical, Jesus means Peter to understand that he must forgive always.

This emphasis on forgiveness and charity rather than on the tribunal is stronger still within the context in which the gospel of John places this saying of Jesus. The Johannine setting is in a post-resurrection appearance which lays particular stress on such themes as 'peace' and 'joy' and 'forgiveness' and does so by showing these gifts of the Holy Spirit to be obtained for us by the passion of Christ and given to the community of the resurrection: the first phrase, 'Jesus came and stood among them' (Jn 20.19), is parallel to the promise, 'I am in the midst of them' (the future tense is not used in the promise phrase because it is written after the promise had been fulfilled and the promise has become a present reality for the community of the evangelist). The passage in John continues with the gift of community: 'Peace be with you' (Jn 20.20), and the reminder that it is through suffering that this peace of the Lord comes: 'When he had said this, he showed them his hands and his side' (Jn 20.20). Peace is followed by happiness: 'Then the disciples were glad when they saw the Lord. Jesus said to them again, Peace be with you. As the Father has sent me so I send you' (Jn 20.21).

The peace we have and the happiness we have are not for ourselves, they are not even simply for the small community within which we receive the gifts, they are for all men. The suffering of Christ was a redemption for all men; those who learn this have a responsibility to participate in the Church's missionary activity. All who are baptized are sent.

Of course the missionary activity of the Church cannot take place unless it be done in the Spirit. This is the meaning of Pentecost. This was well understood within the tradition that formulated John's gospel. The community's activity is initiated by the coming of the Spirit: 'And when he had said this, he breathed on them, and said to them, "Receive the Holy Spirit" ' (20.23), and the first result of the Church's mission, the first result of the bringing of the Spirit to men, is the remission of sins: 'If you forgive the sins of any, they are forgiven; if you retain the sins of any, they are retained' (20.23).

It is important to notice that the 'binding' and 'retaining' spoken of in these passages does not mean the refusal to absolve. This, if it were the case, would certainly mean that the Church had adopted a juridical attitude towards the sinner. As Professor Karl Rahner remarked in his consideration of Penance, in *Theological Investigations*, II, 'a great deal of formal juridical acumen is often summoned up in order to show that such a refusal of absolution . . . represents a truly positive judicial act which creates a new legal situation' (p. 141). He goes on to show (p. 142) that 'binding' in this context might be paraphrased as 'revealing the reality of the sinner's situation' which is that while the sinner seems from outward appearances to be alive because within the living body of Christ which is filled with the life-giving Spirit, he is really dead, and he sums up:

'Binding' and 'loosing' are not two sides of an alternative, but two phases of the one reaction whereby the Holy Church answers the sin of one of her members. At least this is so in the intention of the Church. When she binds she binds in order to be able to loose. Only once the truth, which is covered up by the outward appearances of the belonging to the Church, has been brought to light on the visible plane of the Church, can the guilt towards the Church and God be lifted or 'loosed' again on the same plane, i.e. on the sacramental plane.

The whole saying, therefore, recorded in John and Matthew is directed towards the forgiveness of sin within the visible context of the Church.

If we now return to the original passage about the incestuous Corinthian for a minute, we can see that the context is exactly that which is described by Matthew and John. The community is to assemble for the forgiveness of the sinner, they are the people who have been renewed 'in the Spirit of our God' (I Cor. 6.11) and they represent the whole Church of Christ. Paul himself says, according to the usual translation, that he is 'present in spirit', and it may well be that this should be translated 'in the Spirit' (as also in Col. 2.5 where the conjunction of 'in spirit' with 'rejoicing' is an echo of the idea described in the incident of the Ethiopian eunuch who after receiving baptism 'went on his way rejoicing'). And the assembly is, as the Church, to pronounce the reality of the situation in order that the sinner may repent and be absolved, they are to bind in order to loose. What form did this ceremony take?

There is a suggestion in the passage that the ceremony took place before the Sunday Eucharist in the Corinthian meeting-place and was directed to the celebration of the paschal meal by the 'saints'. Paul writes to them: 'Cleanse out the old leaven that you may be a new lump, as you really are unleavened' (I Cor. 5.7, RSV). They are to recognize that appearances must conform to the reality of their situation before they go on to the Eucharist: 'For Christ, our paschal lamb, has been sacrificed. Let us, therefore, celebrate the festival, not with the old leaven, the leaven of malice and evil, but with the unleavened bread of sincerity and truth' (5.7–8).

The Corinthians had been told by Paul in a previous letter 'not to associate with immoral men' and they had understood this to mean that they should erect a ghetto for themselves, attempting to get 'out of the world'. But Paul tells them this time that he did not mean that they should not share the meal with those who, although to all appearances were living in the Church, were by their way of life refusing to be members of the Church. It was not the governor and the merchant and the sailor of Corinth that they had to avoid—to these indeed they had been sent—but the man who by his incest denied his baptism: 'I wrote to you not to associate with any one who bears the name of brother if he is guilty of immorality' (5.11). They are to refuse his company not on all occasions—this is not a formal excommunication such as developed for a time in the Church as a juridical weapon—but on the occasion of the Eucharist. He tells them they are not 'to eat with such a one'. Whether this is a direct reference to the Christian meal or simply to those meals ordinarily taken within the family makes little difference to the argument, since for the first community all meals were a reminder of the fellowship of the Last Supper and the Eucharist a climacteric reminder which was the reality.

That there is nothing here of the popular notion of the excommunication idea can be seen in the next verse in which Paul asks the community: 'Is it not those *inside* the church whom you are to judge?' The incestuous man is 'inside' the church and therefore comes within the context of the assembly pronouncement. The others are described by Paul as 'outsiders'. This usage is reflected in the explanation Jesus gives the disciples of the parable of the sower, and of parables generally: 'To you has been given the secret of the kingdom of God, but for those outside everything is in parables' (Mk. 4.11, RSV). The distinction is important. It refers to the sacramental economy and the irradicability of the baptismal union of the Christian with Christ through the Spirit of God.

We have then the context of a pre-Eucharist meeting of the community. What happened at the meeting? It is generally agreed that the oldest part of the Christian liturgy is a complex of psalm singing and lections. Eric Werner is his discussion of this in *The Sacred Bridge* (p. 130) quotes the *Apostolic Constitutions*, which, while admittedly of the fourth century, seem to reflect a much earlier tradition and to retain some features of the pre-Christian synagogue worship: 'After each two lessons [someone other than the cantor] shall chant the hymns of David.' And it is significant, I think, that this earliest reference to liturgical forms of this kind testifies also to the refrain-manner in which the psalms were sung: 'and the people shall join in singing the last words of the verses'. This was the Jewish synagogue custom and the Jewish services retained the pattern while other forms of psalmody were developed in the Christian community from this primitive usage.

It is evident that this method of refrain-recitation is responsible for the present shape of Psalm 136 where, alternately with the narrative praise of God's redemptive work at the Exodus, comes the line: 'for his steadfast love endures for ever' which was sung by the people between the cantor's verses. Similarly it appears from Exodus 15 that the Canticle of Moses had a refrain which was first taught to the people before the recitation of the song. The first verse: 'I will sing to the Lord, for he has triumphed gloriously; the horse and the rider he has thrown into the sea', was repeated by the people to the accompaniment of timbrels.

This refrain recitation was retained even by heretical Jewish sects like those of the Therapeutae in Alexandria who were said by Philo in his *De Vita Contemplativa* to perform the liturgical rites in this manner: 'whilst one sings gracefully with a certain measure, the others, listening in silence, join in the singing of the final clauses of the hymns'. Eusebius, commenting upon this (*Ecclesiastical History*, II, 17), and taking into account the contemporary practice of the Christian assembly thinks that Philo must be describing the first Christian community because this practice is so strong in the Christian Church in his day: 'that Philo, when he wrote these statements, had in view the first heralds of the gospel, and the original practices handed down from the apostles, must be obvious to all.'

Somewhat later, Chrysostom testifies to the use of his community. Psalms 42 and 43 were sung in the refrain manner with the more complicated pattern of alternate use of two refrains: 'men say to me continually: Where is your God?' and 'Hope in God; for I shall again praise him, my help and my God.' I think that there is some evidence in the New Testament that such practices had not died out and were in particular used at a ceremony of 'binding', or of 'handing over to Satan' and destruction.

In Mark 9, Jesus is speaking of the punishment of sin; especially those who cause others to sin are to be punished severely: 'it would be better for him if a great millstone were hung round his neck and he were thrown into the sea.' Then comes a passage which has obvious likenesses to the kind of repetitive psalmody discussed earlier:

If your hand causes you to sin,
cut it off;
it is better for you to enter life maimed
than with both hands to go to Gehenna,
to the unquenchable fire,
where the worm does not die,
and the fire is not quenched.

If your foot causes you to sin,
cut it off;
it is better for you to enter life lame
than with two feet to be thrown into Gehenna,
where the worm does not die,
and the fire is not quenched.

If your eye causes you to sin,
pluck it out;
it is better for you to enter the kingdom of God with one eye
than with two eyes to be thrown into Gehenna,
where the worm does not die,
and the fire is not quenched (Mk. 9.42–7, RSV).

Apart from the explicable variant in verse 3 of the song (that is, verse 46 of Mark 9), the structure of the verses and refrain can clearly be discerned in this setting out of the text.

If we adopt the hypothesis that the first part of the song was sung by a cantor and the last two lines by the people we can understand that this looks very like the liturgical texts of the psalter, and it does not seem unlikely that this is a 'binding' text which while referring to the sin of the offender is also cast in the form of a warning to all the members of the community. That such a usage is behind the formal structure of the verses is confirmed by the context in which we find them in Mark's gospel. They occur in conjunction with the parallel passage to Matthew 18.15 ff. and Luke 17.3 f. which deal with the community's method of speaking to a sinner, bringing him before the Church and forgiving him seventy times seven. That is, the very passage which we have seen is reflected in the structure of the incestuous Corinthian incident in Paul's letter demanding a 'binding' ceremony. We have here if not the actual words of the community at the binding ceremony at least something like them, perhaps words from such a ceremony in another community, or perhaps a generalized and formalized complex put together from various traditions by the evangelists. That not all manuscripts have exactly this form here may be explained in terms of various community traditions. The gospel records the contemporary understanding of the Christian life in this matter. It would seem to me that this is eminently a passage which exhibits the characteristic of the evangelists mentioned in the Biblical Commission's Instruction of April 1964: '[the New Testament writers] explicated as they kept in mind the situation of the churches.' The contemporary binding ceremony shaped the gospel narrative of Christ's words and this was proper to the evangelists because they realized that the contemporary ceremony fulfilled the intention behind the words.

The words of the refrain have themselves an origin in the liturgical considerations of the prophet Isaiah (whoever wrote Isaiah 66.23–4). His book contains a picture of the congregation coming out of the Temple worship in Jerusalem after the service looking over the walls of the city into the valley of Gehenna where the rubbish of the city rotted and smouldered in a perpetual incineration: 'from sabbath to sabbath all flesh shall come to worship before me, says the Lord. And they shall go forth and look on the dead bodies of the men that have rebelled against me; for their worm shall not die, their fire shall not be quenched.' The people come from the worship of God and understand the death of those who have no part in the liturgy.

We have now the beginnings of a framework for the binding ceremony suggested in I Corinthians 5. It is a meeting of the people before the Sunday Eucharist directed towards the forgiveness of the sinner and expressed in a warning refrain. Does the New Testament offer any further indication as to how the ceremony was conducted? I think that there may be some relic of such a ceremony in the account in Acts 5 of the condemnation of Ananias and his wife Sapphira. These two sold a piece of land and offered half the proceeds to the community in Jerusalem while pretending that they offered the whole of the money which it had fetched. The people are assembled round Peter when the money is brought in, and at once the narrative takes on the form of a condemnation. Peter tells Ananias (who is introduced separately from his wife, perhaps because there is a reminiscence of their cases being dealt with separately?) that he had handed himself over to Satan and offended the Spirit of God. Paul in I Corinthians links immorality with greed as the two principal sins

211

of the community he knows. The incestuous man is an example of a Christian giving way to the one, Ananias of one who gives way to the other. Peter says to him: 'You have not lied to men but to God. When Ananias heard these words he fell down and died. And great fear came upon all who heard of it. The young men rose and wrapped him up and carried him out and buried him' (Acts 5.4–6, RSV). Similarly with Sapphira. Her incident can be analysed thus:

(i) the woman tells a lie;
(ii) she is condemned to death: 'they will carry you out';
(iii) the community rejects her: 'they carried her out and buried her';
(iv) the community is full of dread: 'and great fear came upon the whole church and upon all who heard of these things.'

This is an account of the coming of death to those who attempt to play the community false and to refuse truth to God. I want to put beside it an account of a miracle which is concerned with the giving of life. I shall discuss the story of Dorcas in Acts 9. I take an example from Acts because it will have been through any Lucan editorial revision to which the Ananias and Sapphira story has been subject. I think it can be shown to follow the common pattern of miracle stories that I have presented earlier.

Now there was at Joppa a disciple named Tabitha, which means Dorcas or Gazelle. She was full of good works and acts of charity. In those days she fell sick and died; and when they had washed her, they laid her in an upper room. Since Lydda was near Joppa, the disciples, hearing that Peter was there, sent two men to him entreating him, 'Please come to us without delay'. So Peter rose and went with them. And when he had come, they took him to the upper room. All the widows stood beside him weeping, and showing coats and garments which Dorcas made while she was with them. But Peter put them all outside and knelt down and prayed: then turning to the body he said, 'Tabitha, rise'. And she opened her eyes and when she saw Peter she sat up. And he gave her his hand and lifted her up. Then calling the saints and widows he presented her alive. And it became known throughout all Joppa and many believed in the Lord (36–42, RSV).

The Dorcas miracle has a structure which conforms to the miracle pattern, it works out thus:

(i) the woman does many works of charity;

(ii) the woman is dead;
(iii) her friends entreat for her;
(iv) she is told to rise;
(v) she rises and is given back to her friends;
(vi) the community rejoices and many believe.

The structure therefore is completely the reverse of the Ananias and Sapphira structure. Both are concerned with community relationships which are realized in death or resurrection. The miracle story in both cases is a paradigm of the Christian life and demonstrates the necessity for living within the people. Ananias and Sapphira are remembered not primarily for the melodramatic incident but as images of the death of the sinner. The death they die is thought of at first as the guilt of sin and the exclusion of the sinner from the community. The account of their deaths is a warning for all men of the kind of reality that sin sets up in a man's life. This is not of course a judgement on the historicity of the incident as described in Acts, an historical event may become a symbol with little difficulty—a man may meet his Waterloo at any moment. But it is to say that event or no event the story was interpreted by the early Christians, and this interpretation was given a definitive shape in Acts, the event became the lesson that exclusion from the community is brought about by sin and is death to the Christian. It is only within the community that the Christian is told to rise, and is able to rise, with the resurrected life of Christ.

If this is the meaning of the Acts narrative then we have something akin to the structure and intent of the binding of the sinner—that is, we have a declaration of an excluding act having been performed which entails death.

There are further indications that this passage may be linked with the Marcan refrain-passage and that both may be concerned with a binding ceremony. I would not, however, wish to put very great stress on these.

The Marcan passage offers the straight alternative of entering 'into life' and going to Gehenna which characterizes all these narratives and which is evidently too commonplace a Christian thought to be used as a support for any particular parallelism. What is interesting in this connection is the way in which the alternative is expressed. The chorus passage speaks ever in terms of giving up half one's possessions in order to enter life; one hand, one eye, one foot, is to be sacrificed for the good of man. There is something here, possibly, which echoes Peter's comment that Ananias could have divided the proceeds of the sale quite legitimately—the money was his since the field had been his—and given half only to the community and been accepted as a full member of the community.

It may be that the best thing is to give the whole of one's property to the community. Luke certainly records our Lord as suggesting this: 'Sell all that you have and distribute to the poor, and you will have treasure in heaven' (Lk. 18.22, RSV), and it is this evangelist who describes several times the primitive communism of the Jerusalem Christians: 'Now the company of those who believed were of one heart and soul, and no one said that any of the things he possessed was his own, but they had everything in common' (Acts 4.32, RSV). But at the same time it is Luke and only Luke among the evangelists who sets down a narrative which demonstrates the generosity of giving half one's goods to the community of the poor. The narrative of Zacchaeus who climbed into a sycamore tree and became the friend of Christ leads up to a climax in which precisely this lesson is taught: 'And Zacchaeus stood and said to the Lord: "Behold, Lord, the half of my goods I give to the poor; and if I have defrauded any one of anything, I restore it fourfold." And Jesus said to him: "Today salvation has come to this house, since he also is a son of Abraham. For the Son of Man came to seek and to save the lost." ' (Lk. 19.8–9, RSV).

The fourfold restitution seems to be an adaptation of the ruling of Exodus, Leviticus and Numbers in the Jewish code; the particularly Christian element of Zacchaeus' solemn declaration is the giving of half his goods away, it is this which is salvific. It is this which is described as salvific in the Marcan refrain-passage and it is this which would have been salvific for Ananias. The two passages are thus linked together, and this would strengthen the suggestion that both are to be understood as echoes of the community binding ceremony even if their present shape is not totally dependent upon their liturgical use.

If the story of Ananias and Sapphira is a binding story then one of the difficulties in interpreting it in a Christian sense is removed. It is difficult, when the story is taken by itself, not to be surprised that the sinners were given no time at all to repent but were suddenly struck dead at the word of Peter. They tell their lie and die with their sin upon them. They are caught like Hamlet's father. But if their story is the first half of a binding and loosing structure then the declaration of their death is done in order that they may repent, it is the binding element, it declares, in Rahner's terms, the reality of the sinful situation, it makes it possible for the situation to be dealt with in a Christian manner. Once the sin and its guilt are recognized by the sinner then the community can pass to forgiveness.

We have, then, in the Ananias story, either an account of a pair of sinners who did not repent and were therefore left in their death outside the community, or the first half of an effort on the part of the community to bring the pair back into the life of Christ, the second half of which is either lost to us now or was for some reason never recorded.

Something of the rubrics of this lost liturgy may be concealed in the description of the activities of the 'young men' of the community who carry out the bodies. Who are these young men?

It is not only in Acts that we find the young men in the New Testament. They appear in the final exhortations of I Peter to various groups within the Christian community. Whether this is an actual account of a liturgical celebration, as has been suggested by many authors, particularly of course Dr F. L. Cross who sees in the text many elements of an Easter Vigil service with its attendant baptisms, or whether it is two letters which have been interwoven by later editors, it cannot be denied that the last section is a series of commissions to various members of the community to play their proper part in the assembly. One group to which the author addresses himself is that of the 'younger men', who are told to be subject to the 'elders'. Since 'elders' is certainly a liturgical term describing the presbytery, it would seem likely that the 'young men' is also a specific liturgical group here, some officers assisting the elders in the community, not deacons certainly, since there was a word for them, but minor acolytic types. Who are these young men who appear in the Ananias account?

'The young men' seem to be a group distinct from the 'whole church' in the account. Their function in this story is evidently to exclude the unwanted from the community. They act as doorkeepers. They fulfil the command to remove the man and this command must have been somewhat in the form Paul takes over from the liturgy described in Deuteronomy 17 where a man or woman who has gone over to the worship of false gods is to be shut out from the community and put to death: 'Let him who has done this be removed from among you. . . . "Drive out the wicked person from among you".' Paul is not thinking of the death of the incestuous man in the sense of a lynching or an execution, but in the sense of his removal from the visible life of the community.

Perhaps in the Ananias story the young men fulfil the same role of janitors.

The young men have perhaps another function in the community and this connected with the refrain singing of the liturgy. Eric Werner (*op. cit.*, pp. 135–6) quotes a Jewish account of liturgical singing in the Exilarchate of Babylon which may depend on Christian practices, in his view. The account speaks of three parts of the recitation of the psalms and hymns: the hazan, leader, the congregation, and between them 'the young men'. He mentions too the notice of Aetheria Silvia on her visit to Palestinian Holy Places in the fourth century which seems to refer to some similar group. It may be that at the binding ceremony the young men sang the refrain and then shut the doors.

We can now put together the various elements of the passages adduced so far. The evidence in favour of their being connected with a binding ceremony varies, of course, from passage to passage, but they seem to fit well together:

(i) The meeting of the assembly before the Sunday Eucharist;

(ii) the questioning of the accused sinner, perhaps apart from those accused with him;

(iii) the recitation or singing of a psalm-like liturgical song with refrain taken up by the people, perhaps alternately with the 'young men';

(iv) the pronouncement of the president of the assembly of the reality of the situation, and the nature of the sin and guilt as excluding the accused from the eucharistic assembly;

(v) the expulsion of the sinner from the visible assembly fulfils externally the interior exile which the sin involved—the young men turn the sinner out;

(vi) an expression of sorrow by the community who understand the man to be dead.

216

This concludes the binding ceremony. What happens after this? Ananias and Sapphira are, as I have suggested earlier, doubtful cases. It may be that they repented and were received back into the living community again, or it may be that they stand as fearful examples of those who die refusing to accept the reality of their offence. It does seem that the latter is the more likely interpretation of the text. There is no indication of their repenting their sin and their death is not described in terms which suggest the death of the Christian who is to rise again. It would seem that the Marcan quotation from Isaiah which was used in the refrain song is completed for them: 'they shall be an abhorrence to all flesh' (Is. 66.24).

The evidence in the case of the incestuous Corinthian gives rather more justification for optimism. There is some indication that the binding ceremony was followed, as Paul had designed it to be followed, by a loosing ceremony and a return to the eucharistic assembly.

Modern writers have generally understood the passage in II Corinthians 2 as referring to the restoration to the community of a man who has offered a personal insult to Paul, but the traditional view of patristic authors (except Tertullian in his Montanist rigorist reaction) is that the passage described the return of the incestuous man denounced in the first epistle. I think that the traditional view agrees better with the general ecclesiastical situation in the Corinthian church and I find it superfluous to suggest the existence of such an insult when the passage can be explained well enough on the supposition that it deals with the already known incestuous man.

Since the binding ceremony was so much involved with imagery of death we should expect that the loosing ceremony to which it was directed would be spoken of in terms of the resurrection. This would link up immediately with the living faith in the risen Lord that is evident in the miracle narratives and which was the critical element in Christian understanding of reality. Origen, writing *Contra Celsum* (III, 51), testifies to the use of such imagery at least in his time: 'The distinguished school of Pythagoreans built cenotaphs to those who turned back from their philosophy, reckoning that they had died. But Christians mourn as dead men those who have been overcome by licentiousness or some outrageous sin, because they have perished and died to God. They admit them some time later as though they had risen from the dead, provided that they show a real conversion.'

It would seem that the loosing ceremony must have taken something of the following shape:

    (i) a command to open the door;
    (ii) the young men open the doors and the man is let into the assembly;
    (iii) the people sing a song about coming 'into life' and the relation of forgiveness to the resurrection;
    (iv) they celebrate the Eucharist.

It is difficult to make a suggestion concerning the point at which the penitent would be asked to declare his sorrow for sin. There would be no use at all in starting the ceremony unless the president of the assembly had an assurance that the man was ready and anxious to return to the community. There must, therefore, have been some preliminary 'soundings', and these may well have been regarded as sufficient for the community to accede to the request. We may be touching here the beginnings of some form of 'private confession' but this is too complicated a matter for my present purpose. On the other hand if the binding had been public and official it would seem that the loosing should be also. Perhaps there was an official questioning of the penitent either before or after the people's song. It is difficult, however, to accept that the primitive community was so concerned with official procedures that having first discovered the facts they would indulge in a further ritual questioning. At any rate the situation seems to require a rite including at least the elements I have outlined.

Of these elements there is no direct evidence, but some parts of the New Testament may reflect such a structure.

    (i) It is noteworthy that one of the three phrases preserved in the Aramaic form Jesus spoke is the command *Effeta*, which means 'open up.' It may be that this releasing, curing, word of Christ was retained in the liturgy for the reconciliation of the penitent.

    (ii) There may just possibly be a more than linguistic connection between the 'young men' who take their part in the liturgy, and the 'young man' who in Mark's account of the resurrection and the opening of the door of the tomb sits to proclaim to the disciples: 'He is risen'. Those who shut the door are those who open and show the way to the resurrected life.

(iii) It is evident that the resurrection is the setting for the forgiveness of sin. In John's gospel the apostles' commission to forgive is pronounced at a resurrection appearance. It is impossible to point to a song for the people at this point but it may well be that they could use the baptismal song preserved in I Corinthians 15: 'Christ died for our sins, according to the scriptures; he was buried and was raised on the third day, according to the scriptures'. This could give the refrain form like that of the Marcan song, and so would be suitable for congregational singing. It also selects as the dominant points of the tradition from which Paul received it, the forgiveness of sins and the rising from the dead—that is, the two themes with which the loosing ceremony would be concerned.

(iv) It is inconceivable that after such a community event as the return of a sinner that they would not celebrate with a meal. The Christians would obviously join in the Eucharist. Such a reaction is typified by Luke's parable of the Prodigal Son and his welcome back into the family. The meal and the resurrection shape the welcome. 'It was fitting to make merry and be glad, for this your brother was dead and is alive; he was lost and is found' (Lk. 15.32, RSV).

In his next letter to the Corinthians Paul seems to speak of the return of the incestuous man to the assembly. He bids them take back the sinner: 'If any one has caused pain, he has caused it not to me, but in some measure—not to put it too severely—to you all' (II Cor. 2.5, RSV), and therefore the whole community must show forgiveness and welcome: 'For such a one this punishment of the many is enough; so you should rather turn to forgive and comfort him, or he may be overwhelmed by excessive sorrow. So I beg you to reaffirm your love for him' (II Cor. 2.6-8).

The community having bound the man is told to show love and forgiveness and to loose him. The penitence of the man has brought him into the kingdom. It is not simply that he has been found out and is sorry for the discovery but he has found himself, he has recognized reality and therefore can accept all the factors of reality, that is he is penitent and loving: 'For godly grief produces a repentance that leads to salvation and brings no regret, but worldly grief produces death' (II Cor. 7.10, RSV). The man who simply looks in on himself and is self-pitying remains dead after the binding and cannot be loosed into the resurrection life.

This pattern of binding and loosing as a resurrection event is a truth presented in pictorial form in the Johannine narrative of the raising of Lazarus: the man is dead and bound, he is released by Christ from the trappings of sin and death: 'The dead man came out, his hands and feet bound with bandages, and his face wrapped with a cloth. Jesus said to them: "Unbind him, and let him go"' (Jn 11.44, RSV).

V

Lazarus

LAZARUS come from the grave is not simply a paradigm of Christ's loosing power over sin, he is the man who shows us what being a Christian means. In this final section I mean to recapitulate the main themes of this study with particular reference to the story of Lazarus.

I have suggested that a way into the understanding of the New Testament witness to Christ could be found by means of three guides —the use of the Old Testament in the writings of the new community, the way in which the resurrection of Christ gives value to the whole of Christ's ministry, especially his ministry of healing, and the way in which the continuing presence of Christ's life and resurrection was celebrated in the sacramental liturgy of the community. These three ideas are discoverable in the Johannine account of the raising of Lazarus at Bethany, which is placed in the fourth gospel as the climax of Jesus' ministry and as the event which determined the Jewish leaders to compass the death of the Lord. It is no side-issue or trivial incident but a central event which I take to exhibit the general themes I have already suggested.

I will consider first those elements in the Lazarus narrative which seem to indicate that we ought to take this man from the tomb as the paradigm of the Christian. Of course Christ is the only true exemplar for the Christian but this does not prevent our being presented with subsidiary examples of how to conform to the perfect image of the Father given us in Christ. In the New Testament several Christians are described in terms which suggest that we should take them for our patterns in the imitation of Christ. Of these men it can be said that Christ lives in them. Just as in the seven sacraments we have seen how Christ continues to act as he acted in Galilee and Judaea and Jerusalem during his ministry, his passion and resurrection, so in such men we can see how Christ acts in the totality of human life now as he has acted in his earthly experience. Such a man is the deacon Stephen who, at his martyrdom, is shown as crying out in the Lord's own words: 'Do not count this sin against them' (Acts 7.60), and another is Paul who is prepared to say to the Galatians: 'Christ lives in me' (Gal. 2.20), and who regards his preaching as the continuation of Christ's preaching, as he tells the Corinthians: 'Christ is speaking in me' (II Cor. 13.3, RSV).

Paul knows himself to be called to be Christ now, called to 'share abundantly in Christ's sufferings' and to be 'crucified with Christ' (Gal. 2.20), and who is so conformed to Christ in his passion that he can say: 'I bear on my body the marks of Jesus' (Gal. 6.17, RSV), and who at last in dying like Christ will rise like Christ, as he tells the Philippians: 'becoming like him in his death . . . I may attain the resurrection from the dead' (3.10, RSV).

Paul's mission is to show other men how Christ can live in their lives. He tells the Galatians: 'I am in travail until Christ be formed in you' (4.19, RSV). Each Christian is to be Christ in his world. We are each to die his death in fulfilment of our baptism: 'those who belong to Christ Jesus have crucified the flesh' (Gal. 5.24), and we are each to rise because we share in the Spirit of Christ: 'If the Spirit of him who raised Jesus from the dead dwells in you, he who raised Christ Jesus from the dead will give life to your mortal bodies also through his Spirit who dwells in you' (Rom. 8.11, RSV).

Once we have realized that we must conform ourselves to the suffering Christ we shall be on the way into the kingdom: 'If any man would come after me, let him deny himself and take up his cross and follow me' (Mk 8.34, RSV).

God, when we were dead in sin, 'made us alive together with Christ and raised us up with him and enthroned us with him in the heavens' (Eph. 2.6).

We are become heirs of the kingdom with Christ. It is to be noted that in our baptism we are conformed to Christ not simply in his public ministry, which historically followed immediately upon his baptism by John in the Jordan, but we are conformed to Christ in the whole procession of events which was entailed in this acceptance of baptism by Christ. At his baptism Christ made himself one with us as a sinful people. He took on himself a community with a sinful

222

race. At his baptism, therefore, the sinful people were given a community with the divine Lord. He shares our human condition and we are to share his redeeming work. The vocation of Christ and the vocation of Christians are one in that they are to be inheritors of the kingdom through accepting the office of the suffering servant. Our baptism is our dying with Christ and our rising with him. Our baptism has not had its full effect until we have risen in Christ. As Paul wrote to the Colossians; 'you were buried with him in baptism, in which you were also raised with him' (2.12). Our rising is therefore to be looked at in two ways. It has both happened by our entering into the community of the Lord here on earth, and it is yet to happen with his manifestation as Lord of all creation in glory. Here and now and not simply in the future glory we are sharers in the resurrection life. This is the meaning of the Lazarus narrative to which I shall now turn. Lazarus is the man who has been baptized and wrenched from the power of death and sin into the life of the community of Christ. The emphasis here is on the continuing present of Christ's action in the whole life of those whom he raises in baptism.

The account of Lazarus begins with a deliberate disturbance of John's chronology: 'It was Mary who anointed the Lord and wiped his feet with her hair, whose brother Lazarus was ill' (Jn 11.2, RSV). Even Mgr Knox was unable to make this sentence read smoothly in translation, and in the original it is a very awkward construction. It suggests that John was determined to wrest both syntax and chronology in order to introduce the incident of Mary's wiping the feet of the Lord before the incident of the raising of Lazarus. The anointing of Jesus before the Entry into Jerusalem is the first of the royal motifs employed by John to point to the kingly nature of Christ's fulfilment of the messianic prohecies in the great week. The incident leads through the use of the royal Davidic ass in the Entry and the acclamations of the populace: 'Hosanna to the Son of David', and the throwing down of the cloaks as they were thrown before Jehu, to Christ's response to Pilate: 'I am a king' (18.37).

John takes this action out of its temporal sequence in order to suggest that the event which is introduced by this royal symbolism is part of the manifestation of Christ's reign. This is confirmed by the immediate comment of Christ on hearing that Lazarus is ill: 'The end of this sickness is not death; it is meant for God's honour, to bring honour to the Son of God' (11.4). The Son is to be manifest because of this death, this is to be, as the next verses show, an opportunity for men to recognize the light of the world.

Lazarus dies and is buried and Christ comes to his grave. Such is the confidence of the believer, the disciples, that Thomas can say that he wishes himself in the grave rather than separated from Christ: 'Let us go too and be killed along with him' (11.16).

To John's readers, many of whom of course would already know the story of Lazarus and others of whom must have been fully aware of the meaning of Christian baptism as it had been explained to them by Paul and the other missionaries, Thomas would be suggesting that it is only possible to be with Christ if one dies with him. Dying with Christ, as the miracle narratives I discussed earlier tended to show, is vastly different from dying apart from Christ. Martha says to Jesus: 'Lord, if thou hadst been here my brother would not have died' (11.21), and Jesus replies in resurrection terms: 'Thy brother will rise again' (11.23).

Martha, like most of us, accepts this, but notionally, she cannot quite realize the truth that wherever Christ is, there is the kingdom of heaven, and whenever Christ is, then is the Day of the Lord. We separate the Last Day from today, we separate the resurrection of the dead from the presence of Christ here and now. Martha says to him: 'I know well enough that he will rise again at the resurrection when the last day comes' (11.24). And in reply Christ presents Martha, and us, with the truth of the last great realization of an image. Christ is the light of the world, he is the fountain of living water, he is the vine of the feast. Jesus said to her: 'I am the resurrection and life; he who believes in me, though he is dead, will live on, and whoever has life, and has faith in me, to all eternity cannot die' (11.25–6).

At this point John ceases to be tied down to the actual temporal context of his narrative and he opens out the scene so that it becomes contemporary with his readers rather than with Mary and Martha. The generation for whom John wrote looked anxiously for the second coming of Christ and were continually alert for the manifestation of the Lord. When Jesus asks Martha if she believes what he has said, she replies in a sentence which by its combination of tenses shows how our faith is both in the present Christ and the one expected at the parousia: 'Do you believe this? Yes, Lord; I believe that you are the Christ, the Son of God, he who is coming

into the world' (11.27, RSV). The speech of Martha here may well
be a quotation from some early Christian credal formula, perhaps
a baptismal confession of faith in the Lord 'who is coming'. The
present tense occurs in similar situations in John, for example in
the affirmation of Nathanael, and that of the Samaritan villagers.
On the other hand it may simply be that John uses the present tense
here to emphasize the continuous activity of the ever present Christ.
Lazarus is the sign of the baptized man. In the discussion of the
primitive baptismal liturgy I suggested that the pericopes in the
New Testament which speak of a man waking up into light, for
example the description of the rescue of Peter from prison by the
angel, derived their vocabulary from the rite of baptism. Such a
vocabulary characterizes the Lazarus story. At the very beginning
Jesus says of the dead man: 'Lazarus is at rest now; I am going
there to awake him' (11.11). So the primary meaning of the narrative is that the baptized man will be raised in Christ. Together
with this goes the secondary sacramental associations of the defeat
of sin in the act of resurrection which is again a participation in
Christ, as Paul writes to the Ephesians: 'Our sins had made dead
men of us, and he, in giving life to Christ, gave life to us too' (Eph.
2.5). And it is a life maintained by our participation in the food
Christ gives to men. Lazarus who has come from the grave is to
share in the meal of the community with Christ: 'a feast was made
for him there . . . and Lazarus was one of his fellow guests' (John
12.2).

The resurrection of Lazarus is a sign of the effects of baptism and
penance and leads to the eucharistic sign of the meal. The sacraments with which we have been concerned earlier are all brought
into one complex in the Lazarus story, as they are in the life of every
member of the community of Christ.

To share in the community, to take part in the sacramental life
of the community, is to be called to be a member of the witnessing
community. The man raised by baptism is to bring other men to
the life of Christ. This is also shown by the Lazarus account: 'A
great number of the Jews heard that he was there and went out . . .
to have sight of Lazarus, whom he raised from the dead' (John 12.9).
The resurrection life in Lazarus is so effective a witness that he
comes into precisely the same clash with the authorities of the
Jewish community as Christ himself: 'the chief priests made a plot

225

against Lazarus' life too, because so many of the Jews, on his account, were beginning to go off and find faith in Jesus' (John 12.10).

The witness of Lazarus to the way in which Christ can work in a man is a creative witness, it begets other witnesses: 'There were many who had been with him, when he called Lazarus out of the tomb and raised him to life, and these too bore witness of him' (John 12.17). And it is shown as a universal witness. The Christian proclamation is irresistible, it is meant to appeal to all kinds and conditions of men: 'the Pharisees said to one another: Do you see how vain are our efforts? Look, the whole world has turned aside to follow him' (12.19). In particular the Lazarus story is effective in breaking down the barrier against the Gentiles. John suggests that the witness will produce an universal reign of Christ by introducing the account of the coming of the Gentile Greeks to the apostle Philip, saying: 'Sir, we desire to see Jesus' (12.21). Philip went to find Andrew and they went together to tell Jesus. This is an indication that the witness of the Christian must always be part of the community witness to Christ. It is noticeable how often John asserts that men came to Jesus because of Lazarus. He is the means to Christ. The witness of the community member leads other men not to any other but to Christ. It is because of the work of Jesus in Lazarus, not because of the work of Lazarus for Jesus, that men become Christians. Similarly Philip does not take charge of events for himself, he leads the Greeks, with another member of the community, to Christ. We have seen, therefore, how Lazarus' story is a paradigm of the sacramental life and its effects, and how it is a paradigm of the Christian vocation to be a witness to the resurrecting life of Christ. In what way does this story indicate that the witness of Lazarus is one which is connected with the Old Testament witness? To answer this question will be to move for a moment back into the kind of question dealt with summarily in the first introductory section of this study.

Lazarus does not simply take part in the active witness of the community, he becomes himself part of the passive material of the community witness. He does not simply bring other men to Christ through his proclamation of what God has done for him, his story is told by others. Evidently John in retelling the Lazarus story shaped his narrative to bring out certain aspects of the Christian life. Some commentators have suggested that the story has been subject to so much Johannine editing that we cannot now discover the original event which lies behind our account. Others have even suggested that since it is incredible that such a manifest example of Jesus' power should have been either unknown to or ignored by the communities which produced the synoptic traditions, the absence of the story from the gospels deriving from these traditions means that the Lazarus story is a pious fraud of the fourth evangelist. Some have argued further that the source of the invented narrative lies in the Lucan parable of the beggar Lazarus and the rich man. In this parable the resurrection of Lazarus is suggested by the rich man in order that his brothers who are living the kind of careless selfish life that he led before arriving in torment should be warned. But the reply comes: 'They have Moses and the prophets, let them listen to these' (Lk. 16.29). The rich man knows that the Old Testament witness has not been enough to convert his brethren: 'They will not do that, but if a messenger comes to them from the dead, they will repent' (Lk. 16.30). But the reply comes again: 'If they do not listen to Moses and the prophets, they will be unbelieving still, though one should rise from the dead' (Lk. 16.31).

It is suggested that John took this parable and imagined what would happen if a Christian did rise from the dead and confirmed the parable's teaching by representing the Jews and their leaders as still, many of them, unbelieving. The Conversion of the Jews is spoken of in terms of 'life risen from the dead' in Romans 11.15, a text which might be brought into the discussion of this complex.

I do not think that such a radical accusation of invention need be made in this instance. It would seem at least as likely from the texts, and much more in harmony with the way we know the creative tradition of the community worked, to suppose an entirely other explanation of the similarities between the parable and the miracle narrative. The community reverenced the eye-witness, as we noted in the opening sections of this study, and is unlikely to have confused the authority of the eye-witness by introducing invented material as if it had the same credentials. The texts would be similar if a factual narrative were used as the basis of a parable and a theologically developed narrative, or if a parable and a theological viewpoint were brought together in a fictional account, but the devices would be quite different and the attitudes of those employing them would be quite different. I think it probable that the tradition has derived a parable and a theologically developed narrative from the original account of the actual raising of Lazarus by Christ. Whether this is the case, or whether those who suppose the miracle narrative to be a late invention of the community are right, the intention behind the narrative is still the same. It is concerned with explaining how we can in this life share the resurrection of the Lord in the Christian community. Of the original provenance of the story not much can be said, though linguistic considerations persuaded Dr Black to put forward in his *Aramaic approach to the Gospels and Acts* the possibility that it was first shaped in the community of Syrian Antioch. However, assuming that the actual raising was the impulse for various stories in the tradition, of which the parable of the rich man and Lazarus is a development of the incident on the basis perhaps also of a piece of oral teaching of Christ, and the miracle narrative is a theologically developed account, and that these may be representative of a much larger group no longer extant, what connection has the parable with the main themes of the miracle narrative?

Three main features are common to the passages. First, Lazarus has done nothing to merit the happiness which comes to him. We are not told that the beggar was peculiarly virtuous in his acceptance of his suffering, nor that the brother of Martha and Mary shared the gifts of either, we are simply told that the beggar was given a place in heaven, and the man of Bethany was raised to life because it was the will of the Father. The stress in both accounts is on the freedom of God's good will to men. The parable and the miracle narrative both emphasize the truth expressed earlier in John's gospel: 'Just as the Father bids the dead rise up and gives them life, so the Son gives life to whomsoever he will' (5.21). It is not insignificant, given the interest of the author of the fourth gospel in the qualities of words, that the etymology of 'Lazarus' is 'God helps.' Secondly, Lazarus is in both passages thought of as a witness to God. In the parable he is suggested as the messenger to tell the rich man's five brothers of God's eternal decrees, in the miracle narrative he becomes a witness to Christ's life-giving power to the Jews who come from Jerusalem to see him. Thirdly, it is stressed in both that those who are unconvinced by the general work of God in the world remain unconvinced by his particular work of resurrection. In the parable

Abraham says that those who have the Scriptures and yet withhold their service from God will not be converted by Lazarus coming from the grave, and in the miracle narrative John emphasizes the continuing hardness of heart of the Pharisees. The men of death see in the resurrection of Lazarus and the declaration of Christ's resurrection character, a real threat to their way of death, their standard of dying: 'From that day forward they plotted his death' (11.53). They have no intention of listening to Lazarus either. T. S. Eliot has expressed this indifference to the message of the resurrected man with customary exactitude. He asks would it have been worth while for anyone with such tremendous news

> To say: 'I am Lazarus, come from the dead,
> Come back to tell you all, I shall tell you all'—
> If one settling a pillow by her head,
>> Should say: 'That is not what I meant at all.
>> That is not it, at all'.

The community tells the story of Lazarus in order that men should care and should understand that in the sharing of the resurrection life is the meaning of existence.

In addition to its similarities to the gospel story, the parable contains one specific feature which is of great interest in my present concern. It gives an indication of the character of the resurrected man's testimony. Abraham is represented as saying that the testimony of Lazarus and the testimony of Moses and the Prophets, that is, of the Old Testament, are to be considered as equivalent as far as the listener is concerned. The witness of the Christian living the life of the risen Lord is identical *as witness* with the witness of the Old Testament which points to this life in the new community. The Jews will listen neither to Moses nor to Lazarus because they say the same thing. The one is as cogent as the other in speaking of the Lord but both have to be attended to with the same open heart. If we continue to assume both that the parable and the miracle narrative derive from one common source in the community tradition about the event, and that the Lazarus account in John is theologically developed into a paradigm of the Christian's present situation, we have the following schema of content:

(i) The witness of the Christian is intimately related to that of the Old Testament writings;

229

  (ii) the central event of the Christian life is the sharing in the life of the risen Lord;

  (iii) this sharing is brought about through the Christian's participation in the sacramental activity of the new community.

The Lazarus writings, therefore, taken together, present us with the general pattern on which I have based this exposition of some aspects of the community witness to Christ, and therefore I have some assurance that I have considered those aspects which are not the least important.